Families in Community Settings: Interdisciplinary Perspectives

The *Marriage & Family Review* series:

• *Cults and the Family*, edited by Florence Kaslow and Marvin B. Sussman

• *Alternatives to Traditional Family Living*, edited by Harriet Gross and Marvin B. Sussman

• *Intermarriage in the United States*, edited by Gary A. Crester and Joseph J. Leon

• *Family Systems and Inheritance Patterns*, edited by Judith N. Cates and Marvin B. Sussman

• *The Ties that Bind: Men's and Women's Social Networks*, edited by Laura Lein and Marvin B. Sussman

• *Social Stress and the Family: Advances and Developments in Family Stress Theory and Research*, edited by Hamilton I. McCubbin, Marvin B. Sussman, and Joan M. Patterson

• *Human Sexuality and the Family*, edited by James W. Maddock, Gerhard Neubeck, and Marvin B. Sussman

• *Obesity and the Family*, edited by David J. Kallen and Marvin B. Sussman

• *Women and the Family*, edited by Beth B. Hess and Marvin B. Sussman

• *Personal Computers and the Family*, edited by Marvin B. Sussman

• *Pets and the Family*, edited by Marvin B. Sussman

• *Families and the Energy Transition*, edited by John Byrne, David A. Schulz, and Marvin B. Sussman

• *Men's Changing Roles in the Family*, edited by Robert A. Lewis and Marvin B. Sussman

• *The Charybdis Complex: Redemption of Rejected Marriage and Family Journal Articles*, edited by Marvin B. Sussman

• *Families and the Prospect of Nuclear Attack/Holocaust*, edited by Teresa D. Marciano and Marvin B. Sussman

• *Family Medicine: The Maturing of a Discipline*, edited by William J. Doherty, Charles E. Christianson, and Marvin B. Sussman

• *Childhood Disability and Family Systems*, edited by Michael Ferrari and Marvin B. Sussman

• *Alternative Health Maintenance and Healing Systems for Families*, edited by Doris Y. Wilkinson and Marvin B. Sussman

• *Deviance and the Family*, edited by Frank E. Hagan and Marvin B. Sussman

• *Transitions to Parenthood*, edited by Rob Palkovitz and Marvin B. Sussman

• *AIDS and Families: Report of the AIDS Task Force Groves Conference on Marriage and the Family*, edited by Eleanor D. Macklin

• *Museum Visits and Activities for Family Life Enrichment*, edited by Barbara H. Butler and Marvin B. Sussman

• *Cross-Cultural Perspectives on Families, Work, and Change*, edited by Katja Boh, Giovanni Sgritta, and Marvin B. Sussman

• *Homosexuality and Family Relations*, edited by Frederick W. Bozett and Marvin B. Sussman

• *Families in Community Settings: Interdisciplinary Perspectives*, edited by Donald G. Unger and Marvin B. Sussman

Families in Community Settings: Interdisciplinary Perspectives

Donald G. Unger
Marvin B. Sussman
Editors

The Haworth Press
New York • London

Families in Community Settings: Interdisciplinary Perspectives has also been published as *Marriage and Family Review*, Volume 15, Numbers 1/2 1990.

The Haworth Press, Inc., 10 Alice Street, Binghamton, New York 13904-1580
EUROSPAN/Haworth, 3 Henrietta Street, London WC2E 8LU England

Library of Congress Cataloging-in-Publication Data

Families in community settings : interdisciplinary perspectives / Donald G. Unger, Marvin B.
    Sussman, editors.
        p.   cm.
        "Has also been published as Marriage and family review, volume 15, numbers 1/2 1990" –
T.p. verso.
        Includes bibliographical references.
        ISBN 1-56024-004-0 : $34.95
        1. Family – United States. 2. Social networks – United States. 3. Community psychology –
United States. I. Unger, Donald G. II. Sussman, Marvin B.
HQ536.F3336   1990
306.85'0973 – dc20   90-31991
                                                                                                                              CIP

Families in Community Settings: Interdisciplinary Perspectives

CONTENTS

Acknowledgements   xi

Contributors   xiii

Introduction: A Community Perspective on Families   1
Donald G. Unger
Marvin B. Sussman

THE COMMUNITY AS PLACE

The Community Context of Child Abuse and Neglect   19
Joan I. Vondra

The Ecology of Child Maltreatment   20
Considerations for Intervention   28
Directions for Future Research   33

The Significance of Home and Homelessness   39
Leanne G. Rivlin

Incidence of Homelessness   40
Forms of Homelessness   41
The Loss of a Home   44
The Significance of Settings   45
Attachment to Place   49
The Homeless Existence   50

Rural Families and Health Care: Refining the Knowledge Base   **57**

Clarann Weinert
Kathleen Ann Long

Concepts of Health   57
Health Concepts Among Rural Populations   59
Health Care Needs of Rural People   61
Adapting Services to Rural Needs   64
Summary   71

ORGANIZATIONS AND FAMILIES

Corporate Responses to Family Needs   **77**
Dana E. Friedman

The Rationale for Corporate Support   78
Why Do Companies Resist Responding?   82
Who Is Responding to Family Needs?   83
Corporate Responses to Child Care   83
Corporate Responses to Elder Care   88
Corporate Responses to Flexibility   90
Conclusion   93

School and Family Connections: Theory, Research, and Implications for Integrating Sociologies of Education and Family   **99**
Joyce L. Epstein

Theoretical Advances in School and Family Connections   100
Research Results and Directions   105
Implications for Linking Sociologies of Education
and Family   118

Low-Income Families and Public Welfare Organizations   **127**
Catherine S. Chilman

The Nature of Human Services Organizations   128
Families in Poverty   129
Existing Public Programs for Poor Families   132

Some Implications for Programs and Policies   139
Summary and Discussion   143

**The Responsiveness of Early Childhood Initiatives
to Families: Strategies and Limitations**   **149**
    Douglas R. Powell

Strategies   151
Needed Directions   162
Concluding Comment   167

**SOCIAL NETWORKS AND PERSONAL
COMMUNITIES**

**The Role of Formal and Informal Groups in Providing
Help to Older People**   **171**
    Eugene Litwak
    Peter Messeri
    Merril Silverstein

Theories Explaining the Unique Role of Primary Groups
    and Formal Organizations   175
Task Specific Theory and Organizational Contingency
    Theory   177
Theory Explaining How Groups with Structural Conflict
    Can Exist Simultaneously   181
Some Programmatic Consequences of the Task Specific
    Theory   183
When Primary Group Support Is Not Available   187
Conclusion and Summary   189

The Place of Kinfolk in Personal Community Networks   **195**
    Barry Wellman

Communities as Networks   195
Are Sisters and Cousins Reckoned by the Dozens?   197
Over the River and Through the Woods   205
Brothers' Keepers   209
W(h)ither Kin in Networks?   217

Family, Religion, and Personal Communities: Examples from Mormonism   **229**
>   *Marie Cornwall*
>   *Darwin L. Thomas*

Introduction   229
Religion, Family, and Personal Communities   230
Examples from Mormon Family Research   239
Religion and Family in the Post-Modern World   245

INTERACTIONS ACROSS SETTINGS AND OVER TIME

A Theory of Competencies × Settings Interactions   **253**
>   *Luciano L'Abate*

Developmental Competencies   254
Settings   260
Priorities   264
Theoretical and Practical Implications   265
Conclusion   266

Paradise Through the Sands of Time: The Human Yearning for Community   **271**
>   *Kris Jeter*

Introduction   271
The Desert   272
Nexus Points at the Desert Crossroads   272
Judaism   277
Christianity   280
Islam   283
Conclusion   285

ABOUT THE EDITORS

Donald G. Unger, PhD, is Assistant Professor in the Department of Individual and Family Studies at the University of Delaware. Dr. Unger has published articles on social support and resource programs for teen parents, neighborhood support systems, and services for families of children with special needs. He serves on the Board of Directors of the Delaware Children's Trust Fund, and is a member of the American Psychological Association, the National Council on Family Relations, and the Society for Research in Child Development.

Marvin B. Sussman, PhD, is Unidel Professor of Human Behavior Emeritus at the College of Human Resources, University of Delaware. A member of many professional organizations, he was awarded the 1980 Ernest W. Burgess Award of the National Council on Family Relations, as well as a life-long membership for services to the Groves Conference on Marriage and the Family in 1981. In 1983, he was elected to the prestigious academy of Groves for scholary contributions to the field. Dr. Sussman has published widely on areas dealing with family, community, rehabilitation, organizations, sociology of medicine, and aging. Dr. Sussman is the editor of *Marriage and Family Review*.

Acknowledgements

The editors would like to thank the following interdisciplinary group of scholars for their helpful comments: Ellen Bassuk, Larry Cohen, Marcia Cooley, Raymond Coward, Nan Crouter, William D'Antonio, Deborah Daro, Jeff Davidson, Marilou Hyson, Jean Ann Linney, Terry Marciano, Debra Rog, Michael Sosin, Howard Stein, Arland Thornton, and Pat Voydanoff. Additionally we would like to thank Kay Pietras who provided excellent secretarial assistance. I (D.U.) would also like to thank Sharon Jacobs for her continual support. Finally, we thank the authors for their time, energy, and perspectives that they contributed to this volume.

Contributors

Catherine Chilman, PhD, School of Social Welfare, University of Wisconsin-Milwaukee, Milwaukee, WI 53201

Marie Cornwall, PhD, Department of Sociology and Acting Director, Women's Research Institute, Brigham Young University, Provo, UT 84602

Joyce L. Epstein, PhD, Principal Research Scientist, Director, Effective Middle Grades Program, & Professor of Sociology, Center for Research on Elementary and Middle Schools and the Center for Research on Effective Schooling for Disadvantaged Students, The Johns Hopkins University, 3505 N. Charles Street, Baltimore, MD 21218

Dana E. Friedman, EdD, Co-President, Families and Work Institute, 330 Seventh Avenue, New York, NY 10001

Kris Jeter, PhD, Director, Programs & Communication, The Possible Society, Newark, DE 19711

Luciano L'Abate, PhD, Department of Psychology, Georgia State University, Atlanta, GA 30303

Eugene Litwak, PhD, School of Public Health, Division of Sociomedical Sciences, Columbia University, 600 West 168th Street, New York, NY 10032

Kathleen Long, PhD, RNCS, FAAN, College of Nursing, Montana State University, Bozeman, MT 59717

Peter Messeri, PhD, School of Public Health, Division of Sociomedical Sciences, Columbia University, 600 West 168th Street, New York, NY 10032

Douglas Powell, PhD, Department of Child Development and Family Studies, Purdue University, West Lafayette, IN 47907

Leanne Rivlin, PhD, Environmental Psychology Program, Graduate Center, City University of New York, New York, NY 10036

Merril Silverstein, MA, School of Public Health, Division of Sociomedical Sciences, Columbia University, 600 West 168th Street, New York, NY 10032

Marvin B. Sussman, PhD, Department of Individual & Family Studies, University of Delaware, Newark, DE 19716

Darwin Thomas, PhD, Department of Sociology, Brigham Young University, Provo, UT 84602

Donald G. Unger, PhD, Department of Individual and Family Studies, University of Delaware, Newark, DE 19716

Joan Vondra, PhD, Department of Psychology & Education, 5C01 Forbes Quadrangle, University of Pittsburgh, 230 South Bouquet Street, Pittsburgh, PA 15260

Claraan Weinert, SC, PhD, RN, College of Nursing, Montana State University, Bozeman, MT 59717

Barry Wellman, PhD, Centre for Urban and Community Studies, University of Toronto, 455 Spadina Avenue, Toronto, Canada, M5S 2G8

Introduction:
A Community Perspective on Families

Donald G. Unger
Marvin B. Sussman

There is an increasing recognition that we need policies and programs which will support families. Family structures are changing, more families are faced with the care of their elderly parents, and children are increasingly being raised in single parent families. The incidence of divorce and remarriage remains at high levels. Alarming numbers of children continue to live in poverty.

Understanding the life situations of families, identifying their problems, and developing new solutions require an ecological framework that recognizes that families are embedded in a matrix of relationships within community and larger social systems (Bronfenbrenner, 1979). Although there has been a great deal of interest in recent years in understanding families from an ecological perspective (Pence, 1988), relatively little is known about the relation of families with their communities. Available research, however, leaves few doubts that characteristics of community settings such as schools and the workplace can have a significant impact on family functioning and child development (Bronfenbrenner, Moen, & Garbarino, 1984; Crouter, 1984a; Litwak & Meyer, 1974). This paper highlights the role of community settings for family functioning and serves as an introduction to the work of an interdisciplinary group of scholars which is presented in this volume. The papers discuss the importance of the family/community interface across a range of family issues.

INTRODUCTION

The relations between families and their communities has become increasingly complex. From an historical perspective, Keniston (1977) suggests that many of the functions of the family began to change as a result of industrialization. The workplace moved out of the home, educational responsibilities were given to the schools, and many social welfare responsibilities were assumed by the community. More recently, women play a prominent role in the workforce, resulting in increasing numbers of children in child care settings (Mortimer & London, 1984). The number of single mother families is also on the increase. Between 1970 and 1984 the number of families headed by a female increased by 107% (Kamerman, 1985). This trend has placed new demands on child care and public support programs (Garfinkel & McLanahan, 1986). These are but a few of the changes which have placed families today in the role of the "weakened executive" (Keniston, 1977). When a family cannot provide direct services to its members, much of its time is spent negotiating with institutions and trying to coordinate services for family members (Sussman, 1977).

The importance of cooperative relations among community settings becomes particularly salient when a family member has special needs. A handicapped child, an elderly parent, or a parent on public assistance, for instance, requires that families interact with a range of different community settings (Berger & Foster, 1986; Chilman, this volume; Friedman, this volume; Litwak, this volume).

While families are intricately involved in their communities, the "myth of the self sufficient family," and the idealized conception of the family as a refuge from the stressors of the world still persist as common beliefs (Keniston, 1977). Not only do these myths result in feelings of inadequacy and distress for families, but they contribute to the failure of families to prepare their members for interactions with bureaucratic institutions (Hareven, 1989). Hareven suggests that "the tendency of the family to shelter its members from the social institutions has weakened its ability to affect the structure of or to influence the programs and legislation that public agencies have directed at the family" (p. 53).

The family's relations with different community settings present opportunities for growth as well as developmental risk (Garbarino, 1982). For instance, when there are good relations between home and school such that parents and teachers are cooperating with each other, children are likely to perform better in school (Epstein, 1987). However, when home-school relations are weak, the potential for developmental problems is greatly increased (Garbarino & Asp, 1981; Lightfoot, 1978). It is this interaction between family members and community settings as illustrated in Figure 1 which we believe provides an important perspective in understanding variations in family functioning (see also Berger & Wuescher, 1975).

COMMUNITY SETTINGS

Communities play a significant role in the lives of families. Community settings can be defined in terms of place and/or a set of relationships and resources (cf. Heller, Price, Reinharz, Riger & Wandersman, 1984; Sarason, 1972). Neighborhoods, for example, are a type of setting defined by physical location which often have great diversity in relationships and resources. In some communities, neighboring results in receiving and giving emotional and instrumental support, socializing family childrearing practices and beliefs, and providing a sense of community and a feeling of attachment to place (Powell, 1979; Unger & Wandersman, 1985). The importance of neighborhood ties for families often becomes more salient when there is a threat to the safety of families due to events such as an increased rate of crime or toxic leakage from a local landfill (Edelstein, 1988; Wandersman, Jakubs, & Giamartino, 1981). When families live in close knit neighborhoods, they frequently empower themselves and become potent constituencies for political and social change.

In other neighborhoods when there is an obvious lack of social ties among neighbors, the community setting will play different roles in the lives of families. Warren and Warren (1977), for example, have described these settings as "diffuse" or "anomic" neighborhoods. In such neighborhoods, families are often faced with high rates of crime and delinquency. Without community ties, families may find it difficult to accomplish family tasks and, under extreme distress, they may be at risk for child maltreatment (Vondra, this volume).

Vondra, defining child abuse as a community problem, discusses the risk factors and dynamics which account for the "ecology of

Figure 1: Families and Their Communities

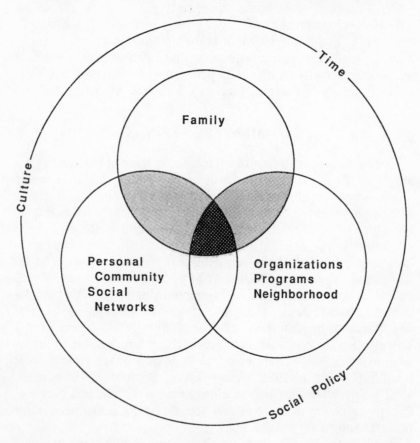

maltreatment.'' This ecology represents an interaction between individual and community characteristics. Social isolation, lack of
social control, economically deprived neighborhoods, unemployment, inadequate social services and psychological functioning,
poverty, and community values and norms are several of the factors
associated with child abuse and neglect. Vondra stresses the importance of broad scale community based programs of support for the
prevention and treatment of child abuse, highlighting the central
role of schools.

The impact of the absence of family ties to a neighborhood community setting is dramatically seen in homeless families (Rivlin, this volume). Rivlin presents the functions of the home and its loss for different forms of visible, invisible and hidden homelessness. An attachment to place and the impact of homelessness is discussed in the context of the significance of settings and the importance of a sense of personal space and personal places. Rivlin proposes that a longitudinal approach to an "ecology of homelessness" is needed to understand the events leading to the loss of a home and the experiences of homeless families within and after leaving shelters. Understanding the impact of homelessness and the significance of personal places and privacy could inform policy makers and help identify those policies which exacerbate the problems of homeless families.

Rural/Urban Settings

The differences between rural and urban settings present different demands and opportunities for families. Rural families are more likely to have fewer employment opportunities and lower economic well-being, less formal education, and lower-quality housing than urban families (Tremblay, Walker, & Dillman, 1983). Acquiring adequate health care and social services is also a major problem for rural families (Jurich, Smith, & Polson, 1983). Rural communities have the nation's highest rates of maternal and infant mortality and fewer medical personnel, particularly specialists, as compared to urban areas (Coward & Jackson, 1983). Urban areas, in contrast, are noted for their higher crime rates, impersonal ties, and higher density and noisier living conditions (Karp, Stone, & Yoels, 1977; Cohen, Glass, & Singer, 1973).

Weinert and Long (this volume) discuss the unique health beliefs, practices, and needs of rural families. They present ways in which community-based, hospital care, and mental health care can be adapted for the delivery of rural health care. Some special considerations include blending formal and informal helping systems, preparing health care personnel as broad based generalists for work in rural hospitals, developing incentives to retain personnel, and assisting primary health care providers in the identification of mental health problems and resources.

Rural and urban areas may differ in the opportunities for family members to assume positions of responsibility and to feel a sense of belonging in their communities. Barker & his colleagues (Barker, 1968; Barker & Schoggen, 1973) have shown that people behave differently based upon characteristics of the settings in their communities. Of particular importance to their theory of "behavior settings" is the concept of under- and overmanning. Manning refers to the number of responsibilities and positions available in a setting relative to the number of potential participants. In undermanned settings, there are more opportunities for children and adults to become involved in a wide range of tasks and to take positions of responsibility (Wicker, 1979). This theory would suggest that children and families living in rural/small towns have more opportunities for responsible involvement than those in urban areas; such opportunities could positively influence a child's development and family life. Research, however, is not currently available to address the impact of manning on family functioning (Bronfenbrenner et al., 1984).

Community settings, broadly defined, also include those settings which provide services to children and families such as schools, public welfare organizations, early childhood programs, self-help/mutual support groups, and family advocacy organizations. The workplace is a setting whose primary objective is not to serve families yet it has an important influence on family life.

ORGANIZATIONAL SETTINGS AND FAMILIES: ISSUES OF RESPONSIVENESS

Family members spend large amounts of time working in organizations and receiving services from a diversity of programs. The "myth of separate worlds" (Kanter, 1977) of work and family has been exposed. Work settings can have a profound effect on families and families, in turn, can influence work (Mortimer & London, 1984). Inflexible work schedules and job stress may interfere with family functioning. Family members, with few exceptions, bring home with them the travails, sorrows, and joys of the workplace. Stress not only "spillsover" from work to family, but family difficulties may influence employee productivity (Crouter, 1984a,

1984b). The rise in single parent and dual-earner families has cata-
lyzed companies to respond to family needs in order to maintain an
effective work force (Friedman, this volume).

Friedman reviews the responsive and innovative strategies which
corporations have used to address the needs of family members in
the workplace. Family members not only have child care needs but
caregiving needs across the lifespan as more families are caring for
elderly parents. While corporations are recognizing the economic
benefits of responding to these family concerns, there is still resistance in a majority of companies. Friedman proposes reasons for
such opposition and discusses ways for corporations, human service
systems, government agencies, and scientists to improve the work/
family interface.

Changes in the work environment of the *community* can also have
significant influences on the family (Elder, 1974). When the availability of jobs decreases, for example, the rate of child maltreatment in the community has been shown to rise (Steinberg, Catalano, & Dooley, 1981). On a family level, loss of the earner role
may result in increased financial hardship and family distress
(Piotrkowski, Rapoport, & Rapoport, 1987; Voydanoff, 1983).

Educational organizations in the 20th century have struggled with
the role of parental involvement. While relations between home and
school have improved, especially in middle class neighborhoods,
there is still a pressing need for more cooperative ties. This is a
result of more educated parents, greater federal regulations and
funding for parent involvement, and a heightened sensitivity of single parents and working mothers to the quality of their children's
education (Epstein, 1987). Research suggests that greater overlap
between these settings results in improvements in the quality of
education. Opportunities for increased communication and parent
involvement have resulted in parents learning new ways to help
their children at home, greater parent satisfaction with teachers,
more positive feelings by teachers about teaching and their schools,
and increases in children's reading skills (Epstein, this volume).
Epstein presents a social-organizational model of family-school relations and a typology of five major types of parent involvement
that would facilitate family and school connections. She stresses the
importance of understanding how diverse family structures and con-

cerns can more effectively overlap with teacher practices and school structures.

The relationship between families and community settings is often tenuous. Low income families frequently spend much of their time interacting with a complicated and overburdened system of public welfare organizations (Chilman, this volume). A family that has multiple family problems is almost assuredly going to have multiple organizational problems. The specialization of service providers results in family members receiving assistance from numerous providers of services. The lack of coordination among these different human service organizational settings is likely to further add to the difficulties of the multiple problem family (Selig,1976). Chilman (this volume) highlights the trends in poverty among families and discusses the problems that have developed in governmental programs which interfere with the ability of these programs to be responsive to low-income families. She emphasizes the ecological nature of this problem, citing larger systemic influences which have shaped public welfare policies.

There is a great deal of interest in making early childhood programs more responsive to families and their communities. Powell (this volume) identifies five major strategies which may strengthen the ability of programs to serve families with young children. These strategies include: enhancing program-family communication, providing opportunities for parent choice of early childhood programs, conducting needs assessments of program participants, altering staff roles and using indigenous community residents, and empowering parents to be involved in making decisions regarding their child's program. Powell stresses that research is needed to determine the processes which influence the success or failure of these strategies in improving family/program relations.

Family therapists have only recently recognized the need to understand the interface of the family and its intergenenerational relationships with community settings. Imber-Black (1988) suggests that

> Families and larger systems frequently become engaged with one another in unfortunate ways, ways that impede growth and development in family members and contribute to cynicism

and burnout among helpers. All too frequently, little attention is paid to the patterns that emerge between families and larger systems, resulting in the replication and reification of unsatisfactory relationships at multiple levels. (p. 2)

Schwartzman and Kneifel (1985) propose that shared beliefs and practices between families and institutions will influence their interaction; within this relationship, helping institutions often replicate family dynamics.

L'Abate (this volume), a family psychologist, has developed a theory of developmental competence. According to the author, family functioning depends upon the ability of family members to successfully negotiate and accommodate to the demands of various settings within which family members interact. His theory proposes that specific task characteristics and demands in settings interact with specific skills and abilities of family members. A practical implication of this theory is the improvement of functioning through skill development.

The relation of families to organizations has also been studied in the context of social networks. Social networks are those ties that individuals have with a particular individual or family member. They provide a way of describing social relationships, linkages or patterns of ties, and the flow of resources between individuals (Wellman, 1981). Social networks can play an important role in a client's decision to use services by acting as an information and referral system (Birkel & Reppucci, 1983; Powell & Eisenstadt, 1983). Social networks may also influence a client's participation in parenting programs and services for parents and their children. Several studies, for instance, have shown that parents are more responsive to home-based parent education programs when the parents have more extensive family ties and support (Badger, 1981; Kessen & Fein, 1975; Powell, 1984; Unger & Wandersman, 1988).

Linkage and task specific theories provide a useful way of conceptualizing the interface between organizations, families, and the social ties of family members. Linkage theory proposes that families and the settings in which they live have unique qualities which influence their problem solving abilities. Primary groups such as families are more competent in performing nonuniform tasks while bureaucratic organizations can better handle uniform demands. For instance, in uncertain situations, bureaucracies often have difficulty in responding quickly and in accord with the individual needs of family members. Decisions are likely to be made based on general policies while families can respond in a more flexible manner. With more uniform tasks, organizational personnel are better suited to respond with their technical expertise and skills. Coordination between the family and organizational settings optimize their specific capabilities (Sussman, 1977).

Litwak, Messeri, and Silverstein (this volume) indicate that family/organization relations can best be understood by focusing on the *structure* of the group and the *nature* of the task. Using task specific theory, they view organizations and primary groups as best suited to manage tasks which match their structure. They show how tasks can be classified according to the same dimensions characterizing structures. It is this match between task and structure which can be used to optimize family/organization relations in responding to family needs. Primary groups and formal organizations are interdependent because most goals require both technical and everyday knowledge. These authors propose that in the face of structural conflict between organizations and primary groups, they can work towards common goals. These ideas are discussed as they apply to families and formal organizations caring for the elderly.

Berger and Neuhaus (1977) identified the importance of "mediating structures" in facilitating the interface between individuals and families with larger social systems. Sussman (1972) has referred to this connecting mechanism as a "linkage group" whose purpose is to reduce the social distance between families and larger systems by establishing effective communication and interaction networks. In the Love Canal Crisis in Niagara Falls, New York, when there were conflicting stories from the "authorities," the neighborhood organization served as an important, reliable source of information for families. The organization conveyed information from the state and various sources about toxic waste which was not readily available to residents (Gibbs, 1983). Sussman (1972) suggests that families need not passively respond to the demands of bureaucratic organizations. When family members learn how to effectively take on "linking roles" and utilize linkage groups, they can empower their families, using their skills and knowledge of bureaucratic organizations to meet their family's needs and objectives.

The church may serve this same role as a mediating structure in many communities. The church can be a source of support, a major influence in value transmission, a source of social control, and a provider of family education (Dunnington, 1988). In many communities, the church plays an active role in providing social welfare services to families in need. Shinn (1987), for instance, describes a home visiting program run by several religious organizations where families at risk for parenting difficulties and residential placement work with a supportive and empowering paraprofessional.

Reiss (Reiss & Klein, 1987) has proposed a paradigm theory which has been used to predict the quality of fit between families and institutions. Families can be described according to their paradigms or underlying assumptions and beliefs that family members hold in common about their social environment. For example, families differ in their beliefs that the world has a pattern or order in which events can potentially be mastered. Organizations have their own paradigms or "organizational objectives" which refer to a shared understanding of the task to be accomplished by the organization and the corresponding values which guide implementation. Reiss suggests that the "fit" between the family and organization will depend upon the match between the family's and the organization's paradigms. A family that believes the world regards them as a "group" will be prone to drop out of treatment in a psychiatric facility, for example, when that facility places a priority on viewing mental health problems as a breakdown of a physical or psychological "mechanism" rather than a breakdown of human relationships.

PERSONAL COMMUNITIES

Community settings are not restricted to a physical location. Community settings can involve relationships or social networks that go beyond place. Communities are often "communities without propinquity," not limited by their geographical boundaries (Wellman, 1979). These social networks have been shown to have important effects on family functioning (Milardo, 1988; Ramey,

1978; Unger & Powell, 1979). Wellman (this volume) has found that within these "personal communities," social network members play unique helping roles. The family kin network has historically aided families in problem solving (Sussman & Burchinal, 1962). Wellman points out that while families have undergone significant changes, immediate kin still serve as important social network members, providing support for families. His research in Toronto communities indicates that kin form both a distinct social network and are part of a broader personal community network. Kin often have socially close ties and are even confidants; these kinship ties tend to be more actively maintained over a distance than friendship ties. Wellman discusses the determinants of kinship ties, their uniqueness in a family's larger personal community network, and the consequences of these contacts for families.

Ogbu (1988) suggests that communities may extend beyond network ties to a "cognitive community." Minorities and ethnic groups belong to communities that are defined by collective historical experiences distinct from the rest of society. The collective community contributes to a child's and family's definitions of life's possibilities and problems and of appropriate means and strategies to achieve individual and family goals. Reiss and Oliveri (1983) suggest that families in communities develop a "community frame" through interactions with and observations of other families. This community framework represents a community's shared understandings of events and families. The community frame is proposed to play an important role in defining whether an event is stressful for a family and how the event is responded to by the family. These frameworks provide for an understanding of the structure and meaning of events. They also help determine the impact of events on families which compose specific communities.

The religious community has ties not only to a place of worship but also to a larger cognitive community of beliefs, values, and traditions (Cornwall & Thomas, this volume). Cornwall and Thomas' findings suggest that religious identities are sustained within personal religious communities which can be understood separately from institutional religious participation. The personal religious community develops through interaction with others who also have a similar faith. Personal religious communities among Mormon families have a significant influence on the socialization of adolescents and are positively related to the well-being of families. These networks carry out institutional religious influences in families. Cornwall & Thomas argue for the importance of the personal religious community in today's complex society, emphasizing the need to understand the unique roles of religious personal communities and participation in religious programs for families.

A personal religious community is very similar to what has been called a psychological sense of community. This "human bond" is characterized by a sense of membership and influence, and a sharing of values and emotional connection. A psychological sense of community is not limited by geographical boundaries (McMillan & Chavis, 1986). Through membership, families develop a sense of belonging, relatedness, and personal investment. Influence can result in social conformity as well as the ability to exert power in larger systems. A sharing of values allows individuals and families to express and fulfill their beliefs. Finally, through a common history and identity, a shared emotional connection can develop. Jeter (this volume) suggests that the search for community has been a central theme throughout history. She traces this search using examples from ancient history and mythology. A sense of community, historically and today, is an important component of a support system for families (Unger & Nelson, 1989).

COMMUNITY SETTINGS ACROSS CULTURES AND TIME

No discussion of families and community settings would be complete without mention of cultural differences among settings. Scientists have used cross-cultural research to compare families across geographical, political and ethnic boundaries (Larzelere & Klein, 1987). Cultural differences among families may have an important impact on the fit between families and the community settings within which they interact. Weinert and Long (this volume) point out the unique concerns and beliefs of rural families regarding health care. Wellman (this volume) argues that personal community networks function differently, for example, in Third World and First World countries. Numerous examples can be found in the literature which point out the challenges that both ethnic families and human service professionals confront as they interface in different community settings (e.g., Williams, 1988; Green, 1982). Fandetti and Gelfand (1978), for instance, found that traditional mental health centers and their programs were frequently not recognized as an appropriate source of help by urban Italian and Polish families. Powell (this volume) argues that it is important to not make over-generalizations about different cultural groups. What is needed is a recognition of "within-group variations in generating a differentiated grid of matches between program design and population characteristics." Community based service delivery models which are culturally sensitive to minority, ethnic, and religious communities and class differences within these groups are very much in need (Biegel, 1984).

The importance of different community settings for family members will change over the life span and generations of the family. However, issues such as making programs more responsive to families are just as relevant for families with young children (Powell, this volume) as they are for families caring for elderly parents (Litwak et al., this volume). The relations of families to their communities will also evolve as they respond to life course, social policy, and economic systemic changes (Hareven, 1989).

THIS VOLUME

This volume brings together an interdisciplinary group of scholars to address key issues facing families and their communities from different perspectives. The fields of family sociology, urban and community studies, education, social policy, community psychology, ancient history, environmental psychology, family studies, early childhood education, family psychology, and social welfare are represented. Had space permitted, we would have welcomed the inclusion of other disciplines. It is hoped that the work of the authors presented in this volume will stimulate further study of families in the context of their communities. Understanding the family/community interface will help us move forward in developing policies and programs which can strengthen and support children and families.

REFERENCES

Badger, E. (1981). Effects of a parent education program on teenage mothers and their offspring. In K.G. Scott, T. Field, & E.G. Robertson, (Eds.), *Teenage parents and their offspring*, (pp. 283-310). NY: Grune & Stratton.

Barker, R.G. (1968). *Ecological psychology: Concepts and methods for studying the environment of human behavior*. Stanford, CA: Stanford University Press.

Barker, R.G. & Schoggen, P. (1973). *Qualities of community life*. San Francisco: Jossey-Bass.

Berger, M. & Wuescher, L. (1975). The family in the substantive environment: An approach to the development of transactional methodology. *Journal of Community Psychology*, *3*, 246-253.

Berger, M. & Foster, M. (1986). Applications of family therapy theory to research and interventions with families with mentally retarded children. In M.M. Gallagher & P.M. Vietze (Eds.), *Families of handicapped persons*, pp. 251-260. Baltimore: Brookes.

Berger, P.L. & Neuhaus, R.J. (1977). *To empower people*. Washington, D.C: American Enterprise Institute for Public Policy Research.

Biegel, D.E. (1984). Help seeking and receiving in urban ethnic neighborhoods: Strategies for empowerment. In Rappaport, J., Swift, C., & Hess, R. (Eds.), *Studies in empowerment*, pp. 119-143. NY: Haworth.

Birkel, R.C. & Reppucci, N.D. (1983). Social networks, information-seeking, and the utilization of services. *American Journal of Community Psychology*, *11*, 185-205.

Bronfenbrenner, U. (1979). *The ecology of human development: Experiments by nature and design*. Cambridge, MA: Harvard University Press.

Bronfenbrenner, U., Moen, P., & Garbarino, J. (1984). Child, family, and community. In R.D. Parke, R.N. Emde, H.P. MacAdoo, & G.P. Sackett (Eds.), *The family*, pp. 283-328. Chicago: University of Chicago Press.

Cohen, S., Glass, D.C., & Singer, J.E. (1973). Apartment noise, auditory discrimination, and reading ability in children. *Journal of Experimental Social Psychology*, *9*, 407-422.

Coward, R.T. & Jackson, R.W. (1983). Environmental Stress: The rural family. In H.I. McCubbin & C.R. Figley (Eds.), *Stress and the family*, Vol. 1, pp. 188-200. NY: Brunner/Mazel.

Crouter, A.C. (1984a). Participative work as an influence on human development. *Journal of Applied Developmental Psychology*, *5*, 71-90.

Crouter, A.C. (1984b). Spillover from family to work: The neglected side of the work-family interface. *Human Relations*, *37*, 425-442.

Dunnington, S.F. (1988). The interface of church, family, and community. Unpublished manuscript, Department of Individual and Family Studies, University of Delaware.

Edelstein, M.R. (1988). *Contaminated communities*. Boulder, CO: Westview.

Elder, G.H. (1974). *Children of the great depression*. Chicago: University of Chicago.

Epstein, J.L. (1987). Toward a theory of family-school connections: Teacher practices and parent involvement. In K. Hurrelmann, F.X. Kaufmann, & F. Losel (Eds.), *Social intervention: potential and constraints*, pp. 121-136. NY: Walter de Gruter.

Fandetti, D.V. & Gelfand, D.E. (1978). Attitudes towards symptoms and services in the ethnic family and neighborhood. *American Journal of Orthopsychiatry, 48,* 477-486.

Garbarino, J. (1982). *Children and families in the social environment.* NY: Aldine.

Garbarino, J. & Asp C.E. (1981). *Successful schools and competent students.* Lexington, MA: Lexington Books.

Garfinkel, I. & McLanahan, S.S. (1986). *Single mothers and their children.* Washington, DC: The Urban Press.

Gibbs, L.M. (1983). Community response to an emergency situation: Psychological destruction and the Love Canal. *Journal of Community Psychology, 11,* 115-126.

Green, J.W. (1982). *Cultural awareness in the human services.* Englewood Cliffs, NJ: Prentice-Hall.

Hareven, T.K. (1989). American families in transition: Historical perspectives on change. In A.S. Skolnick & J.H. Skolnick (Eds.), *Family in transition* (6th Ed), pp. 39-57. Boston: Scott, Foresman and Co.

Heller, K., Price, R.H., Reinharz, S., Riger, S., & Wandersman, A. (1984). *Psychology and community change.* Homewood, IL: Dorsey Press.

Imber-Black, E. (1988). *Families and larger systems: A family therapist's guide through the labyrinth.* NY: Guilford Press.

Jurich, A.P., Smith, W.M., Polson, C.J. (1983). Families and social problems: Uncovering reality in rural America. In R.T. Coward & W.M. Smith (Eds.), *Family services*, pp. 41-66. Lincoln, NE: University of Nebraska Press.

Kamerman, S.B. (1985). Young, poor, and a mother alone: Problems and possible solutions. In H. McAdoo & T.M. Parham (Eds.), *Services to young families*, pp. 1-38. Washington, D.C.: American Public Welfare Association.

Kanter, R.M. (1977). *Work and family in the United States: A critical review and agenda for research and policy.* NY: Russell Sage Foundation.

Karp, D.A., Stone, G.P., & Yoels, W.C. (1977). *Being urban.* Lexington, MA: D.C. Heath.

Keniston, K. (1977). *All our children.* NY: Harcourt Brace Yovanovich.

Kessen, W., & Fein, G. (1975). *Variations in home-based infant education: Language, play and social development.* New Haven, CT: Yale University (ERIC Document Reproduction Service No. ED 118233).

Larzelere, R.E. & Klein, D.M. (1987). Methodology. In M.B. Sussman & S. Steinmetz (Eds.), *Handbook of marriage and the family* (p. 125-155). NY: Plenum.

Lightfoot, S.L. (1978). *Worlds apart: Relationships between families and schools.* NY: Basic Books.

Litwak, E. & Meyer, H.J. (1974). *School, family and neighborhood: The theory and practice of school-community relations*. NY: Columbia University Press.

McMillan, D.W. & Chavis, D.M. (1986). Sense of community: A definition and theory. *Journal of Community Psychology, 14*, 6-23.

Milardo, R.M. (1988). Families and social networks: An overview of theory and methodology. In R.M. Milardo (Ed.), *Families and social networks*, pp. 13-47. Beverly Hills, CA: Sage.

Mortimer, J.T. & London, J. (1984). The varying linkages of work and family. In P. Voydanoff (Ed.), *Work and family: Changing roles of men and women*, pp. 20-35. Palo Alto, CA: Mayfield.

Ogbu, J.U. (1988). A Commentary. In S.F. Hamilton, *The interaction of family, community, and work in the socialization of youth*. NY: William T. Grant Foundation.

Pence, A.R. (Ed.). (1988). *Ecological research with children and families*. NY: Teachers College Press.

Piotrkowsku, C.S., Rapoport, R.N., & Rapoport, R. (1987). Families and work. In M.B. Sussman & S. Steinmetz (Eds.), *Handbook of marriage and the family*, pp. 251-283. NY: Plenum.

Powell, D.R. (1979). Family-environment relations and early childrearing: The role of social networks and neighborhoods. *Journal of research and Development in Education, 13*, 1-11.

Powell, D.R. (1984). Social network and demographic predictors of length of participation in a parent education program. *Journal of Community Psychology, 12*, 13-20.

Powell, D.R. & Eisenstadt, J. (1983). Predictors of help-seeking in an urban setting: The search for child care. *American Journal of Community Psychology, 11*, 401-422.

Ramey, J. (1978). Experimental family forms. *Marriage and Family Review, 1*, 1-9.

Reiss, D. & Klein, D. (1987). Paradigm and pathogenesis: A family-centered approach to problems of etiology and treatment of psychiatric disorders. In T. Jacob (Ed.), *Family interaction and psychopathology* (p. 203-255). NY: Plenum.

Reiss, D. & Oliveri, M.E. (1983). Family stress as community frame. In H.I. McCubbin, M.B. Sussman, & J.M. Patterson (Eds.), *Social stress and the family*, pp. 61-83. NY: Haworth Press.

Sarason, S.B. (1972). *The creation of settings and the future societies*. San Francisco: Jossey-Bass.

Schwartzman, H.B. & Kneifel, A.W. (1985). Familiar institutions: How the child care system replicates family patterns. In J. Schwartzman (Ed.), *Families and other systems: The macrosystemic context of family therapy*, pp. 87-107. NY: Guilford Press.

Selig, A. (1976). The myth of the multiproblem family. *American Journal of Orthopsychiatry, 4*, 526-532.

Shinn, M. (1987). Expanding community psychology's domain. *American Journal of Community Psychology, 15,* 555-574.

Steinberg, L., Catalano, R., & Dooley, D. (1981). Economic antecedents of child abuse and neglect. *Child Development, 52,* 975-985.

Sussman, M.B. (1977). Family, bureaucracy, and the elderly individual: An organizational/linkage perspective. In E. Shanas & M.B. Sussman (Eds.), *Family, bureaucracy, and the elderly,* pp. 2-20. Durham, NC: Duke University Press.

Sussman, M.B. (1972). Family, kinship, and bureaucracy. In A. Campbell & P.E. Converse (Eds.), *The human meaning of social change,* pp.127-158. NY: Russell Sage Foundation.

Sussman, M.B. & Burchinal, L. (1962). Kin family network: Unheralded structure in current conceptualizations of family functioning. *Marriage and Family Living, 24,* 231-240.

Tremblay, K.R., Walker, F.S., & Dillman, D.A. (1983). The quality of life experienced by rural families. In R.T. Coward & W.M. Smith, Jr. (Eds.), *Family services,* pp. 26-40. Lincoln, NE: University of Nebraska Press.

Unger, D.G. & Nelson, P. (1989, June) *The community context of parenting: Empowering parents.* Paper presented at the Biennia Community Research and Action Conference, East Lansing, MI.

Unger, D.G. & Powell, D.R. (1979). Supporting families under stress: The role of social networks. *Family Relations, 29,* 566-574.

Unger, D.G. & Wandersman, A. (1985). The importance of neighbors: The social, cognitive and affective components of neighboring. *American Journal of Community Psychology, 13,* 139-170.

Unger, D.G. & Wandersman, L.P. (1988). A support program for adolescent mothers: Predictors of participation. In D.R. Powell (Ed.), *Parent education as early childhood intervention.*, pp. 105-130. Norwood, NJ: Ablex.

Voydanoff, P. (1983). Unemployment: Strategies for family adaptation. In C.R. Figley & H.I. McCubbin (Eds.), *Stress and the Family, V.II: Catastrophic Stressors,* pp. 90-102. NY: Brunner Mazel.

Wandersman, A., Jakubs, J.F., & Giamartino, G.A. (1981). Participation in block organizations. *Community Action, 1,* 40-47.

Warren, R.B. & Warren, D.I. (1977). *The neighborhood organizer's handbook.* Notre Dame, IN: University of Notre Dame Press.

Wellman, B. (1979). The community question: The intimate networks of East Yonkers. *American Journal of Sociology, 84,* 1201-1231.

Wellman, B. (1981). The application of network analysis to the study of support. In B. Gottlieb (Ed.), *Social networks and social support,* pp. 171-200. Beverly Hills: Sage.

Wicker, A.W. (1979). *An introduction to ecological psychology.* Belmont, CA: Wadsworth.

Williams, K. (1988). Cultural diversity in family support: Black families. In S.L. Kagan, D.R. Powell, B. Weissbourd, & E.F. Zigler (Eds.), *America's family support programs* (p. 295-307). New Haven, CT: Yale University Press.

The Community Context of Child Abuse and Neglect

Joan I. Vondra

Abuse and neglect of children and youth in this country occurs daily. It occurs in the privacy of the home and in formal institutional settings including schools, day care centers, shelters, and detention centers. It occurs among the most destitute and among the wealthiest of families. Although many would prefer to view child abuse and neglect as relationship or family problems, it is increasingly clear that they are also community problems. This paper will consider the role of community in the incidence, identification, and prevention of child maltreatment.

By now, there are few communities in which children have not been reported for some form of maltreatment. Of nearly 2,100,000 children reported one or more times for child abuse and neglect in 1986 (American Humane Association, 1988), 55% were reported for neglect (defined as deprivation of necessities), 28% were reported for major or minor physical injury, and 16% were reported for sexual abuse. At least 17% of these reports involved more than one form of maltreatment, and it is arguable that every case involved emotional maltreatment (Garbarino & Vondra, 1987).

Community concern for child maltreatment is evident in the fact that the largest proportion of reports (34%) originated from friends, neighbors, relatives, or the perpetrator. School personnel and childcare providers accounted for another 18% of the reports. Whether it is neighbors, law enforcement officers, or medical personnel who alert officials to the possibility that a child is being maltreated, they are almost always members (functional, if not residing, members) of the same neighborhood or community as the perpetrator. Identification of maltreated children, in other words, is a function of the community. So too, however, is the incidence of child maltreatment.

Significantly, both the number and the severity of cases are greatest among those who are *poorest* off, in economic, social, and psychological terms (Pelton, 1978). Furthermore, physical neglect is the single most predominant form of child maltreatment, and it is most closely linked to social and economic conditions. Cases characterized by notable poverty, social deprivation, and chaotic living conditions most often come to the attention of community agencies, and represent at least half the cases documented nationally. It should be noted, however, that the incidence of sexual abuse continues to increase, and that this form of maltreatment is *least* associated with either family poverty or a perpetrator who is a member of the immediate family.

A number of common risk factors, many of them relevant at a community-level analysis, characterize families involved in and circumstances surrounding maltreatment. Together, these risk factors and the dynamics that cause them to converge in a powerful negative cycle comprise what some have termed the "ecology of child maltreatment" (Belsky, 1980; Garbarino, 1977). Consistent with both the empirical literature and the incidence data, discussion of risk factors will focus on parents and stepparents who demonstrate inadequacies of caregiving that range from persistent failure to meet the psychological and developmental needs of their children to briefer incidents of life-threatening behavior.

THE ECOLOGY OF CHILD MALTREATMENT

Understanding the necessary and sufficient causes of maltreatment requires consideration of broad and interacting sets of factors that contribute to individual instances of abusive behavior or, more commonly, a pattern of chronic emotional maltreatment and neglect of the physical and/or psychological needs of the developing infant, child, or adolescent. These factors arise from within and outside the family, converging to create a family situation characterized by both extreme need and an inability to develop or maintain the external supports that could help bolster this fragile system. Indeed, research has consistently demonstrated that recurrent maltreatment is *not* the outcome of any single factor—whether parental psychopathology or maltreatment history, child temperamental or behavioral deviance, marital conflict or violence, economic hardship and job stress, inadequate social supports, or sociocultural mores that encourage punitive, authoritarian parenting (Belsky & Vondra, 1989).

Nevertheless, by examining each factor in turn, it becomes clearer how these multiple factors interact and coalesce to produce circumstances conducive to abusive and/or neglectful parenting. In this sense, the focus is on an "ecology" of child maltreatment—the etiological context that is shaped by an interaction of *both* individual and environmental characteristics.

Social and Economic Factors

In a series of analyses aimed at community-wide influences on family functioning, Garbarino (1976; Garbarino & Crouter, 1978; Garbarino & Sherman, 1980) demonstrated how the concept of "risk" could be applied at the community level. Rates of child maltreatment could be predicted across different communities on the basis of family income, presence of single-parent households, transience of residents, and number of working mothers with young children. Even when communities were comparable in socioeconomic level and demographic character, they often differed considerably in rates of child maltreatment. These differences were associated with a number of indices of social impoverishment *among* families from high-risk neighborhoods and with poorer evaluations of the neighborhood *by* these same families as "a place to raise children."

Whether socially and economically deprived families migrate to poor neighborhoods to obtain cheap housing, or are left behind when families with resources desert declining neighborhoods, the neediest families reside in communities with the fewest resources. Relevant community "quality of life" markers here include high-quality childcare and education, recreational facilities, libraries . . . and the organization and participation of neighborhood members. Not only are these elements typically lacking in "risk" neighborhoods, but the high cost and unavailability of public transportation usually represents an additional form of deprivation and isolation. When families in need then come to depend upon a limited circle of needy others for resources, the resulting resource drain may put an end to "neighborly" exchanges of goods and services (Stack, 1974) . . . and ultimately, a sense of community.

Given these circumstances, it is not surprising that families in high-risk neighborhoods perceive their communities to be less caring and less connected in a social sense. Whereas only 8% of families in a low-risk neighborhood of Garbarino's study reported "never engaging in neighborhood exchanges," some 32% of families in a high-risk neighborhood reported the same (Garbarino & Sherman, 1980). Families in the high-risk neighborhood also reported fewer individuals whom they felt took an interest in their children, and fewer neighborhood children who served as regular playmates for them. What is lacking in these neighborhoods, in other words, is a sense of community involvement, mutual caring, and social cohesion.

Social Support and Social Isolation

It is critical to point out that a neighborhood at risk is, in part, an outcome of individuals and families at risk. Data on maltreating families support this contention. Social isolation is perhaps the single most common finding of studies comparing maltreating families with low-income comparisons (Egeland & Brunnquell, 1979; Kotelchuck, 1982; see also Garbarino & Gilliam, 1980). Crittenden (1985) suggests, however, that social *isolation* — a pattern of few friends, short-term friendships, and dissatisfaction with relations with kin — may be more characteristic of neglectful parents, whereas social *conflict* — arising from enmeshed, asymmetric relationships involving over- or underdependency on both friends and relatives—may be more characteristic of abusive parents. In either case, the low-income, high-risk families most in need of instrumental and emotional support from friends, neighbors, and community (Stack, 1974), are the least likely to have (or at least perceive that they have) the kind of interpersonal ties that provide support.

Inadequate social support undermines the functioning of parents, both as individuals and as caregivers. Parents need the emotional support and instrumental assistance furnished by social networks for their own day-to-day functioning and feelings of well-being (Colletta, 1983; Levitt, Weber, & Clark, 1986; Whittaker & Garbarino, 1983). These needs are compounded when childcare demands add to the burden of meeting personal and familial needs. Parents who are dissatisfied with the support provided by friends, neighbors, and relatives tend to be dissatisfied with their caregiving role, to engage in less optimal caregiving, and to provide a poorer quality home environment for children (Crnic, Greenberg, Ragozin, Robinson, & Basham, 1983; Stevens, 1988).

Dissatisfaction with social network support, less contact with friends, more exclusive contact with relatives who are likely to be needy themselves, and greater reliance on institutional support agencies are common patterns in at-risk and/or actively maltreating families (Colletta, 1983; Crittenden, 1985). They highlight the possibility of selection factors at work when these same families are found in the least supportive of neighborhoods, and/or perceive those around them as uncaring and unsupportive. Crittenden (1985) noted that the maltreating mothers of her study were "likely to avoid or offend potential sources of help" (p. 1310). Egeland and his colleagues (Egeland, Breitenbucher, & Rosenberg, 1980) put it this way: "These [mothers who provide inadequate care] were reported to be easily frustrated and annoyed and quick to respond to their frustration in a hostile and aggressive fashion. They tended to annoy and alienate their families and friends rather than using these relationships to help in dealing with problems and crises" (p.203). The existence of high-risk communities may, in part, reflect the presence of high-risk parents who have difficulty in developing and maintaining health-promoting social bonds.

In addition to offering limited social support, Garbarino (& Gilliam, 1980; & Sherman, 1980) suggests that the social networks of maltreating families fail to provide the social control functions that would normally set limits on extremes of parental behavior. The social cohesion these families and communities lack is in some ways a prerequisite for social control. In the absence of interpersonal trust and informal social visits and exchanges, neighbors have less opportunity to observe what goes on in a maltreating home and fewer chances to offer suggestions or feedback. Thus, the impoverished social relations of maltreating families offer neither positive standards or role models (Cochran & Brassard, 1979) nor any lifeline or safety net to families in need.

Social Class and Socioeconomic Status

The majority of chronically maltreating families fall within the lowest social echelons (Pelton, 1978). Economic, sociocultural, and interpersonal factors act jointly in these families to create a situation of severe economic stress, hardship, and dependency that has been cited as the single greatest threat to adequate family functioning (Garbarino & Gilliam, 1980; Gil, 1970; Siegal, 1982).

Decades of research support the link between low socioeconomic status and styles of childrearing that emphasize authoritarian control, encouragement of conformity, and punitive disciplinary techniques, all of which increase the probability of child maltreatment. Lower-class mothers of below-average education are consistently found to provide home environments and to employ childrearing strategies associated with poorer developmental functioning and lower educational achievement among children (e.g., Bradley & Caldwell, 1984; Bronfenbrenner, 1958; Kohn, 1977).

Parental job characteristics and work conditions have also been related to styles of parenting likely to contribute to the perpetuation of low-status employment across generations. In particular, when parents hold jobs that emphasize subordination to authority and offer little self-direction, they tend to emphasize authoritarian values of compliance, conformity, and physical punishment with their children at home (Mortimer & Kumka, 1982; Piotrkowski & Katz, 1982; see also Bronfenbrenner & Crouter, 1982).

Job loss and economic instability, circumstances likely to exist in families reported for maltreatment (Gil, 1970; Steinberg, Catalano,

& Dooley, 1981), may be especially detrimental to family function-ing (Elder, Nguyen, & Caspi, 1985; Lempers, Clark-Lempers, & Simons, 1989). Increased irritability, conflict, and physical punish-ment are common parental responses to economic stressors. As Siegal (1982) notes, "Perhaps there is no better single example of the importance of studying the socioeconomic conditions underly-ing parent-child relations than child abuse" (p. 16). Child maltreat-ment and family social *and* economic impoverishment often go hand in hand (Pelton, 1978; Straus, Gelles, & Steinmetz, 1980).

Socioeconomic conditions and resources for economically dis-tressed families have obvious community links. In depressed areas, unemployment — especially among minority families and those of low SES — may be a pervasive and relatively enduring family cir-cumstance. Support services for families may be overburdened and underfunded . . . or absent altogether. Job-training programs, day-care facilities, low-cost housing, and substance abuse centers may be inadequate to serve the individual and collective needs of the community, or may be out of reach of families with limited access to transportation. Furthermore, reliance on these institutionalized support services in the absence of or lack of participation in *infor-mal* support services based in churches, youth groups, and other neighborhood networks may have an undermining effect on paren-tal or family functioning (Colletta, 1983). Family social and eco-nomic empowerment, as opposed to dependency, may depend on a combination of formal and informal support (Miller & Whittaker, 1988). Research suggests that competent child functioning in the context of family and community poverty is linked to an active sense of family embedded in strong church ties and strict family rules (Baldwin, Baldwin, & Cole, in press).

Sociocultural Values and Mores

Many have argued persuasively that maltreatment of children is predicated on sociocultural mores that condone the use of physical force and that view children as private property (Garbarino, Stock-ing, & Associates 1980; Gil, 1970; Zigler, 1981). The notion that parents have the right to rear children as they see fit, in the privacy of their home, is a deeply-rooted tradition in American history.

Public scrutiny and, worse, public intervention into private lives are almost universally frowned upon. However, the combination of this zealous defense of family privacy with the belief that children are the property of their parents, opens the way for child victimization (Garbarino, 1977). In the context of high-volume expression of violence in the media, the probability that child care will drift into child maltreatment no doubt increases proportionately.

Societal factors also play a role in the fact that a disproportionate number of the children reported for maltreatment nationally (one third) are from single, female-headed households (American Humane Association, 1988). The increasing proportion of such families now living below the poverty line is well-documented. On the one hand, economic pressures send both willing and reluctant low-income mothers into the full-time job market, typically into lower-status, lower-paying jobs that help to perpetuate economic hardship. At the same time, it is expected that the full-time employed mother should continue to function as the full-time housekeeper and childcare provider. Quality—or even reliable—childcare services are either unavailable or unaffordable in many communities. At a societal level, fathers are neither expected nor required, for the most part, to take an equal role in household labor and in childrearing when present in the home, or to support their families in real financial terms when absent. Among the population of young, low-income, black fathers, the demoralization and powerlessness of chronic unemployment may preclude family support even when there is willingness to become involved.

Each of these larger social issues represents a community risk condition for family functioning. The availability and quality of substitute childcare, the presence of parents to care for children in the home after school, the proportion of single-parent households, mean family income, and crime and delinquency rates have all been used as indices of the quality of the community as a context for healthy childrearing (Garbarino, 1982). Whether or not individual families "select" themselves into socially impoverished neighborhoods—and certainly when parents are lacking psychological resources and/or interpersonal skills—opportunities for community support need to be more abundant and more accessible, not less so.

Parental Psychological Functioning

Within the maltreating family, interpersonal difficulties and/or disturbances have been found to characterize multiple family members as well as multiple family relationships. Maltreating adults appear to share a common history characterized by insecure, unstable, and/or pathological relations with their parent(s) (Altemeier, O'Connor, Vietze, Sandler, & Sherrod, 1982; Engfer & Schneewind, 1982; Rutter, Quinton, & Liddle, 1983). Impoverished relations are typically reflected in other intimate relationships as well. Of particular importance are deficiencies in relations of maltreating parents with spouses and partners (Engfer & Gavranidou, 1988; Rosenbaum & O'Leary, 1981; Straus et al., 1980). The instability of intimate partner relationships often noted among maltreating parents has been related in non-clinical samples to less adequate parental care and less optimal child development (Crockenberg, 1987; Pianta, Egeland, & Hyatt, 1986). Taken together, these and other findings strongly suggest that attachment issues form the crux of the maltreating family's interpersonal problems (Crittenden & Ainsworth, 1989; DeLozier, 1982).

Not every child who experiences even severe attachment disruptions or disturbances, however, will mistreat or even have troubled relations with his or her own children. Retrospective prediction to maltreatment is invariably more accurate than is prospective prediction. A childhood history of troubled attachment relations can, for example, serve as the basis for *rejecting* harsh parental attitudes and practices. Indeed, data suggest that open acknowledgement and criticism of painful attachment experiences may be the "decoupling" mechanism that halts the progression of disturbed parent-child relations (including official "maltreatment") across the generations (Main & Goldwyn, 1984).

Generally, however, as a result of preexisting attachment issues, the maltreating parent will be less effective in coping with day-to-day difficulties and, perhaps more importantly, in garnering the support needed to buffer the resulting stresses. The deficits in support will likely be manifest in the quality of marital/intimate relationships established, in the ability to develop and maintain close, supportive friendships, and in the ability to use formal and informal community resources effectively.

An additional implication of this attachment perspective are the alternative strategies of coping with stress that these parents may be likely to use. In the absence of close, stable relationships with others, parents already at risk for child maltreatment may be especially vulnerable to substance abuse as a means for combatting stress, anxiety, and depression. Although the evidence for causal links between alcohol abuse, for example, and child maltreatment is equivocal (Epstein, 1977; Orme & Rimmer, 1981), it is not the case that substance abuse has no bearing on child abuse and neglect. This is especially true when one considers the potentially more damaging experience of emotional maltreatment, arising from very inconsistent, hostile or withdrawn, and verbally abusive care by addicted parents (Russel, Henderson, & Blume, 1985). Experiences of this sort may never make it to the official report filed on a family, or may not be reported to authorities at all. Thus, reporting statistics may say little about both the role of alcohol and drugs in the lives of maltreating families and the impact of alcohol and drugs on the lives of many other children from families at risk.

CONSIDERATIONS FOR INTERVENTION

In view of the attachment issues just indicated, "normal" stresses associated with poverty, low social status, and joblessness are likely to be magnified in their impact on parents who lack or feel they lack support. So too are the stresses of raising children with behavior problems resulting from poor care (including prenatal care). If personality characteristics such as anxiety, depression, and negative affectivity (Watson & Clark, 1984) are adult manifestations of attachment disturbances, then almost any negative circumstance or event may well be magnified in its impact.

At the same time, resources that *are* available on an individual, relational, and community level may be ignored or misused. This is abundantly evident from the intervention literature. Successful intervention with chronically maltreating families is typically accomplished with only the most active, persistent, and coordinated mobilization of services (see Cicchetti & Toth, 1987; Fraiberg, 1980;

Greenspan et al., 1987). Part of the difficulty is a direct result of the hostility, avoidance, and reluctance of maltreating parents to be engaged by helping professionals. The infrequent success stories, both at the prevention and remediation levels, almost invariably seem to be linked to approaches that bring empathic, non-threatening service providers into the home for regular visits (e.g., Olds & Henderson, 1989; Whittaker, 1986).

Community-based programs of support may have to reach out persistently to overcome initial skepticism, resistance, and mistrust on an individual level to secure participation (Fraiberg, 1980). The most effective resources, therefore, may be those that promote *and help maintain* informal social ties within the community (Whittaker & Garbarino, 1983). Miller and Whittaker (1988) describe a number of family support programs blending professional and "lay" services that have been successful in providing social support to families and reducing the risk of child maltreatment. These programs serve to strengthen already existing, "natural" support networks available to families, and/or to cultivate new social resources through such avenues as self-help groups, skills training, and personalized connections with service agencies.

Family service providers need access to a variety of basic social services that can be offered to families in need. Substance abuse treatment programs, shelters for battered women, crisis nurseries and low-cost childcare services, unemployment agencies and job-training programs, health clinics, and temporary housing facilities are some examples. But few of these services may be utilized if a trusted spokesperson for the family is not on hand to enlist parental cooperation and guide family members through the intricacies of the system. The "Homebuilders" program model (Whittaker, 1986) has effectively demonstrated how such coordination and personalization of services can be accomplished. Part of its success has been in meeting the interpersonal challenges of "connecting" socially disconnected families to formal and informal support systems. The success of other family and community interventions also depends on meeting these challenges.

> To break [the] cycle of destructive family-community relationships and to encourage the community to assume a more re-

sponsible and responsive role toward families, we need to intervene on the community level: first, to stop the social amplification of high risk and maltreatment; and second, to utilize the community resources on behalf of intervention with families . . . In a cost-benefit sense, the gains to communities that adopt an active role in developing a coordinated, comprehensive approach to reducing . . . maltreatment will be measured in the healthy growth and development of their children. (Garbarino, Guttmann, and Seeley, 1986, pp.156-178)

The foregoing principles are equally relevant from a prevention standpoint. Both the number and breadth of factors placing families at risk, and the difficulty of creating and maintaining long-term change in maltreating families, argue for implementing family support strategies on a broader scale. "Mini-interventions" requiring minimal institutional cost and effort that could be incorporated into the workplace, the school system, day-care centers, hospitals and clinics, and family planning agencies have been proposed as another strategy for "reaching out" to a wider segment of the population (Belsky & Vondra, 1989; Garbarino, 1982). An advantage to this approach is its routine application to *all* families during periods of stress or transition, thereby avoiding "risk" analyses that label individuals or families. More intensive efforts may then be targeted at those in greatest need, without ignoring families that would benefit from only temporary support and encouragement.

Whether the focus is prevention *or* treatment, the vehicle for successful efforts are social connections that begin at the individual level and broaden to encompass the larger community. When community programs and services—ranging from well-baby clinics to technical training projects—expand and enhance opportunities for individualized social connections and for signals of caring to families on an individual level, each contact becomes a mini-intervention. It is at this level that individuals and families develop a sense of investment in the neighborhood and community, and at this level, initially, that community social support translates into social cohesion within the community. In the following section, this approach is illustrated within a primary community-level setting, the local school system.

The Role of the Schools

If identifying children who may be experiencing abuse and neglect is a community enterprise, it is also, to a considerable extent, a school enterprise (Garbarino & Gilliam, 1980). The largest proportion of reports nationally from any single professional source were provided by school personnel. School personnel and childcare providers accounted for some 18% of all reports, in contrast with law enforcers, who accounted for only 13%, and medical personnel, who accounted for 11% (American Humane Association, 1988). Yet the most recent National Incidence Study indicates that the former are *least* likely to report the cases they identify (Westat Associates, 1987). Training and advocacy efforts need to focus more on educational and childcare professionals.

Both schools and daycare centers are in a unique position to identify children who show physical and/or behavioral evidence of mistreatment. Child symptomology indicative of dysfunctional family relationships and/or maltreatment can be quite pronounced (see Garbarino et al., 1986). By preschool age, for example, it is already possible to distinguish maltreated children by deficits and abnormalities in their social interactions with peers and adults (George & Main, 1979; Hoffman-Plotkin & Twentyman, 1984). By school age, these children also demonstrate poorer cognitive and academic performance, are more likely to be retained a grade or receiving special educational services, and have lower self-esteem than low-income peers (Barahal, Waterman, & Martin, 1981; Oates, Forrest, & Peacock, 1985; Vondra, Barnett, & Cicchetti, 1988, 1989).

Troubled and/or disruptive children performing poorly in school are often fairly accurate indicators of troubled or disturbed relationships at home. Teachers and other school staffpersons who deal with the children regularly, and have at least occasional opportunities to interact with family members, are often aware of problems in the home. In extreme cases, at least, we know they file maltreatment reports. On the other hand, they are also in a position to identify families in need, and to foster initial links with troubled, isolated families. Without burdening already overburdened systems, it is still possible to connect schools and daycare centers more effectively into coordinated community social services (Garbarino & Gilliam, 1980).

Referrals to family support programs, information about community resources for parents and children, modeling of behavior management strategies and other useful childcare techniques, and efforts to encourage parents to make school/center contacts are all small ways to begin drawing troubled families into the community. When teachers, counselors, daycare center directors, and childcare providers have ties to family support programs — perhaps fostered through instruction and demonstration in-service modules — their efforts can be supported and expanded by others. No one individual is then expected to work unaided at developing and maintaining what may be some of the first tenuous links between a struggling, resistant parent or family and the neighborhood resources.

The potential for schools — and for communities — to serve as a coordinated support system for *prevention* of child maltreatment is even more unlimited. An innovative program in Philadelphia, called "Education for Parenting," (Heath & Meyer, 1988) offers just one example. In addition to parent education for adults, Education for Parenting has established model parent education programs in selected private and city schools. These involve trained volunteer teachers and several hundred students from kindergarten through eighth grade. The school programs provide modeling and hands-on experience in caring for infants and toddlers, in learning about the responsibilities of parenthood, and in understanding child development. Similarly innovative programs have been developed to assist teen parents in completing school *and* improving their parenting skills, to involve teen and adult fathers in the early care of their infants, and to bring parents in need together with experienced parents in the community (see Weiss & Jacobs, 1988).

There is no dearth of creative prevention/enhancement programs instituted at the family and community levels. The issue is to make such programs *routinely* available in every community, forging the links with parents and families who wouldn't otherwise participate, and coordinating whatever human services are already available to bring them to those in need. It is not enough for a community to have its arsenal of formal programmatic resources. It is the bonds between individuals, families, and social institutions, it is the perceived opportunities for individual growth and family cohesion, and it is the collective sense of responsibility for child care and child rearing that determine whether a community will contribute to an ecology of family health or an ecology of child maltreatment.

DIRECTIONS FOR FUTURE RESEARCH

Numerous approaches have been described for enhancing community support for families. Many have been implemented in one form or another, often on a small scale and in an isolated, sometimes haphazard, manner. Much more limited, however, is the availability of rigorous data demonstrating not only *whether* a particular intervention works, but *when* and *how* it does so. Until there is greater collaboration between those who design and implement such programs and those who have the knowledge and skills to assess them, the initiative, funding, and commitment to operate these programs systematically will remain elusive.

Even at the most basic level of understanding, there are unanswered questions about the relative effectiveness of community-based interventions. Can single programs make a discernable group difference or will changes come about only as a result of cumulative and/or coordinated interventions? Can one generate the community support that fosters active church involvement, effective social networking, and participation in human service programs in high-risk neighborhoods, or does support of this kind emerge only in the context of already existing family and community strengths? Does an emphasis on individualized services coordinated through a single contact person make a measurable difference in encouraging families to use the resources that are available?

Applied research that is linked with program models would be an invaluable contribution to the field. A pilot effort to open a school-based day care center, for example, offers an ideal opportunity to study the impact of a "practicum in parenting" for school-age children and adolescents. A program model introducing case conferences in the school that utilize representatives from schools, family support programs, and child welfare agencies can provide data about the effectiveness of training teachers to identify children at risk. It can also serve as a vehicle for basic research about the incidence of family disturbance among children identified for school behavior problems. Implementation of an institutional or community-wide "mini-intervention" allows researchers to assess not only improved functioning of individuals and families considered at low-risk for disturbances, but also improved identification and referral of families at higher risk.

In every case, the greatest profit is gained when there is active collaboration between researcher and practitioner. By joining forces early in the planning stages, a more convincing case can be offered to funding agencies, a better designed program can be instituted, and more useful information can be gained and disseminated. Practitioners considering program development or change should be active in seeking out research collaborators; applied researchers should maintain vital working networks with the service community. Together, their efforts are significantly more potent for both research and real-life communities than either could be in isolation . . . and neither community can afford lost opportunities.

REFERENCES

Altemeier, W.A., O'Connor, S., Vietze, P.M., Sandler, H.M., & Sherrod, K.B. (1982). Antecedents of child abuse. *Journal of Pediatrics, 100*, 823-829.

American Humane Association (1988). *Highlights of official child neglect and abuse reporting, 1986*. Denver, CO: The American Humane Association.

Baldwin, A., Baldwin, C., & Cole, R.E. (in press). Stress-resistant families and stress-resistant children. In J. Rolf, A. Masten, D. Cicchetti, K. Neuchtherlin, & S. Weintraub (Eds.), *Risk and protective factors in the development of psychopathology*.

Barahal, R.M., Waterman, J., & Martin, H.P. (1981). The social cognitive development of abused children. *Journal of Consulting and Clinical Psychology, 49*, 508-516.

Belsky, J. (1980). Child maltreatment: An ecological integration. *American Psychologist, 35*, 320-335.

Belsky, J. & Vondra, J. (1989). Lessons from child abuse: The determinants of parenting. In D. Cicchetti & V.K. Carlson (Eds.), *Child maltreatment: Theory and research on the causes and consequences of child abuse and neglect*. New York: Cambridge University Press.

Bradley, R.H. & Caldwell, B.M. (1984). 174 children: A study of the relationship between home environment and cognitive development during the first five years. In A.W. Gottfried (Ed.), *Home environment and early cognitive development* (pp. 5-56). New York: Academic Press.

Bronfenbrenner, U. (1958). Socialization and social class through time and space. In E.E. Maccoby, T.M. Newcomb, & E.L. Hartley (Eds.), *Readings in social psychology* (pp. 400-425). New York: Henry Holt.

Bronfenbrenner, U. & Crouter, A.C. (1982). Work and family through time and space. In S.B. Kammerman & C.D. Hayes (Eds.), *Families that work: Children in a changing world* (pp. 39-83). Washington, D.C.: National Academy Press, 1982.

Cicchetti, D. & Toth, S.L. (1987). The application of a transactional risk model to intervention with multi-risk maltreating families. *Zero to Three*, Bulletin of the National Center for Clinical Infant Programs, 7, 1-8.

Cochran, M. & Brassard, J. (1979). Child development and personal social networks. *Child Development, 50*, 601-616.

Colletta, N.D. (1983). At risk for depression: A study of young mothers. *Journal of Genetic Psychology, 142*, 301-310.

Crittenden, P.M. (1985). Social networks, quality of childrearing, and child development. *Child Development, 56*, 1299-1313.

Crittenden, P.M. & Ainsworth, M.D.S. (1989). Attachment and child abuse. In D. Cicchetti & V. Carlson (Eds.), *Child maltreatment: Theory and research on the causes and consequences of abuse and neglect*. New York: Cambridge University Press.

Crnic, K.A., Greenberg, M.T., Ragozin, A.S., Robinson, N.M., & Basham, R.B. (1983). Effects of stress and social support on mothers and premature and full-term infants. *Child Development, 54*, 209-217.

Crockenberg, S. (1987). Predictors and correlates of anger toward and punitive control of toddlers by adolescent mothers. *Child Development, 58*, 964-975.

DeLozier, P.P. (1982). Attachment theory and child abuse. In C.M. Parkes & J. Stevenson-Hinde (Eds.), *The place of attachment in human behavior* (pp. 95-117). New York: Basic Books.

Egeland, B., Breitenbucher, M., & Rosenberg, D. (1980). Prospective study of the significance of life stress in the etiology of child abuse. *Journal of Consulting & Clinical Psychology, 48*, 195-205.

Egeland, B. & Brunnquell, D. (1979). An at-risk approach to the study of child abuse: Some preliminary findings. *Journal of the American Academy of Child Psychiatry, 18*, 219-235.

Elder, G.H., Jr., Nguyen, T.V., & Caspi, A. (1985). Linking family hardship to children's lives. *Child Development, 56*, 361-375.

Engfer, A. & Gavranidou, M. (1988). *Prospective identification of violent mother-child relationships*. Paper presented at the Third European Conference on Developmental Research, Budapest.

Engfer, A. & Schneewind, K.A. (1982). Causes and consequences of harsh parental punishment. *Child Abuse and Neglect, 6*, 129-139.

Epstein, T. (1977). Alcohol and family abuse. In *Alcohol casualties and crime*, NIAAA Report. Rockville, MD: U.S. Department of Health and Human Services, National Institute on Alcohol Abuse and Alcoholism.

Fraiberg, S. (1980). *Clinical studies in infant mental health: The first year*. New York: Basic Books, Inc.

Garbarino, J. (1977). The human ecology of child maltreatment: A conceptual model for research. *Journal of Marriage and the Family, 39*, 721-727. (a)

Garbarino, J. (1977). The price of privacy in the social dynamics of child abuse. *Child Welfare, 56*, 565-575. (b)

Garbarino, J. (1982). *Children and families in the social environment*. New York: Aldine Publishing Company.

Garbarino, J. & Crouter, A.C. (1978). Defining the community context of parent-child relations. *Child Development, 49*, 604-616.

Garbarino, J. & Gilliam, G. (1980). *Understanding abusive families*. Lexington, MA: D.C. Heath & Co.

Garbarino, J., Guttmann, E., & Seeley, J.W. (1986). *The psychologically battered child*. San Francisco: Jossey-Bass.

Garbarino, J. & Sherman, D. (1980). High-risk neighborhoods and high-risk families: The human ecology of child maltreatment. *Child Development, 51*, 188-198.

Garbarino, J., Stocking, S.H., & Associates (1980). *Protecting children from abuse and neglect: Developing and maintaining effective support systems for families*. San Francisco: Jossey-Bass.

Garbarino, J. & Vondra, J. (1987). Psychological maltreatment of children and youth. In M.A. Brassard, R. Germain, & S.N. Hart (Eds.), *The psychological maltreatment of children and youth* (pp. 24-44). New York: Pergamon Press.

George, C. & Main, M. (1979). Social interactions of young abused children: Approach, avoidance, and aggression. *Child Development, 50*, 306-318.

Gil, D. (1970). *Violence against children: Physical child abuse in the United States*. Cambridge, MA: Harvard University Press.

Greenspan, S.I., Wieder, S., Nover, R., Lieberman, A., Lourie, R., & Robinson, M.G. (Eds.) (1987). *Infants in multirisk families*. Madison, WI: International Universities Press.

Heath, H.E. & Meyer, S. (1988). *Learning about parenting, learning to care: A curriculum for elementary students*. Research presented at the Annual Meeting of the National Council on Family Relations, Philadelphia, November.

Hoffman-Plotkin, D. & Twentyman, C.T. (1984). A multimodal assessment of behavioral and cognitive deficits in abused and neglected preschoolers. *Child Development, 55*, 794-802.

Kohn, M.L. (1977). *Class and conformity: A study in values*. Chicago, IL: The University of Chicago Press.

Kotelchuck, M. (1982). Child abuse and neglect: Prediction and misclassification. In R.H. Starr, Jr. (Ed.), *Child abuse prediction* (pp. 66-89). Cambridge, MA: Ballinger Publishing Co.

Lempers, J.D., Clark-Lempers, D., & Simons, R.L. (1989). Economic hardship, parenting, and distress in adolescence. *Child Development, 60*, 25-39.

Levitt, M.J., Weber, R.A., & Clark, M.C. (1986). Social network relationships as sources of maternal support and well-being. *Developmental Psychology, 22*, 310-316.

Main, M. & Goldwyn, R. (1984). Predicting rejection of her infant from mother's representation of her own experience: Implications for the abused-abusing intergenerational cycle. *Child Abuse and Neglect, 8*, 203-217.

Miller, J.L. & Whittaker, J.K. (1988). Social services and social support: Blended programs for families at risk for child maltreatment. *Child Welfare, 67*. 161-174.

Mortimer, J.T. & Kumka, D. (1982). A further examination of the "occupational linkage hypothesis." *The Sociological Quarterly, 23*, 3-16.

Oates, R.K., Forrest, D., & Peacock, A. (1985). Self-esteem of abused children. *Child Abuse and Neglect, 9*, 159-163.

Olds, D.L. & Henderson, C.R. (1989). The prevention of maltreatment. In D. Cicchetti & V. Carlson (Eds.), *Child maltreatment: Theory and research on the causes and consequences of child abuse and neglect*. New York: Cambridge University Press.

Orme, T.C. & Rimmer, J. (1981). Alcoholism and child abuse: A review. *Journal of Studies on Alcohol, 42*, 273-287.

Pelton, L.H. (1978). Child abuse and neglect: The myth of classlessness. *American Journal of Orthopsychiatry, 48*, 608-617.

Pianta, R.C., Egeland, B., & Hyatt, A. (1986). Maternal relationship history as an indicator of developmental risk. *American Journal of Orthopsychiatry, 56*, 385-398.

Piotrkowski, C.S. & Katz, M.H. (1982). Indirect socialization of children: The effects of mothers' jobs on academic behaviors. *Child Development, 53*, 1520-1529.

Rosenbaum, A. & O'Leary, D. (1981). Marital violence: Characteristics of abusive couples. *Journal of Consulting and Clinical Psychology, 49*, 63-71.

Russel, Henderson, & Blume (1985). *Children of alcoholics*. New York: Children of Alcoholics Foundation.

Rutter, M., Quinton, D., & Liddle, C. (1983). Parenting in two generations: Looking backwards and looking forwards. In N. Madge (Ed.), *Families at risk* (pp. 60-98). London: Heinemann.

Siegal, M. (1982). Economic deprivation and the quality of parent-child relations. In *Fairness in children*. New York: Academic Press.

Stack, C.B. (1974). *All our kin: Strategies for survival in a black community*. New York: Harper & Row.

Steinberg, L., Catalano, R., & Dooley, D. (1981). Economic antecedents of child abuse and neglect. *Child Development, 52*, 975-985.

Stevens, J.H. (1988). Social support, locus of control, and parenting in three low-income groups of mothers: Black teenagers, black adults, and white adults. *Child Development, 59*, 635-642.

Straus, M.A., Gelles, R.J., & Steinmetz, S.K. (1980). *Behind closed doors: Violence in the American family*. New York: Anchor Press.

Vondra, J., Barnett, D., & Cicchetti, D. (1988). *Perceived and actual compe-*

tence among maltreated and comparison school children. Unpublished Manuscript, University of Rochester.

Vondra, J., Barnett, D., & Cicchetti, D. (1989). *Child maltreatment and perceived competence in school children.* Research presented at the Biennial Meeting of the Society for Research in Child Development, Kansas City, MO.

Watson, D. & Clark, L.A. (1984). Negative affectivity: The disposition to experience aversive emotional states. *Psychological Bulletin, 96,* 465-490.

Weiss, H. & Jacobs, F. (Eds.) (1988). *Evaluating family programs.* Hawthorne, NY: Aldine Press.

Westat Associates (1987). *Study of National Incidence and Prevalence of Child Abuse and Neglect: Final Report.* Washington, D.C.: National Center on Child Abuse and Neglect, U.S. Department of Health and Human Services.

Whittaker, J.K. (1986). *Improving practice technology for work with high-risk families: Lessons from the "Homebuilders" social work education project.* Seattle, WA: University of Washington.

Whittaker, J.K. & Garbarino, J. (1983). *Social support networks: Informal helping in the human services.* New York: Aldine Publishing Co.

Zigler, E. (1981). Controlling child abuse: Do we have the knowledge or the will? In G. Gerbner, K. Ross, & E. Zigler (Eds.), *Child abuse: An agenda for action.* New York: Oxford University Press.

The Significance of Home
and Homelessness

Leanne G. Rivlin

In 1978, I began a year-long study of Grand Central Terminal in New York City, along with students in the program in which I teach. In the course of our observations of the waiting room and other areas, we found some homeless persons who were spending large portions of their days in the terminal surrounded by their possessions usually in shopping bags. In one case, a large steamer trunk served as a life support system for an elderly man, with a battery-run coffeepot, food, clothing, linen and an assortment of other personal items neatly arranged inside. Even then the homeless were not well-received. Periodically, the terminal's security police would sweep through the waiting room banging their nightsticks against the shoes of sleeping homeless persons. Sitting was permitted, not sleeping.

At that time I did not fully comprehend why these people had no homes. In fact, my interests in nomadic groups and gypsies had led me to believe that these urban nomads had chosen their homeless life style, that they preferred to be on the streets. It took me some time to disabuse myself of these misconceptions. In the intervening years I have seen many different kinds of homeless people in various parts of the world. Since 1984 I have been looking at the ways homeless persons cope with their lives, how they address their basic needs and the supportive communities they have created. Studies of homeless self-help groups (Rivlin & Imbimbo, 1988), research on

This paper reports research that was funded, in part, by a PSC CUNY Research Award (#667474). An earlier version of the paper was presented at the panel on Multidisciplinary and Cross-Cultural Perspectives on Shelter at the annual meeting of the Society for Applied Anthropology, Tampa, FL, April 1988.

39

people's attitudes toward homelessness (Benedict, Shaw & Rivlin, 1988) and work, now in progress, following the lives of homeless families from their time in shelters and after they are rehoused, have provided opportunities to recognize the significance of the loss of a home and what a homeless existence is like.

INCIDENCE OF HOMELESSNESS

The more carefully we look at homeless people their diversity and their skills become apparent. We hear so often of their needs that it becomes easy to take on a stereotypic picture of the people involved. Influenced by the kind of persons the media publicize, there is a common view that most homeless persons are disordered people, former psychiatric patients who are incapable of managing their lives or people unwilling to work. This narrow view is inaccurate, unfair, and dangerous because it leads to simplistic thinking and limited approaches to a very complex issue.

Many different kinds of persons have lost their homes. They include single heads of households, unemployed or underemployed men and women, immigrants (some undocumented), poor elderly, victims of domestic violence, substance abusers, deinstitutionalized psychiatric patients and the so-called "new poor" who have suffered from the double adversity of unemployment and the absence of low-cost housing (Hopper & Hamberg, 1984). Members of minority groups are particularly over-represented among the homeless and families are among the fastest growing group of homeless persons (U.S. Conference of Mayors, 1987).

By the nature of their life styles homeless persons are difficult if not impossible to count. Most statistics either are estimates or rely on counts of the various agencies providing services for homeless persons. But not all homeless persons use public or private services. The figures run as low as those of the much-criticized survey by the U.S. Department of Housing and Urban Development (1984) of between 250,000 and 350,000 homeless per night to the estimates of the total numbers of homeless persons over a year which reach two to three million (see, for example, Axelson & Dail, 1988; Hombs & Snyder, 1982; Hopper & Hamberg, 1984). Perroff (1987) offers a comprehensive critique of the statistical data and the difficulties in counting the homeless population. She points out findings in some of the surveys which suggest that some persons are homeless for a limited period of time while others are homeless occasionally, that is on an "episodic basis" (p. 44). The fluidity of homelessness, its transient nature and the invisibility of homeless persons make both direct and indirect counts of their numbers suspect. The U.S. Bureau of the Census plans a more comprehensive approach to cover the homeless population in their 1990 counts. However, it is unreasonable to expect that they will reach all of the different types of homeless persons that presently exist.

FORMS OF HOMELESSNESS

While recognizing the dangers of categorization, it is helpful to address the diversity of the homeless first by acknowledging that both the distinctions and the statistics are based on the visible homeless. Many of the homeless either are *invisible*, that is, able to pass as people with homes (Rivlin, 1986a; Ropers, 1988), or are *hidden*, able to find temporary, marginal shelter with family or friends. Others are *potentially* homeless, people who have housing but of such poor quality that it is likely to deteriorate to the point where the residents will be forced to leave. This *underhoused* population, in both rural and urban areas, has contributed to the homeless totals over the years.

In earlier work I have found it useful to distinguish different forms of homelessness on the basis of the time dimension that is involved (Rivlin, 1986b). This distinction considers chronic, periodic, temporary and total homelessness.

Chronic homelessness, a type best epitomized by the "Bowery Bum" stereotype. It is a form associated with alcoholism and drugs. These homeless persons, largely males, spend considerable time on the streets begging and hanging out, often in the company of others in a similar state. Generally, they are able to pay for a "flophouse" bed at night. This type of life can be quite social, with communities of men "hanging out" together. This kind of homelessness has existed for many years representing an "underclass" that has been documented by novelists, journalists and historians (see, for example, Allsop, 1967; Jackson, 1987; Kusmer, 1987 & Rabon, 1985).

Periodic homelessness occurs for many different reasons. Personal and family pressures may force people to leave their homes, but the homes are there when the person feels ready to return. Migrant workers experience a form of periodic homelessness when they leave home to follow the crops. Although some have their families with them, and they do have temporary housing provided near the work sites, they are periodically uprooted and their lives and those of their families are disrupted. We might add any people who regularly relocate to this group. The process of moving temporarily creates a kind of homelessness until the new dwelling becomes a home. Military personnel and some corporate executives fall into this group.

Gypsies and nomads may appear to be periodically homeless but their homes travel with them. Their paths generally are habitual ones with familiar places and people along the route. In many cases they have homes in a place to which they regularly return.

Temporary homelessness is limited in time, the result of a "natural" crisis—a hurricane, flood, earthquake, tornado—or a human crisis—a fire, chemical spill, nuclear accident, an eviction for nonpayment of rent or condemnation of a dwelling. If there is sufficient housing stock, a new home can be located. However, today the vacancy rate for inexpensive housing is extremely low in many communities making it near to impossible to find affordable housing.

Moving creates another form of temporary homelessness that exists until roots are established in a new residence. However, once the crisis ends or the new home acquired, people can resume their roles and create or re-create a home. Their roots may be damaged but they are not destroyed, despite the pain that they may suffer. Affiliations with others, friends and family, may help in the adjustment process.

Total homelessness is the most traumatic form. It is both chronic and pervasive, resulting from the complete loss of a home and contacts with the community in situations where the creation of a new home is undermined. The reasons are much the same as those precipitating the temporary, periodic and chronic forms—natural disasters, mental illness, loss of jobs, economic upheavals, family conflicts, condemnation of housing and fires. However, in this case the homebuilding abilities and social and community supports have disappeared along with loss of the home.

In looking at the persons involved we find that children are frequent victims of homelessness. Some of them are part of homeless families but others are on their own. Examining the situation of homeless children on an international scale we find horrendous and increasing numbers — considered to be between 30 million (Agnelli, 1986) and 90 million (Jupp, 1985). These statistics are estimates but there is little doubt of the scale of the problem which we hear of especially in South and Central America, Africa, India, Thailand, Bangladesh and the Philippines. In industrialized countries, most of the street children are "victims of inner-city decay, inherited deprivation, chronic unemployment, impossible housing markets, extraordinarily high divorce rates and claustrophobic stress" (Agnelli, 1986, p. 36).

As we might expect, there are different kinds of homeless children. A widely cited typology applied to the international scale distinguishes "children *on* the street," "children *of* the street" and "*abandoned*" children (Jupp, 1985). Most common are "children *on* the street" estimated at 60% of the total population of homeless children, according to Felsman (1981; 1984). They engage in various forms of work on the streets still maintaining contacts with their families. About 30% of the homeless children live independently with occasional family contacts and are the "children *of* the streets." "*Throwaway*" children constitute about 7% of the total and are the group abandoned by their families. Although they may find some shelter off the streets they do not have the security of stable, long-term homes. It does not seem unreasonable to add to this category youths in the United states who reach 18 years of age while in foster care. Many are left to their own resources once they reach their majority.

In the United States, especially but not exclusively in large cities, there are enormous numbers of children living in shelters, welfare hotels and motels and in their families' automobiles. Runaway children are largely on the streets and in public areas, with the fortunate ones finding places like Covenant House, in New York, the city's largest shelter for runaway children. Many fend for themselves surviving on their earnings as prostitutes or selling drugs, living in the dangerous edges of society, camping out in vacant apartments.

In each of the different forms of homelessness there may be family-like relationships among a few homeless youths but often they are exploited by adults such as violent pimps and drug dealers. For the runaways an extraordinary and very sad profile can be found. Here, too, the image of a voluntary nomad, a adventurer can be put to rest. Most runaways have been identified as "victims" of "dysfunctional" family units and are running away from threatening and stressful situations (Hersch, 1988). They are escaping from physical and sexual violence, drug- and alcohol-abusing parents and many are children who literally have been thrown out of their homes. It has been estimated that there are between 20,000 and 40,000 runaway and homeless adolescents in New York City and as many as 1.2 million in the United States (Hersch, 1988). The increasing numbers challenge the view that children and youths — indeed all people — have a right to a stable, safe and secure home, nourishment, schooling, health care and protection. The absence of these basic necessities has serious consequences that need to be addressed.

THE LOSS OF A HOME

Losing one's home is a profoundly, traumatic situation. Regardless of the quality of the housing, a person's home is the central organizing structure for the stream of activities that constitute a life. For children this loss is most threatening since it occurs at a time when they are developing a sense of themselves, of their identity, of what they are capable of doing and of their own self-worth. The lack of consistency of setting threatens the acquisition of personal identity for children and challenges the identity and strength of adults.

From many different sources, we are aware that loss of a home is painful. These range from images of the agonized faces of victims of fire, floods and earthquakes that leap at us from newspapers and television to the research on urban relocation as a result of various slum clearance projects, all over the world. Fried's study of the reactions of residents of Boston's West End who were relocated because of urban renewal found depression and grief expressed by many as a result of the destruction of their neighborhood (Fried, 1963). Even for people placed in housing that planners considered to be superior to what they had before, the sense of loss remained. This same kind of reaction has been identified by other researchers (Marris, 1961; 1975; Willmott & Young, 1966; Young & Willmott, 1957). Although most people are able to establish new homes in time, the power of the original sense of loss must be acknowledged. Why loss of a home is so devastating relates to the significance of settings to people.

THE SIGNIFICANCE OF SETTINGS

In recognizing the significance of settings it is important to remind ourselves that all experiences are grounded in places, settings filled with people, objects, vegetation, animals, with sights, smells, sounds, tastes and textures. In psychology, an emphasis has been placed either on the human participants or on minute stimuli in the environment. The physical qualities are also components of a person's lifeworld, but they often have been overlooked. From the time of birth, and even before, people's surroundings influence their lives, their personalities, their cognitive, social, and emotional development. While it is clear that nurturing persons play central roles, these interpersonal experiences also are place-bound. In the infant's early experiences of distinguishing the self from the surroundings, the personal and cultural attributes of the people who shape the settings all help to define the world. Two aspects of this process are important to describe in understanding the significance of the home: the development of a sense of *personal space* and the emergence of *personal places*.

Personal space is a term that Hall (1966) used to describe the "small protective sphere or bubble that an organism maintains between itself and others" (p.119). This bubble, which is shaped by experiences in a particular culture, remains part of a person, defining the comfort zone of close and distant contacts. From the experiences within the intimate zone that is a part of the personal space emerge the most detailed and articulated sense of the world as children touch, taste, hear and smell their immediate surroundings. Stimulation within this zone is essential to development and stimulus deprivation can seriously damage the child (Provence & Lipton, 1962). But there also is evidence that too much stimulation can be injurious, for example, the kind of noise, confusion and press of bodies that can be found in shelters and hotels for the homeless. There are indications that crowded conditions can seriously impair children's mental health and school achievement (Saegert, 1981).

In their discussion of the environment as a source of stimulation, Wohlwill and Heft (1987) have considered the significance of both focal and background stimulation. They have cited the value of diverse, complex and responsive objects within the immediate context of the child for cognitive development. In examining background conditions they have identified evidence of the threatening nature of too much noise and crowding. These stresses resound with the conditions to which many homeless children are exposed — the sounds and the presence of unfamiliar persons with whom living, eating and bathroom spaces must be shared.

Wachs (1977) has suggested a range into which an optimal level of stimulation falls, too little creating deprivations, too much disruptive of proper development. While this optimal level will be influenced by the individual's past experiences, it nonetheless sets a tolerance level for healthy functioning, a set of expectations as to what is satisfactory and strategies for dealing with this expected level.

Privacy is another quality of personal space that relates to the ability of a person to control inputs from the outside world, the ability to withdraw either physically or psychologically, to develop strategies that make it possible to leave an aversive situation. This is an important need for children and adults. In interviews on privacy with 900 children and adolescents, ages 5 through 17, Wolfe and her associates (Wolfe, 1978; Wolfe & Laufer, 1975) found that children knew what privacy was and that they developed their abstract conceptualizations from concrete experiences. The most commonly mentioned qualities of private situations were "aloneness, information management, the lack of disturbance and interruption of activities, the control over access to spaces, autonomy and quiet" (Wolfe, 1978, p. 196). While the complexity of the children's concepts increased with age, there was an awareness of privacy needs before first grade.

One way of obtaining privacy is to go to a place where interference from the outside ceases, where there is some control over access to space. In our research with children and adults in schools, day care settings and psychiatric hospitals, we have documented the significance of privacy and the use and value of a place to retreat from the stimulation, intensity and surveillance of institutional life (Rivlin & Wolfe, 1985). There was need for a "stimulus shelter" (Wachs, 1973) where relief from the activity levels of the open classroom or the noise and confusion of the day care setting could be obtained. In a children's psychiatric hospital patients told us of feigning an outburst in order to be placed in a seclusion room, the only place in the hospital where they could be alone (Rivlin & Wolfe, 1985). Adults confined to psychiatric wards identified times when their shared bedrooms were likely to be unoccupied and were available for private times; they found places on the unit where privacy was available (Ittleson, Proshansky & Rivlin, 1970; Rivlin, Proshansky, Ittelson, 1969-1970).

If we consider what it is like to be subjected to chronically dense conditions in crowded slum apartments, shelters accommodating hundreds or thousands, or in a single hotel room filled with all family members and their personal possessions, it is clear that there is little opportunity to escape the stimulation or to control the space. Living under these conditions, often in neighborhoods that are, at the very least, unfamiliar and often dangerous, there is little spatial privacy. The ability to maintain a sense of personal space and to control personal places has broad implications for people's lives and offers an understanding of their roles in the world and their own sense of competence.

Personal places are spaces that are identified with a particular individual, places where a person has priority. Adults often control places by virtue of their roles and power. The process of bounding a place and establishing rights there, has been identified as *territoriality* (Altman & Haythorn, 1967; Ardrey, 1966; Proshansky, Ittelson & Rivlin, 1976). However, this concept, borrowed from ethology, biology, ornithology and animal psychology, has some serious limitations. While territoriality is instinctive in animals, it is optional in human beings (Roos, 1968). Useful as a metaphor for a range of space acquisition behaviors it is important to recognize that much of what is identified as a human territory involves private property. Territoriality in people is based on complex social and cultural experiences. Nonetheless, it has some usefulness in Western societies since it helps to explain why the possession and control of personal places are so important over the life span.

Establishing proprietary interests over places and the objects within them in cultures where sharing is limited is one means of obtaining a sense of security, mastering the stimulation and the expectations of others and meeting the social and intellectual demands of the outside world. This appropriation of space contributes to the identity of people whether it is a day care center child retreating to her cubby for some "time out" on a hectic day or an adult closing a bedroom door for a quiet moment. These places can be enhanced by personalization—by defining the space with signals that it belongs to a particular person, even for a limited time. The markers may be signs with the name of the person or toys that provide an identity to an area. But it must be possible to lay out these markers with some assurance that they will remain and that they will be respected. In a welfare hotel or shelter there is little enough room for necessities and no space to appropriate other than a bed. There are few opportunities for personalization, making people anonymous figures in a mass of others like themselves. Possession of places and control over them is a source of conflict rather than the quality of a home in these settings. Residents of shelters frequently complain about the loss of their personal belongings and their reluctance to trust the people around them.

Personalization of spaces and the development of personal places provide tangible signs to people that they are unique. They are part of a process that stimulates a person's "place-identity," a component of self-identity, an environmental contribution to an individualistic sense of self. Place identity is not a "stable and integrated cognitive structure" (Proshansky & Fabian, 1987, p.23). There are changes over time. The inclusion of places as a component of personal identity has developed from the recognition that identity formation is grounded in environmental experiences, shaped by the settings people occupy including their homes, neighborhoods, schools, play and recreational areas, work places, and places where they socialize with friends and family, worship, and participate in clubs and organizations. Each of these supports a range of activities, roles and relationships with people that form our lives and structure our memories endowing them with special characteristics that become part of our sense of self. How all of this happens has yet to be identified in detail, although Proshansky and his associates have laid out the intellectual domain for future empirical research (Proshansky, Fabian & Kaminoff, 1983).

It is possible to uncover some of the contribution of settings to identity by asking people to talk about places that have been important to them, over the course of their lives. These environmental autobiographies point out the powerful and enduring impacts that specific settings have on people, especially their childhood homes (see, for example, studies with adults by Cooper Marcus, 1978). We must question the kinds of memories that shelters, welfare hotels, transitional housing and the street are creating and their contributions to people's identities. They are not the ingredients of strong, positive feelings and a healthy sense of self. They are not likely to foster connections to places that contribute in positive ways to a person's identity. If anything they communicate a message of unworthiness that is threatening rather than supportive.

ATTACHMENT TO PLACE

In one of the homeless communities that I have observed, consisting of people camped out on an empty lot in make-shift shacks that they constructed out of found wood, four of the six residents grew up in the area (Rivlin & Imbimbo, 1988). In explaining why they were living in that place, they talked about their right to be there, that they belonged there, that it was their neighborhood. Not only did they see their precarious hold on the lot as creating a home—for they are, in fact, illegal residents on city-owned property—but they articulated connections to the place that extended back to their childhood years.

Attachments to places, the bonds that develop between people and places over time provide a sense of stability, caring and concern for a setting. Some years ago Firey (1945) described the feelings that people had for Boston landmarks, sentiments that imply emotional connections to places. Fried (1963) found strong reactions of grief on the part of many residents of the West End of Boston when they had to leave their homes (viewed as slums by urban renewal planners), and move to new housing. These strong emotions suggest the power that places have for people. Woven into the geography are complex social networks that compose the substance of people's lives. When people are relocated these connections may be lost along with the housing or they may require considerable effort to rebuild. These attachments and the significance of home must be recognized when looking at the lives of homeless people.

THE HOMELESS EXISTENCE

My understanding of what homeless lives are like comes largely from the stories of others, from journalists' accounts and the research literature (for example, Baxter & Hopper, 1981; Dear & Wolch, 1987; Hombs & Snyder, 1982; Hope & Young, 1986; Kates, 1985; Kozol, 1988; Ropers, 1988), from people I have met as a volunteer since 1984 in a small private shelter and from others on the street and in transitional housing. In the words of one homeless friend, "You can't know what it's like unless you've been there" — and I have never been homeless.

Picture a day when you cannot be certain where you will sleep, how you will clean yourself, how you will find food, how you will hold on to your belongings (in settings where they can be stolen with ease), how you will be safe, how you will dress properly to go to work (for many homeless persons do, indeed, work), and for some, how you will fill up the long hours of a day and do so in places that will tolerate your presence. Ordinary activities become major struggles: finding places to wash hair or clothing, locating toilets when they are needed, surfaces on which to raise swollen feet or finding food, places to keep warm in cold weather and to escape the rain, snow or summer heat.

The welfare hotels and motels that pass for a home for many homeless families offer little more than a small, shabby room with no stoves or refrigerators. Meals are prepared on a hotplate under very difficult circumstances. It took many years for the city administration to move homeless families in New York from the hotels housing them. They had to remain in the hotels for 18 months, later changed to 12 months, before an effort was made to locate apartments for them, something difficult to do oneself in the tight market for low-cost apartments. It was a frightening experience to live in the hotels with the fear of crime and considerable drug dealing rampant in the corridors and stairwells (Kozol, 1988).

Shelters provided by municipalities are equally unsavory. In many cities they are huge gymnasia or armories converted into dormitories. The impersonal service, unsanitary conditions, unfamiliar neighborhoods and threats to person and possessions drive many homeless back onto the streets. Those who remain may eventually become "shelterized," a condition that was described in a study of unemployed Chicago men in shelters, in 1934 to 1935 (Sutherland & Locke, 1936). It identified the narrowing of lives "to a limited sphere of action" where, "after a few months his independence is broken down, his individuality disappears, his identity is lost, his personality becomes reorganized, and he becomes shelterized" (p. 15).

Private agencies have provided emergency shelters that homeless persons regard as less threatening. These facilities deal with small numbers, often including services for the specific needs of their residents: battered women with their children, single men or women, substance abusers, former psychiatric patients. Shelters, however they are set up, are not reasonable housing for more than a few days. Yet, we are developing a huge shelter system in the United States that does not meet people's needs nor provide more than protection from the elements.

In addition, we are finding strong community resistance to these shelters and to other housing solutions. In a study of attitudes of the public toward the homeless, largely sympathetic feelings were expressed toward homeless persons. Despite this concern, people did not want shelters in their neighborhoods, even shelters accommodating fewer than ten persons (Benedict, Shaw & Rivlin, 1988).

In many areas a form of dwelling called "transitional housing" has been set up as a reaction against long stays in emergency shelters and hotels (see Bach & Steinhagen, 1987, for examples). Organized by municipal authorities and private sponsors, these congregate residences provide private bedrooms with various forms of shared kitchens and social spaces. Some offer small, private apartments for residents. They also may specialize in the kinds of residents accepted, with places for single women and their children, drug abusers families, and single persons. Various services may be available on the premises although some expect residents to use agencies located in the community. They vary in scale and degree of resident participation in the upkeep and running of the building. Presumed to be places where residents can regroup their resources and locate apartments, for some this new form of congregate shelter may be more long-term than its name would suggest. There is every danger that the shelter system we have created will be the institutions future generations will struggle to disassemble much like our recent experiences with huge, non-therapeutic psychiatric hospitals.

Complex problems do not have simplistic or singular solutions. There are many creative housing alternatives to shelters that require support. We also need to recognize the efforts of homeless persons, themselves, to provide needed resources. While it is unreasonable to expect that the homeless population must take on the enormous task of providing housing for themselves, their efforts are strengths on which to build. There is great diversity among the population of homeless persons and within this group many capable, creative persons, are struggling to deal with their lives, working and making efforts to provide shelter for themselves. Rarely are the homeless given the help that might lead to permanent housing improvements in places where they are squatting or on lots where they have built makeshift housing. There is considerable sharing and communal concern among the homeless, in some cases self-help efforts to create a home-like environment and survive as a community (Rivlin & Imbimbo, 1988). These are qualities that should be supported in some of the new housing alternatives.

While many policy implications emerge from an examination of homelessness there also are a number of directions needed in future research. The past few years have seen an increase in the empirical evidence on homeless issues started, in large measure, by the ground-breaking research of Ellen Baxter and Kim Hopper and the Community Service Society (Baxter & Hopper, 1981). Efforts also have been made to assess the degree of pathology in the homeless population (Bassuk, 1984; Bassuk, Rubin & Lauriat, 1986). There are many reports on the homeless situation in specific areas (for example, Burt & Cohen, 1988; Molnar, 1988), documenting the numbers of homeless persons and ways homelessness has been addressed in different communities. What is especially needed is an over-time consideration of what might be called the ecology of homelessness, a view of the events leading to loss of a home along with descriptions of the shelter and rehousing experiences of homeless persons. A longitudinal perspective will make it possible to identify the various threats to the children and adults involved, the results of public policies concerning homelessness and the efforts of the homeless people on their own behalf.

Following the experiences of homeless individuals and families will enable an understanding of the ways personal spaces of homeless persons can be supported, as well as policies that respect peoples' needs for personal places and privacy. It will be easier to identify clues to successful strategies and recognize policies and procedures that intensify the difficulties.

Social scientists need to look beyond untested assumptions and journalistic reports into the nature of homelessness. They must examine the impacts of loss of home rather than focus solely on the symptoms of pathology in homeless persons. From these data reasonable, grounded directions for public policy can be developed, policies that emerge from an understanding of the individual needs and personal strengths of the populations affected and the trauma of a homeless existence. It is unlikely that this national crisis of homelessness will be resolved in the near future. We can only hope that measures undertaken will help to improve the situation rather than aggravate it so that our shelter system can become a relic of the past.

REFERENCES

Agnelli, S. (1986). *Street children: A growing urban tragedy. A report for The Independent Commission on International Humanitarian Issues*. London: George Weidenfeld & Nicolson Limited.

Allsop, K. (1967). *Hard travellin': The hobo and his history*. New York: The New American Library.

Altman, I. & Haythorn, W.W. (1967). The ecology of isolated groups. *Behavioral Science, 12*, 169-182.

Ardrey, R. (1966). *The territorial imperative: A personal inquiry into the animal origins of property and nations*. New York: Atheneum.

Axelson, L.J. & Dail, P.W. (1988). The changing character of homelessness in the United States. *Family Relations, 37*, 463-469.

Bach, V. & Steinhagen, R. (1987). *Alternatives to the welfare hotel: Using emergency assistance to provide transitional shelter for homeless families*. New York: Community Service Society.

Bassuk, E.L. (1984). The homeless problem. *Scientific American, 251*, (1), 40-45.

Bassuk, E.L., Rubin, L., & Lauriat, A.S. (1986). Characteristics of sheltered homeless families. *American Journal of Public Health, 79*, (9), 1097-1101.

Baxter, E. & Hopper, K. (1981). *Private lives/Public spaces*. New York: Community Service Society.

Benedict, A., Shaw, J.S., & Rivlin, L.G. (1988). Attitudes toward the homeless in two New York City Metropolitan samples. *Journal of Voluntary Action Research, 17* (3), 90-98.

Burt, M.R. & Cohen, B. (1988). *State activities and programs for the homeless: A review of six states*. Washington, DC: The Urban Institute.

Cooper Marcus, C. (1978). Remembrance of landscapes past. *Landscape, 22* (3), 34-43.

Dear, M. & Wolch, J. (1987). *Landscapes of despair: From deinstitutionalization to homelessness*. Princeton, NJ: Princeton University Press.

Felsman, J.K. (1981, April). Street urchins of Columbia. *Natural History*.

Felsman, J.K. (1984, May, June). Abandoned children: A reconsideration. *Children Today*, 13-14.

Firey, W. (1945). Sentiment and symbolism as ecological variables. *American Sociological Review, 10*, 140-148.

Fried, M. (1963). Grieving for a lost home. In L.J. Duhl (Ed.), *The urban condition* (pp. 151-171). New York: Basic Books.

Hall, E.T. (1966). *The hidden dimension*. Garden City, NY: Doubleday.

Hersch, P. (1988). Coming of age on city streets. *Psychology Today, 22* (1), 28-37.

Hombs, M.E. & Snyder, M. (1982). *Homelessness in America: A forced march to nowhere*. Washington, DC: The Community for Creative Non-Violence.

Hope, M. & Young, J. (1986). *The faces of homelessness*. Lexington, MA: DC Heath.

Hopper, K. & Hamberg, J. (1984). *The making of America's homeless: From skid row to new poor*. New York: Community Service Society of New York.

Ittelson, W.H., Proshansky, H.M., & Rivlin, L.G. (1970). A study of bedroom use on two psychiatric wards. *Hospital & Community Psychiatry, 21*, 177-180.

Jackson, K.T. (1987). The Bowery: From residential street to skid row. In R.

Beard (Ed.). *On being homeless: Historical perspectives* (pp. 69-79). New York: Museum of the City of New York.

Jupp, M. (1985). From needs to rights: Abandoned/street children. *Ideas Forum*.

Kates, B. (1985). *The murder of a shopping bag lady*. New York: Harcourt Brace Jovanovich.

Kozol, J. (1988). *Rachel's children*. New York: Crown.

Kusmer, K.L. (1987). The underclass in historical perspective: Tramps and vagrants in urban America. In R. Beard (Ed.), *On being homeless: Historical perspectives* (pp. 21-31). New York: Museum of the City of New York.

Marris, P. (1961). *Family and social change in an African city*. London: Routledge & Kegan Paul.

Marris, P. (1975). *Loss and change*. Garden City, NY: Anchor Books.

Molnar, J. (1988, March) *Home is where the heart is: The crisis of homeless children in New York City*. A report to the Edna McConnell Clark Foundation. New York: Bank Street College of Education.

Peroff, K. (1987). Who are the homeless and how many are there? In R.D. Bingham, R.E. Green, & S.B. White (Eds.) *The homeless in contemporary society* (pp. 33-45), Newburg Park, CA: Sage Publications.

Proshansky, H.M. & Fabian, A. (1987). The development of place identity in the child. In C. S. Weinstein & T. G. David (Eds.), *Spaces for children: The built environment and child development* (pp.21-40). New York: Plenum.

Proshansky, H.M., Fabian, A.K., & Kaminoff, R. (1983). Place-identity: Physical world socialization of the self. *Journal of Environmental Psychology, 3*, 57-83.

Proshansky, H.M., Ittelson, W.H., & Rivlin, L.G. (1976). Freedom of choice and behavior in a physical setting. In H.M. Proshansky, W.H. Ittelson, & L.G. Rivlin (Eds.), *Environmental psychology: People and their physical settings* (2nd edition), (pp. 170-181). New York: Holt, Rinehart & Winston.

Provence, S. & Lipton, R.C. (1962). *Infants in institutions*. New York: International Universities Press.

Rabon, I. (1985). *The street*. New York: Schocken. (Original work published in 1928)

Rivlin, L.G. (1986A, August). *The nature of homelessness: Some views on the homeless existence*. Paper presented at the meeting of The Society for the Study of Social Problems, New York, NY.

Rivlin, L.G. (1986b). A new look at the homeless. *Social Policy, 16*, 3-10.

Rivlin, L.G. & Imbimbo, J. (1988). Homeless children in New York City: A view from the nineteenth century. *Children's Environments Quarterly, 5* (1), 26-33.

Rivlin, L.G. & Wolfe, M. (1985). *Institutional settings in children's lives*. New York: Wiley.

Rivlin, L.G., Proshansky, H.M., & Ittelson, W.H. (1969-1970). Changes in psychiatric ward design and patient behavior. *Transactions of the Bartlett Society, 8*, 7-32.

Roos, P.D. (1968). Jurisdiction: An ecological concept. *Human Relations, 21*, 75-84.

Ropers, R.H. (1988). *The invisible homeless*. New York: Human Sciences Press.

Saegert, S. (1981). Environment and children's mental health: Residential density and low-income children. In A. Baum & J. Singer (Eds.), *Handbook of psychology and health (Vol. 2)*. Hillside, NJ: Erlbaum Associates.

Sutherland, E.H. & Locke, H.J. (1936). *Twenty thousand homeless men: A study of unemployed men in the Chicago shelters*. New York: J.B. Lippincott. (Reprinted 1971, New York; Arno Press & The New York Times).

U.S. Conference of Mayors. (1987). *A status report on homeless families in America's Cities: A 29 city survey*. Washington, DC: US Conference of Mayors.

U.S. Department of Housing and Urban Development. (1984). *Report to the Secretary on the homeless in emerging shelters*. Washington, DC.

Wachs, T.D. (1973). The measurement of early intellectual functioning. In C. Meyers, R. Eyman, & G. Tarjan (Eds.), *Socio-behavioral studies in mental retardation*. Washington, DC: American Association on Mental Deficiency.

Wachs, T.D. (1977). The optimal stimulation hypothesis and early development. Anybody got a match? In I.C. Uzgiris & F. Weizman (Eds.) *The structuring of experience* (pp. 153-178). New York: Plenum.

Willmott, P. & Young, M. (1966). *Family and class in a London suburb*. London: Routledge & Kegan Paul.

Wohlwill, J.F. & Heft, H. (1987). The physical environment and the development of the child. In D. Stokols & I. Altman (Eds.), *Handbook of environmental psychology* (Vol. 1), (pp. 281-328). New York: Wiley.

Wolfe, M. (1978). Childhood and privacy. In I. Altman & J. Wohlwill (Eds.), *Children and the environment. Human behavior and environment: Advances in theory and research* (Vol. 3), (pp.175-222). New York: Plenum.

Wolfe, M. & Laufer, R.S. (1975). The concept of privacy in childhood and adolescence. In D. H. Carson (Ed.), *Man-environment interactions: Evaluations and applications. Part II*. Stroudsberg, PA: Dowden, Hutchinson & Ross.

Young, M. & Willmott, P. (1957). *Family and kinship in East London*. Glencoe, IL: The Free Press.

Rural Families and Health Care: Refining the Knowledge Base

Clarann Weinert
Kathleen Ann Long

Before one can understand the complex mix implied in the phrase, "rural families and health care," it is necessary to examine both the historical and the current context of the term, health. Over the last century, persons in the United States have shifted their view of, and aspirations regarding, health. Perceptions of health affect the behavior of both health care consumers and providers, and ultimately determine the parameters of their interactions. If health care providers do not understand and address health in a manner which fits with consumers' perceptions, the opportunities for meaningful collaboration between the two groups, and thus effective health care, are greatly reduced. The purpose of this article is to explore the concept of health from the perspective of rural dwellers. Health care needs of persons in sparsely populated areas are examined along with potential strategies to meet the challenge of providing quality care to this segment of the American population.

CONCEPTS OF HEALTH

Smith (1983) in her review of current literature indicated four distinct models related to how consumers and providers view

The authors wish to acknowledge the work of Montana State University, College of Nursing graduate students and faculty. Qualitative data collected and analyzed by them form a basis for portions of this article. Ethnographic data collection and analysis were supported in part by a U.S. Dept HHS, Division of Nursing Advanced Training grant (#1816001649A). Portions of the paper related to survey data of rural dwellers were supported by a Montana State University Faculty Research/Creativity award and grant from NIH/National Institute of Aging (5R23A605245).

health. The *Clinical Model* is perhaps the most familiar. It explains illness as a state in which there is a conspicuous presence of disease symptoms. Health is defined as a state in which the signs and symptoms of disease as identified and diagnosed by medical science are absent. The mechanistic view of the human body on which the Clinical Model is built, has dominated the development of the biomedical sciences and subsequently of health care for the past two centuries (Smith, 1983). It emphasizes the belief that illness is an irregularity or dysfunction of the body, and that health is the absence of such irregularities or dysfunctions.

In the late 1950s, writers and thinkers in the health field began to examine the concept of health anew. The idea of "high level wellness" was introduced (Dunn, 1959) and health was defined as a process of adaptation and taking responsibility for self-regulation (Illich, 1976). Health was portrayed on a continuum from wellness to illness, and health began to be discussed as a state in which the individual's functioning was maximized (Newman, 1986). Alternate models of health have been evolved. The *Adaptive Model* of health was originally drawn from the writings of Dubos (1965), and emphasizes the interaction of the whole person with the environment. Change, as a fact of life, is a central theme in this model. Health is viewed as flexible interaction with, and beneficial adjustment to the environment. In contrast, illness is seen as a state in which the person is unable to make corrective or adaptive responses. This model has contributed to broadened notions of health which include biological, intellectual, and social components. The *Eudiamonistic Model* of health emphasizes the concepts of wholeness, unity, and individuality. The ideals of this model are captured in the writings of Maslow (1962) who discussed levels of needs in relation to health, and identified self-actualization as the ultimate state of health. Within the Eudiamonistic Model health is described as a state of high energy and holistic well-being; illness is a state in which one lacks energy, focuses on basic physiologic needs, and eventually becomes debilitated (Smith, 1983). The *Role Performance Model* of health focuses on the individual's ability or lack of ability to perform key roles, especially those associated with work and family responsibilities. Health is viewed within a social context, and being healthy implies peak performance and high output within one's social roles. The writing of Parsons (1972) emphasized this view, and explicated the "sick role." Being sick or having an illness is seen as being unable to perform one's expected role, for example as a machine operator or housewife. It is this model of health which appears to most closely approximate the view of health which is prevalent among rural populations.

HEALTH CONCEPTS AMONG RURAL POPULATIONS

In recent years several studies, both surveys and ethnographic approaches, have examined the health beliefs and practices of rural people (Lee, 1987; Ross, 1982; Weinert & Long, 1987). One finding which has appeared repeatedly and across numerous and varied rural groups is that rural people tend to associate health with the ability to be productive, to work, and to carry out usual role functions. Long and Weinert (1989) found that rural dwellers in Montana were likely to view themselves as healthy if they were able to work, despite the fact that they might be in pain or be suffering from a chronic or even life-threatening disease. Similarly, Warren (1986) found that rural oil field workers in Montana indicated they were in "good health" if they were currently able to work. Ross (1982) in interviewing women in rural areas of Nova Scotia found that their definition of health reflected the importance of performing expected tasks both within and outside the home. A recent study by Lee (1989) found that men in rural Montana were most closely aligned with the Role Performance Model of health as measured by Laffrey's Health Conception Scale.

The emphasis on work ability in relation to health may relate to the economic necessities of rural life. Many rural occupations, such as ranching and farming, do not provide health insurance, nor do they readily allow for sick days. Thus many rural dwellers may be financially constrained to seek health care only when it is deemed essential, i.e., when it interferes with the ability to earn a living and support one's family. Lee (1987) has speculated on the "hardiness" of rural dwellers, emphasizing that the independent and self-reliant nature of many rural persons may be a factor in their perception of health and their response to illness. Among rural populations that have been studied, it appears that the ability to function is more important than the comfort, cosmetic and life-prolonging aspects of health. There is little evidence, however, that rural persons actually experience less pain and illness than urban dwellers, and in fact there is reason to suspect that some rural groups experience a great deal more (Donham & Mutel, 1982; Levitz & Curry, 1984).

Health-seeking behavior by rural people is strongly influenced by a reliance on informal resources, such as family and neighbors, as well as by considerable distrust of "outsiders" or "newcomers" (Bachrach, 1983; Stein, 1987; Weinert & Long, 1987). Weinert (1983) conducted a study of 181 adults age 50 to 70 years who lived in areas throughout the state of Montana. Those who lived in the more sparsely populated counties (population density of .5 to 5.9 persons per square mile) relied more heavily on informal sources of help for health and other problems than did those living in more "urban" areas of the state. Likewise, they tended to turn to formal resources less often than did the "urban" Montana dwellers or a comparable group of persons living in the greater Seattle area. In a national study of 353 couples living in 41 states, 19% of the participants identified their place of residence as rural farm or rural non-farm. These people turned to professionals for assistance with health problems significantly less than did those persons living in urban settings (Weinert, 1988). It could be argued that this use of informal help is based, at least in part, on the relative unavailability of formal resources in rural areas. However, rural subcultural values of self-reliance and distrust of "outsiders" cannot be discounted. Hassinger and Hobbs (1973) in a study of four rural Ozark communities demonstrated that the use of formal services was not directly related to service availability.

Findings for rural areas as diverse as Maryland's Eastern Shore, Montana, and Nova Scotia indicate that rural people are wary of health care providers who do not know them and their community well (Long & Weinert, 1989; Ross, 1982; Salisbury State College, 1986). Rural persons prefer a known and trusted, although possibly non-expert, health care provider, over an unfamiliar specialist or expert.

Thus, one must consider how health, illness, and health care are *perceived* by those in rural areas. It can be hypothesized that rural environments allow less opportunity for a broad and idealistic perception of health. Rural living may be associated with financial, geographic, and social constraints on the seeking of frequent and sophisticated health care, thus lowering the health expectations of rural persons. In addition, rural lifestyles may challenge persons to function optimally, disregard seemingly minor health problems, and utilize informal, but available, resources for help and support.

HEALTH CARE NEEDS OF RURAL PEOPLE

Differences among rural groups and the unique aspects of segments of the rural population create a need for careful assessment when describing "rural" health care status, needs, and services. A significant segment of our society lives in areas that are commonly considered rural. Census definitions of rural consider places of 2,500 or fewer inhabitants as rural (U.S. Census, 1987). Based on recent estimates, 63.9 million persons or 27 percent of the U.S. population live in rural areas and of these rural residents, 50 million live on farms (Kalbacher & DeAre, 1987). However, the definition of rural is not consistent, and this causes difficulties in accurately describing and quantifying the health needs and problems of rural persons. For example, some government designations define rural as those living outside a Metropolitan Statistical Area (Office of Management and Budget, 1983). In other more sociologically oriented literature, the definition of rural is based on occupational, ecological, and sociocultural factors (Bealer, Willits, & Kuvlesky, 1965). Bachrach (1983) cautioned against rigid designations which fail to take into account the sociological distinctions between rural and nonrural populations. In this article rural is defined as meaning sparsely populated. Within this context states such as Montana which are sparsely populated overall are viewed as rural throughout, despite the existence of some population centers within them. Further, based on this definition, rural regions or areas can be identified within otherwise heavily populated states (Long & Weinert, 1989).

Regional Differences

Regional diversity is an essential consideration when identifying rural health care needs. Miller, Stokes, and Clifford (1987) cautioned that in studying rural health problems there is no homogeneous rural America and that it is reasonable to expect that health differences among various rural areas and subgroups may be pronounced. Miller and associates (1987) concluded that there are many different rural populations defined in different ways and made up of different age, race, and gender groupings, and that ultimately each community will generate its own pattern of health and illness. In a study of the health status of older persons Cutler and Coward (1988) also warned against over-generalization. In their study of various health indicators of elderly persons living in four locations (central city, not central city, nonfarm, and farm), they found that rural *farm* residents were on the whole in the best health while residents of rural *nonfarm* areas were in the poorest health. Their study demonstrated the heterogeneity of rural environments and further emphasized the inadequacy of simple residential dichotomies.

Rural America is generally considered an agrarian society; however, a recent report indicated that a significant portion of rural dwellers are employed in nonagricultural industries (Banks & Kalbacher, 1981) such as servicing recreation seekers, and employment in small industries or service businesses (Carlson, Lassey, & Lassey, 1981). The biggest evolution in rural America in the past two decades is greater diversity (Coward, 1980). This diversity is associated with land use, community structure, employment, educational options, and political activitism. Many rural areas are experiencing population increases associated with industries seeking to provide employees with an attractive environment, Americans searching for rural tranquility, retirees escaping the high costs of urban living, cultural enclaves looking for privacy, and boomtown growth related to energy developments (Carlson et al, 1981; Kushman, Cowper, & Radovic, 1984). While contemporary rural America is undergoing major changes, substantial differences between rural and urban environments and social systems continue to exist (Ford, 1978). This paradox of stability in the midst of change must be considered in attempting to understand rural health care needs.

The Rural Profile

Despite subgroup variations, and the issues of flux and change, it is possible to describe general health care needs and issues which affect most rural people. The profile of health care needs of rural dwellers indicates that they are more likely to suffer from chronic disease conditions such as arthritis, visual and hearing impairments, ulcers, thyroid and kidney problems, heart disease, hypertension and emphysema (Joint Task Force of NACHC/NRHA, 1988). In five of the six groupings used in the National Health Interview Survey, rural persons had higher rates of chronic illness (National Center for Health Statistics, 1986). Likewise, rural persons were more likely than urban dwellers to have limitations in activity as a result of chronic conditions (National Center for Health Statistics, 1986). A recent estimate indicated that more than 13.5 million people in rural America are poor (McDonald, 1986). Non metro unemployment rates have been higher than metro rates since 1979 with a fourth of the non metro counties having rates of 12 percent unemployment or more (Pollack & Pendelton, 1986).

Life in rural America is sometimes thought to be simple and serene, if not idyllic. Yet, environmental and economic stressors take a heavy toll on rural dwellers. Walker and Mountain (1988) in a study of the recent plight of the farmers and the oil field workers in Texas noted the magnitude of the transitions facing rural residents. One fifth of the Iowa farmers responding to a poll on rural life and the impact of the sagging farm economy indicated that they were very concerned about the level of stress in their lives (Cooperative Extension Service of Iowa State University, 1985). Economic conditions are forcing many to change from life-long, multigenerational careers in farming to other types of rural employment. Many rural residents are experiencing a sense of isolation, displacement, a loss of identity, and failure (Farmer, 1986; Stein, 1984). For many farm families the psychological tie to place is so strong that they would rather take unsatisfying work in the local rural community than leave the area. These families often withdraw socially, stop going to church, start avoiding school and community activities and simply don't want to face others, especially their creditors (Farmer, 1986). These stressors affect both the physical and mental health of rural dwellers.

Health Care Constraints

Social, environmental, historical, and economic factors put rural residents in jeopardy in terms of their health and place special demands on health care services. Political and economic constraints operate to limit health services, and there are inadequate public financing mechanisms for health care in rural areas. Rural physicians are reimbursed by Medicare and Medicaid at lower rates than urban physicians. There are fewer public programs aimed at prevention of disease, and a shortage of providers. Rural hospitals are closing at a record-setting pace, while the National Health Service Corps is being disbanded. Rural residents have a 24 percent higher rate of uninsuredness for health care than their metropolitan counterparts (Joint Task Force of NACHC/ NRHA, 1988). Levitz and Curry (1984) pointed out that rural residents are not eligible for many federal health care and welfare programs because criteria and standards have been designed to screen and access needy persons in urban settings.

Rural dwellers are often forced to delay care until chronic conditions become life-threatening (Reilly, Legge, Reilly, 1980; Scharff, 1987). The inadequate health care system in rural areas must deal with extreme environmental hazards, such as toxins, grain dust, and fertilizers and the high injury rates associated with agriculture, timber, oil field, and mining industries. In addition it must handle the unique problems of emergency accident care for urban tourists drawn to rural areas for recreation (Waller & Brink, 1987).

ADAPTING SERVICES TO RURAL NEEDS

As has been made apparent, the health care needs of rural areas are extensive, diverse, and in some respects unique. There are particular challenges associated with tailoring health care services to meet these needs. Special problems arise because the majority of large-scale health care models and programs have been developed with urban populations in mind (Rosenblatt and Moscovice, 1982). A discussion of adapting health care services to meet rural needs must include both community-based care and hospital care. Additional aspects to be considered are mental health needs and the unique role of the rural health care provider.

Community-Based Health Care

The basic and natural component of rural health care is community based care. Informal networks tend to be strong and powerful in rural settings. This results from both a lack of formal and sophisticated resources, and attitudes which foster reliance on self, family, and neighbors. Thus, naturally occurring health care in rural areas is community based: family members care for each other with the support of neighbors and friends. While examples of community-based health care, such as hospice, exist in urban settings this phenomenon appears to be considerably more prominent in rural areas (Lewis, Messner, & McDowell, 1985; Weinert & Long, 1987). In a study by Young, Giles, and Plantz (1982), 80% of rural respondents reported themselves as being active help-givers and receivers within an informal network of family, friends, and neighbors. Similarly, in studying a rural Montana community, Swehla (1986) found that the majority of long-term home health care was provided by friends and relatives, rather than by nurses or other formal providers.

The challenge of adapting community-based health care to rural areas is one of blending the formal network with the existing informal system. Rural residents are unlikely to use a new, more formal, health care service, in place of an established informal resource, even if it were possible to make the new service affordable and accessible. However, if the new service can become linked with existing informal resources, it can serve to expand and upgrade health services for the population.

How do such linkages occur? Of primary importance is the ability of a formal health care service to be accepted by and integrated into the existing informal network. Weinert and Long (1987) discussed ways in which formal health care providers can augment and supplement, but not usurp or replace, informal systems. For example, in many rural areas a local resident, such as the drug store proprietor or volunteer ambulance director, might be the established source of health information, and often the means for referral to formal health care. Nurses or physicians in rural areas should focus on establishing a collaborative relationship with such community leaders, and serve as a resource to him or her. Acting indirectly through this trusted local leader, professionals within the formal health care system are able to provide improved health information and health care to the population. The formal-informal linkage allows for expert health care knowledge from the professional and expert community and cultural knowledge from the local leader. These are blended, resulting in more relevant health care information and referral. A genuine and mutual respect between health care professionals and local leaders is necessary. This requires time and consistency in the formation of collaborative relationships. The development of such lay-professional relationships has been emphasized in the preparation of rural community-health nurses (Lassiter & Goeppinger, 1986), and is increasingly being addressed in the preparation of physicians for rural practice (Stein, 1986; 1987).

The accessibility of formal community based health services is an additional aspect frequently discussed in writings about rural services. While persons will not use services they cannot access, the accessibility equation is more complex. Consideration of location, distance, and cost are primary. However, the emotional and social climate of care providers and settings will also make health care more or less accessible. The ability of rural persons to feel at ease and accepted, to understand what is done and said, and to leave with a maintained sense of dignity and self-reliance will determine both return visits and the informal referral of others. Accessibility further implies organized efforts by providers to inform rural persons about available services, and to assist them in self-assessment and self-care. Formal services can then be used when appropriate and necessary, and avoided when inappropriate or unnecessary. The informal, community-based network of health care and support in rural areas cannot, given existing resources, and should not be replaced by formal services. Informal systems are the core of the rural health care system, and should be supplemented and supported by formal services and providers.

Hospital Care

The provision of hospital care for rural dwellers presents a unique set of barriers and constraints. Costs and the lack of available personnel have combined to make it increasingly difficult for rural hospitals to maintain themselves. Rural hospitals have been particularly adversely affected by changes in the reimbursement system over the past ten years. In addition rural areas for the most part continue to be unable to recruit and retain nurses, physicians, and others necessary to maintain acute care hospital services. Adapting hospital services to meet rural needs requires a variety of innovative strategies. Rural hospitals are converting larger portions of their beds into rehabilitative and nursing home care for persons with chronic illness, particularly the elderly. These services are needed in rural communities, and sometimes provide an economic base for the hospital. Rural populations are aging at rates faster than the country in general (National Center for Health Statistics, 1984); more elderly persons reside in, are drawn to, or are left behind in, rural areas. Chronic illnesses predominate. Local rehabilitative and nursing home services permit residents to retain some ties to family and remain connected to informal community support systems.

Rural hospitals increasingly serve as referral links, stabilizing acutely ill persons for transport to larger hospitals, and receiving them back for prolonged recuperation or rehabilitation. Unfortunately, the present health care reimbursement systems tend to penalize smaller hospitals which serve in these capacities. In general the federal prospective payment system reimburses at lower rates for rural hospitals than urban ones, and it does not provide adequate reimbursement for prolonged stays associated with recuperation and rehabilitation (Moscovice, 1987). Reform in the reimbursement structure will be necessary if most smaller hospitals are to continue meeting rural needs.

Preparing personnel to work in rural hospitals is a major issue. Several graduate level programs in nursing now specifically focus on rural nursing and health care. Residency and subsidized training programs for physicians have existed for several years, but have had limited success in retaining physicians for work in rural areas (Rosenblatt & Moscovice, 1982). Health care providers in rural hospitals need preparation as broad based generalists. Nurses are called upon to function in expanded and diverse roles even within a single work day. A recent study by Scharff (1987) showed that nurses in small rural hospitals might function in areas as different as obstetrics, coronary care, and pharmacy within a typical work shift. Nurses, physicians, and others who will staff rural facilities need not only a broad knowledge base, but specific preparation in providing care despite a lack of sophisticated equipment. They must often make decisions without specialist consultation and are isolated from their professional peers and resources.

Specific system-level strategies can assist professional health care practitioners in rural areas in dealing with these problems as well as help to highlight the rewards of rural practice. Several rural hospitals have devised unique and specific incentives to retain health care personnel. For example, Nantucket Cottage Hospital, a 39 bed facility on an island off the Massachusetts coast, established a reward system for nursing personnel willing to meet the unique needs of this rural hospital. Nurses accrue incentive points when they agree to be on-call as needed, to provide diverse kinds of care, or to permit short-term notice of schedule changes. The incentive points can be used to "purchase" a variety of perks including round trip airfares to the mainland, and pre-paid family or group activities (Fox, 1988). Increasingly, rural hospitals are realizing that in order to maintain quality care, special efforts are required not only to retain physicians, but nurses and other health care personnel as well.

Rural practice has its rewards, and these can include increased independence, the challenge of diverse and frequently changing types of patient care, close relationships with patients and coworkers, and a sense of being needed and belonging in a small community. The latter two aspects can be reinforced and enhanced by rural community members, usually to the benefit of the overall community. Activities aimed at breaking down the "newcomer" and "outsider" barriers for health care professionals can include invitations to civic and social clubs, churches and community social functions. Linking the new professional with an established health care provider, introductory "open house" activities sponsored by community leaders, and efforts to introduce the professional's family members to community schools and businesses are also beneficial. Mutual effort is needed. Not only must professionals be open to the community, but community leaders and groups must reach out to professionals. So doing usually increases the likelihood that the rural community will both retain and utilize the professional as a valuable health care resource.

Mental Health Care

Meeting the mental health needs of persons in rural areas is an aspect of health care with special features and ramifications. Historically, rural dwellers have underutilized mental health care, and this has led to speculation about their degree of mental health problems, and their openness to help with such problems (Bachrach, 1983). There are little data to support the commonly presented myth that rural life, with its slower pace and so-called "low-stress" life style, decreases the likelihood of mental health problems. Rather, there is increasing evidence that rural dwellers may actually be at higher risk then urban dwellers for mental disorders and for related problems such as family violence and alcohol abuse (National Mental Health Association, 1987; Swaim, Beauvais, Edward, & Oetting, 1986; Wagenfeld and Buffum, 1983). Further, isolated rural communities often develop social value systems which encourage tolerance of certain kinds of deviance including mental illness (Bachrach, 1983; Long, 1986; Stern, 1977). For example, in the interest of protecting the citizenry, the "town drunk" or the "touched in the head" may be tolerated or ignored. This process, despite its benign intent, may prevent appropriate referral and treatment for serious problems.

While rural populations are certainly not homogeneous, two major factors, one attitudinal and one situational, appear to effect the provision of mental health services to many rural residents. Self-reliance, including a strong preference to keep "personal matters, personal," makes it very difficult for rural persons to seek help with issues such as depression, marital dysfunction, or substance abuse. While self-reliance has been shown to have positive effects in relation to health (Weinert & Long, 1987), in its more extreme manifestations it can lead to denial of problems, refusal to seek appropriate care and even the active "cover up" of family crises (Long, 1986; Loschen, 1986). A major situational factor, that of decreased anonymity in rural areas, tends to exacerbate these problems. In a large urban area, those seeking mental health services can usually do so without the awareness of friends, coworkers, and even family members. In addition, urban dwellers are not likely to know and see their mental health provider outside of the context of treatment. In contrast, there is less privacy in sparsely populated areas. The mental health provider may be known to the patient as a neighbor, social acquaintance, or friend, thus mixing and complicating the therapist-client roles (Bachrach, 1983).

Several strategies can be helpful in meeting mental health needs in rural areas. Rural dwellers appear to be more likely than urban dwellers to use their primary health care provider for mental health as well as physical health care (Flaskerud & Kris, 1982; Rosen, Locke, Goldberg, & Babigian, 1972). This tendency may relate to issues of trust, availability, and stigma. In a rural practice setting primary providers need to have thorough information about available mental health resources, including pastoral services and support groups, so that well informed referrals can be made. Conversely, rural mental health providers need to locate and utilize as a sponsor, an established and trusted rural nurse, physician, or informal community health care provider. Rural mental health facilities and offices are often best placed in inconspicuous locations and identified with broad titles, such as "family services." Locating mental health offices in multipurpose civic or health care buildings is helpful. These strategies make it easier for residents to access services without being stigmatized.

Rural mental health care providers must be prepared to deal with the exaggerated distrust and discomfort which many rural dwellers will experience in seeking mental health care. This circumstance will be complicated by the fact that rural clients are frequently available only for short-term therapy (Bachrach, 1983). Limited finances for service, and work and distance constraints make numerous and prolonged visits impractical. Crisis intervention approaches, including a specific focus on identifying with the client the desired outcomes of treatment, can be useful. Providers will often be challenged to accept short-term and less-than-perfect treatment outcomes because these fit the client's needs and resources.

In summary, rural mental health services must be accessible without being conspicuous. Providers and their staffs need to be deeply sensitive to issues of stigma and confidentiality. Rural communities need primary providers who know how and when to make appropriate mental health referrals, and whose educational efforts are aimed at increasing rural residents' acceptance of the reality of mental health problems and the appropriateness of seeking mental health services.

SUMMARY

Appropriate models of health care delivery to rural populations must take into consideration what health means to rural consumers and the current accepted practices of particular locales. Several models of health, Clinical, Adaptive, Eudaimonistic, and Role Performance have been discussed. Rural dwellers' definitions of health most closely approximate the Role Performance Model.

While the health care needs of rural families are diverse and complex, aspects of these needs are held in common across rural populations. Other features are unique based on geography, subculture, or idiosyncratic factors. This article, drawing from both qualitative and quantitative data, demonstrates that major features of rural health and health care are: the definition of health as the ability to work, reliance on self and informal systems, reluctance to use the services of "outsiders," and the need for generalist providers. These features have an impact on how rural dwellers seek and utilize health care, and they must be considered in designing health services which can meet the needs of rural Americans. Urban models of health care delivery are often inappropriate and lead to unnecessary expenditures and underutilization by those most rural persons in need of the service. Specific strategies to adapt acute care services, community based agencies, and mental health care have been presented.

The knowledge base for meeting rural health care needs, for so long underdeveloped, has grown dramatically in the past ten years. The challenge ahead is to expand and adapt health resources so that the myth of rural health and well being can more closely approximate the rural reality.

REFERENCES

Banks, V. J., & Kalbacher, J. Z. (1981). *Farm income recipients and their families* (Report No. 30). Washington, DC: U.S. Department of Agriculture, Economic Research Service.

Bachrach, L. (1983). Psychiatric services in rural areas: A sociological overview. *Hospital and Community Psychiatry, 34,* 215-226.

Bealer, R., Willits, F., & Kuvlesky, E. (1965). The meaning of "rurality" in American society: Some implications of alternative definitions. *Rural Sociology, 30,* 255-266.

Carlson, J. E., Lassey, M. L., & Lassey, W. R. (1981). *Rural society and environment in America.* New York: McGraw-Hill.

Coward, R. T. (1980). Rural families changing but retain distinctiveness. *Rural Development Perspectives, 3,* 4-8.

Cooperative Extension Service of Iowa State University. (1985). *The Iowa Farm and Rural Life Poll,* Ames: University of Iowa.

Cutler, S., & Coward, R. (1988). Residence differences in the health status of elders. *The Journal of Rural Health, 4*(3), 11-26.

Donham, K. J., & Mutel, C. F. (1982). Agricultural medicine: The missing component the rural health movement. *The Journal of Family Practice, 14,* 511-520.

Dunn, H. L. (1959). High-level wellness for man and society. *American Journal of Public Health, 49,* 786-792.

Dubos, R. (1965). *Man Adapting.* New Haven, CN: Yale University Press.

Farmer, V. (1986, April). Broken heartland. *Psychology Today,* 54-62.

Flaskerud, J. H., & Kris, F. J. (1982). Resources rural consumers indicate they would use for mental health problems. *Community Mental Health Journal, 18,* 107-119.

Ford, T. R. (1978). Contemporary rural America: Persistence and change. In T. R. Ford (Ed.), *Rural U.S.A.: Persistence and Change* (pp. 3-16). Ames: Iowa State University.

Fox, L. (1988). Employee incentives in a small rural hospital. *Nursing Management, 19*(10), 90.

Hassinger, E., & Hobbs, D. (1973). The relation of community context to utilization of health services in a rural area. *Medical Care, 11,* 509.

Illich, I. (1976). *Medical nemesis.* New York; Bantam Books.

Joint Task Force of the National Association of Community Health Centers and the National Rural Health Association. (1988). *Health care in rural America: The crisis unfolds.* Washington, DC (NACHC), & Kansas City, MO (NRHA).

Kalbacher, J., & DeAre, D. (1987). *Rural and rural farm population: 1987.* Joint Census-ERS annual report on the social and economic characteristics of the farm resident population.

Kushman, J., Cowper, P., & Radovic, E. (1984). *New residents and rural health care.* In Committee on Agriculture, Nutrition, and Forestry United States Senate, *Emerging issues in the delivery of rural health services* (S. Prt. 98-239). Washington, DC: U.S. Government Printing Office.

Lassiter, P., & Goeppinger, J. (1986). Education for rural community health nursing practice. *Family and Community Health, 9*(1), 56-67.

Lee, H. (1987). *Relationship of hardiness and current life events to perceived health in rural adults.* Unpublished manuscript, Montana State University, College of Nursing, Bozeman.

Lee, H. (1989). *Quantitative validation of health perseptions in rural persons.* Unpublished manuscript, Montana State University, College of Nursing, Bozeman.

Levitz, G., & Curry, J. (1984). Rural-urban differences in the determinants of physician utilization. In Committee on Agriculture, Nutrition and Forestry, United States Senate, *Emerging issues in the delivery of rural health services* (S. Prt. 98-239). Washington, DC: U.S. Government Printing Office.

Lewis, S., Messner, R., & McDowell, W. (1985). An unchanging culture. *Journal of Gerontological Nursing, 11*, 21-26.

Long, K. A. (1986). Cultural considerations in the assessment and treatment of intrafamilial abuse. *American Journal of Orthopsychiatry, 56*, 131-136.

Long, K. A., & Weinert, C. (1989). Rural nursing: Developing the theory base. *Scholarly Inquiry for Nursing Practice, 3*, 113-127.

Loschen, E. L. (1986). The challenge of providing quality psychiatric services in a rural setting. *Quality Review Bulletin, 12*, 376-379.

Maslow, A. (1962). *Toward a psychology of being.* Princeton, NJ: Jan Nostrand.

McDonald, T. (1986). Short subjects. *Rural Development Perspectives, 3*(1), 40-41.

Miller, M. K., Stokes, C. S., & Clifford, W. B. (1987). A comparison of the rural-urban mortality differential for deaths from all causes, cardiovascular disease and cancer. *The Journal of Rural Health, 3*, 23-34.

Moscovice, I. (1987). Rural hospitals: A literature synthesis and health research agenda. *Health Services Research, 23*, 891-930.

National Center for Health Statistics, (1984). *Vital and health statistics.* (Series 10, No. 146). Washington, D.C.: U.S. Government Printing Office.

National Center for Health Statistics (1986). *Vital and health statistics.* (Series 10, No. 160). Hyattsville, MD: NCHS.

National Mental Health Association, (1987). Studies on rural mental health issues. *Behavior Today, 18*(44), 1.

Newman, M. A. (1986). *Health as expanding consciousness.* St. Louis: C. V. Mosby.

Office of Management and Budget (1983). *Metropolitan Statistical Areas.* Washington, D.C.: Executive Office of the President. (NTIS No. PB83-218891).

Parsons, T. (1972). Definitions of health and illness in the light of American values and social structure. In E. G. Jaco (Ed.). *Patients, Physicians, and Illness* (pp. 107-27). New York: Free Press.

Pollack, S., & Pendleton, S. (1986). Non-metro unemployment tied to major industry in regions. *Rural Development Perspectives, 3*(1), 38-39.

Reilly, B., Legge, J., Reilly, M. (1980). A rural health perspective: Principles for rural health policy. *Inquiry, 17,* 120-127.

Rosen, B., Locke, B., Goldberg, I., & Babigian, H. (1972). Identification of emotional disturbance in patients seen in general medical clinics. *Hospital and Community Psychiatry, 23,* 364-370

Rosenblatt, R. A., & Moscovice, I. S. (1982). *Rural health care.* New York: John Wiley and Sons.

Ross, H. (1982). Women and wellness: Defining, attaining, and maintaining health in Eastern Canada. (Dissertation, University of Washington, Seattle, WA, 1982). *Dissertation Abstracts International, 42,* (University Microfilm No. DEO 82-2624).

Salisbury State College. (1986, June). *Discussion of Salisbury State College rural health findings.* Presented at the Contemporary Issues in Rural Health Conference, Salisbury, MD.

Scharff, J. (1987). *The nature and scope of rural nursing: Distinctive characteristics.* Unpublished master's thesis, Montana State University, Bozeman, MT.

Smith, J. A. (1983). *The idea of health: Implications for the nursing professional.* New York: Teachers College Press.

Stein, H. F. (1984). The emotional separation syndrome among recent Oklahoma migrants: Description, explanation, and clinical implications. *Oklahoma State Medical Association Journal, 5,* 152-157.

Stein, H. F. (1986, June). *From stereotypes to minute particulars: Some lessons I have learned in rural health care teaching.* Paper presented at conference on contemporary issues in rural health, Salisbury, MD.

Stein, H. F. (1987). Effects of rural/urban stereotypes in medical education. *High Plains Applied Anthropologist, 7*(1), 11-15.

Stern, M. S. (1977). Factors in the utilization of mental health and state hospitals. *Hospitals and Community Psychiatry, 28,* 378-381.

Swaim, R., Beauvais, F., Edwards, R. W., & Oetting, E. R. (1986). Adolescent drug use in three small rural communities in the Rocky Mountain region. *Journal of Drug Education, 16,* 57-73.

Swehla, B. (1986, December). *Health perceptions of a subpopulation of Belt, Montana.* Unpublished manuscript. Montana State University, College of Nursing, Bozeman, MT.

U.S. Bureau of the Census (1987). *Stastical Abstract of the United States: 1988* (108th ed.). Washington, D.C.: U.S. Government Printing Office.

Wagenfeld, M., & Buffum, W. (1983). Problems in, and prospects for, rural mental health services in the United States. *International Journal of Mental Health, 12,* 89-107.

Walker, M., & Mountain, K. (1988, Spring/Summer). The rural Texas environment and its stressors: A comprehensive model for stress management. *Texas Journal of Rural Health,* pp. 39-45.

Waller, J. A., & Brink, S. (1987). Trauma in tourist towns. *The Journal of Rural Health, 3,* 3.

Warren, S. (1986, December). *Ethnographic health perceptions: A study of oil field workers*. Unpublished manuscript. Montana State University, College of Nursing, Bozeman.

Weinert, C. (1983). [Social support: Rural people in their "new middle years"]. Unpublished raw data.

Weinert, C. (1988). [Social support: Families living with long-term illness]. Unpublished raw data.

Weinert, C., & Long, K. A. (1987). Understanding the health care needs of rural families. *Family Relations, 36*, 450-455.

Young, C., Giles, D., & Plantz, M. (1982). Natural networks: Help-giving and help-seeking in two rural communities. *American Journal of Community Psychology, 10*, 457-469.

Corporate Responses to Family Needs

Dana E. Friedman

Today's workplace assumes a far greater role in the family lives of workers than ever before. It is no longer possible for workers to leave their personal problems at home, as company cultures dictate — because someone is rarely home to solve them. Demands for a more "family-friendly" workplace come at a time when business needs to invest more in its people. Concerns about labor shortages, productivity and global competitiveness create the bottom-line reasons for a business response to families.

If companies are to recruit and retain productive workers they must be in touch with the needs and expectations of those workers. With benefit plans and work schedules designed for a male breadwinner, many company policies and practices are out of step with those of dual earner families and single parents, who now comprise 44% of the workforce (Axel, 1988). These employees have needs for child care assistance, elder care support, and greater flexibility in their work schedules in order to be productive on the job and at home.

A growing number of employers have begun responding to the family needs of workers. This article will describe the reasons for their responsiveness and the innovations that yield greatest benefits to both employee and employer. This review is intended to intro-

77

duce to the research community the corporation as a social institution in an attempt to encourage more research on the intersect of work and family life.

THE RATIONALE FOR CORPORATE SUPPORT

John Naisbitt (1982) said in *Megatrends*, "Change occurs when there is a confluence of both changing values and economic necessity, not before." Over the past 20 years, corporate America has been able to absorb more than half of the women over age 18 into the workforce with very few accommodations. Now that the labor pool is shrinking and a growing proportion of new labor entrants will be women, there is an economic imperative for the workplace to change in order to accommodate the family.

Slowed labor force growth is largely due to a decline in birth rates and the aging of baby boomers. Between 1970 and 1985, the labor force increased 40%, or about 2.2% annually. However, between 1985 and the year 2000, the labor force is expected to grow only 15%, or about one percent annually. Slower labor force growth means that economic growth cannot come from merely hiring more people as U.S. companies did in the past. Growth will come more from getting the most out of the people hired (Johnston and Packer, 1987).

About two-thirds of net, new entrants into the workforce are women (Johnston and Packer, 1987). Nearly three-quarters of these women will become pregnant at some point in their work careers (O'Connell and Bloom, 1987). More than half will return to work before their child's first birthday, and an estimated 20% of workers will provide care to an aging relative while employed (Friedman, 1986b).

Although women bear the primary responsibility for family obligations, 60% of men have working wives, and many of these men are taking on more family responsibilities (Pleck, 1989). More men actively participate in childbirth and parenting classes and a growing number are requesting—and getting—custody of their children after divorce (Baruch and Barnett, 1981; Pleck, Staines and Lang, 1980). Research suggests that when men take on family responsibilities, they experience similar work-family conflicts as women (Burden and Googins, 1987; Galinsky, 1988).

The increased labor force participation of working mothers has lead to a heated debate about their value to an employer and their proper place in the organizational hierarchy. This debate has been labeled "the mommy track," and was fueled by a recent article written by Felice Schwartz (1989), President of Catalyst, a national organization committed to advancing the cause of women. The piece was considered heretical, especially because of its opening sentence which stated, "The cost of employing women in management is greater than the cost of employing men." Schwartz suggested that the solution for companies was to create two tracks: one for "career-primary women" who are not expected to have children and who should be promoted aggressively. The other track was for "career-and-family women" who would be expected to make career sacrifices for their families.

The criticisms of this argument, aside from the practical absurdity of determining who is going to have a baby and who is not, is that (1) it focuses on the changes that women must make and ignores the need for corporate cultures to adapt to a changing workforce; (2) it belittles or overlooks the notion that men also cost the company money with greater incidence of heart attacks and substance abuse or that men might be "career-and-family" oriented as well; and (3) it does not consider the cost benefits of providing family-supportive policies, i.e., with accommodations to family needs there need not be an increased cost, but rather a savings to the firm. Feminist Betty Friedan appearing on TV's "Nightline," called the "mommy track" a "new form of discrimination." As the number of working parents grows, these issues will continue to be debated with the likely result that major institutions will come to terms with the profound changes among their workers and the need to change the way they do business.

The attitudes of all employees have shifted as the employee-employer contract has been torn by takeovers, buyouts, mergers, and lay-offs rampant in business today. Employees, less secure in their jobs, have become less committed to a particular firm than to their own careers. Employee loyalty is more difficult to engender today and more targeted efforts are necessary to retain workers (Skelly,

1982). Companies may also be concerned about the morale problem caused by the restructuring and uncertainty in the organization. Family-supportive policies may become "survivor benefits" for those who remain after downsizing.

Companies will be persuaded to change benefit plans and work schedules when it can be shown that family problems create a productivity loss or that family programs yield productivity gains. For instance, company needs assessments have found that companies lose valuable time from employees forced into a cumbersome and time-consuming search for child care (Galinsky, 1987; Emlen and Koren, 1984). When child care is located, parents often find it is of questionable quality and considerable expense, complicating the work-family balance. In a study of employees in 33 companies in Oregon, Emlen and Koren (1984) found that employed mothers with children under age 12 who report difficulty finding child care are likely to make arrangements with which they are dissatisfied, report worry or stress about child care, and say that combining work and family responsibilities is difficult. They almost invariably feel that child care is difficult to continue or maintain. Worries about children result in stress that often leads to other physical problems causing absenteeism and poor work performance (Burden and Googins, 1987; Crouter, 1984).

Parents usually combine several child care arrangements to cover their needs. Several company surveys found 1.7 child care arrangements used per child per week (Friedman, 1989). The more arrangements there are, however the more likely they are to break down. A New Jersey survey of 1,000 employees in three companies found that 40% had missed at least one day in the past three months due to child care breakdown, and 51% had left early or arrived late for the same reason (Galinsky, 1988).

Even when the pattern is established, emergencies, illnesses and snow days are inevitable. Parents tend to be absent five days per year due to sick children (Emlen, 1984). Fernandez (1986) found that sick child care was at the top of the list among 15 possible child care problems. The problem was bigger for women than men, where 45% of women and 17% of men indicated that providing care for a sick child was at least somewhat of a problem.

In a study at a large computer company in New England (Burden and Googins, 1987), women employees were twice as likely as men to have to stay home with a sick child (65% compared to 32%). Whether a parent is absent due to a sick child depends on the nature of the illness, the availability of back-up support, and the personal inclinations of the parent. In a study of employees who had lost time from work due to sick children at Manville Corporation in Denver, 65% did not want to leave their children home alone, 25% did not know a provider, and 22% could not afford one (Friedman, 1989).

Elder care concerns lead to similar conflicts and work loss. In the 1982 Long-Term Care survey conducted by the Department of Health and Human Services (Stone, Cafferata, and Sangl, 1986), 12% of daughters quit their jobs to provide elder care support, 23% reduced their work hours, 35% rearranged their work schedules, and 25% took time off without pay. In a study at Wang Labs (Administration on Aging, 1987), one-third of caregivers said that elder care responsibilities negatively affected their work; caregivers were absent about five days per year due to elder care.

The emotional strain of caring for parents may also affect work performance. Caregivers are three times more likely to be depressed than the relatives for whom they are caring. About one-third of those caring for those with Alzheimer disease use prescription drugs for depression, tension, and sleep disorders—compared to 10% of the general population (Enright and Friss, 1986).

There is very little empirical research to show that when a company responds to these family problems, the negative effects will disappear. Seventeen evaluations of on-site child care centers have been identified (Friedman, 1989), many with serious methodological flaws, no statistical tests, and difficulty in establishing causality. Only six of the studies are empirical, comparing center users to a control group before and after the center opened. Four of the five studies that conducted statistical tests claimed that enhanced recruitment and reduced turnover were the most significant benefits of sponsoring an on-site child care center. There have been virtually no studies evaluating other forms of child care support provided by the company. Other research on employee assistance programs and flextime suggest that these programs have the potential of mitigating some of the negative effects of unmet family problems (Krug,

Palmour, and Ballassai, 1972; Milkovich and Gomez, 1986; Marquart, 1988; National Council of Jewish Women, 1988; Pierce, 1989; Winnett and Neale, 1985; Bureau of National Affairs, 1986).

WHY DO COMPANIES RESIST RESPONDING?

The vast majority of employers have not responded to the family needs or workers. Despite the natural resistance to change, companies are particularly loathe to change in response to family needs because decision-makers believe that the worlds of work and family should remain separate (Kanter, 1977). When only men worked and women stayed home, it was easy for companies to believe that work and family life could be kept separate. But as the sex roles blurred, so did the line between work and family life. The majority of decision-makers, however, still fit the traditional mold with their wives tending to the family's daily needs. These men experience fewer conflicts between their work and family life than those who do not have someone at home tending to their family responsibilities.

The workplace is not yet conducive to speaking up about family problems. Many employees perceive risks associated with mentioning dependent care problems to one's supervisor. As a result, employees do not openly express their family concerns. Without personal experience or employee input, decision-makers remain ignorant of family problems at the workplace.

There are also economic constraints on the corporate response to families. Companies concerned with escalating health care costs are reluctant to augment the benefits package. Many now favor hiring contingent workers, or "disposable workers," who provide temporary, leased, or part-time work without benefits (Freedman, 1989). These employers have not realized the potential return on investment in responding to family needs. They see only the costs associated with child care or parental leave, rather than the potential for keeping valuable employees. Those employers who recognize the potential for a return on investment have already responded to the child care, elder care, and flexibility needs of their workers.

WHO IS RESPONDING TO FAMILY NEEDS?

Larger firms typically are in the forefront of providing family-supportive benefits. A growing number of small- and mid-size companies (less than 500 employees) are also becoming involved. A 1987 Small Business Administration study identified 24 small companies (less than 200) currently providing child care support. These firms were in a tight labor market, were very profitable, and were run by progressive management (Berkeley Planning Associates, 1988). These characteristics of small firms involved with child care are identical for larger companies that currently provide family supportive programs.

Responsive companies are more likely to be female-intensive and non-unionized (Friedman, 1983). More unionized companies are likely to provide or negotiate for family supports as labor steps up its efforts to recruit female office workers. A 1989 AT&T labor-management agreement may also provide momentum to increased inclusion of dependent care in future contract negotiations.

Family-supportive policies are often found in family-owned businesses where family values are incorporated into corporate policy. Many of the companies that produce family-related services and products, such as The Stride Rite Corporation and Johnson & Johnson, have pioneered a variety of family supports.

Perhaps the greatest determinant of corporate receptivity to family issues is the corporate culture — the unspoken mores and values of the organization. Corporate culture is shaped by decision-makers of the firm, whose personal values and experiences are naturally reflected in company values. Decision-makers are more likely to have aging parents than preschoolers, and as a result, there tends to be a more sensitive reaction to elder care than to child care problems.

CORPORATE RESPONSES TO CHILD CARE

Of all the work-family initiatives, child care has probably gotten the most attention during the past ten years. During the 1960s, when corporate social responsibility was in vogue, 18 companies created child care centers for their employees (Friedman, 1983). Only two of those remain open today, the most notable of which is at Stride Rite Corporation in Cambridge, Massachusetts. In 1990, Stride Rite will be a pioneer once again with the opening of an intergenerational day care center to care for the children *and* parents of their employees.

Much of the growth in employer-supported child care during the early 1980s can be attributed to the Reagan Administration. The former president made it both necessary and fashionable for the business community to play a larger role in the child care delivery system. By cutting back on social services, the nonprofit community was forced to look to other funding sources. At the same time, public-private partnerships encouraged by the White House sanctioned business investments in social programs. Between 1983 and 1985, the White House sponsored 33 breakfasts for corporate CEOs to educate them about child care.

These, and other educational efforts as well as an improvement of the economy provided the impetus for significant growth in employer-supported child care during the 1980s, as Table 1 indicates. The rise from 600 employers in 1982, to an estimated 4,100 in 1989, is dramatic in absolute terms, but it represents only 11% of the 44,000 employers with more than 100 employees (Friedman, 1989).

Company responses reflect the inadequacies of the child care market. Employers try to help increase the supply of care with the creation of new services they provide greater access to existing programs through resource and referral services, and they address the affordability of care by providing various types of financial assistance. Through all of these strategies, companies try to improve the quality of services.

Creating New Services

Most people tend to think first of the on-site day care center when contemplating a business role in child care. As shown in Table 2, of the 4,100 employers providing some form of child care support, 1,100 do so by sponsoring a child care center. About 600 of those

Table 1:   Growth In Employer-Supported Child Care

Year	Number of Companies
1982	600
1984	1,500
1986	2,500
1988	3,300
1989	4,000

Source: Dana E. Friedman, The Conference Board, "Update on Employer-Supported Child Care," (Distributed Memo) 1989.

1,000 centers are sponsored by hospitals as a response to a nursing shortage and the need for care during evenings and weekends.

The 200 corporate-sponsored centers are most often contracted out to a profit or nonprofit agency to run for the company. Others are owned and operated by the company, or are owned by the company, but managed by an outside management firm. Several companies may jointly create a center in what is known as a consortium arrangement, where participants share in the costs, risks, and benefits. And many more companies contribute to the creation or expansion of community-based child care centers.

The on-site center is not feasible for the majority of employers.

Table 2: Type of Employer Involvement In Child Care

Type of Child Care

On - or near site child care center		1,000
Hospitals	600	
Corporations	200	
Government	200	
Family day care, school age care, sick child care		50
Referral Services		1,000
Discounts, vouchers		50
Flexible Benefits		<u>2,000</u>
		4,100

Source: Dana E. Friedman, The Conference Board, "Update on Employer-Supported Child Care," (Distributed Memo) 1989.

Many firms are too small and do not have the resources or the labor pool to fill it. While consortium arrangements sound attractive, especially for small firms, they are very difficult to develop. Large urban areas such as New York, Los Angeles, and Chicago, have very few on- or near-site centers because of the high costs of downtown space and the commuting patterns of employees. Parents travelling on public transportation in rush hour are not anxious to bring their preschoolers with them. Finally, some worksites, such as chemical plants, may be inappropriate for children.

Other firms have tried to increase the supply of care by focusing on family day care which is often preferred by parents of children under age three (Kamerman and Kahn, 1987). American Express, for instance, provides funds to family day care associations and to resource and referral (R & R) agencies to recruit, train, and help get licensed new family day care homes.

School-age care is another concern of parents, and therefore of growing concern to companies. It is estimated that between 1.5 and 3 million children return to empty homes at the end of the day (Coolsen et al., 1986). Companies might help by providing phone-in services that children can call when they arrive home, when they need assistance or someone to talk to. These services are important because many parents do not have access to a phone at 3:00 p.m. Other companies offer after-school services in their on-site child care centers or help create such services in schools, YWCAs, and other community agencies.

Sick child care services supported by companies include sick bays in centers or in-home nursing services. Realizing that some parents want to and should be with their sick children, companies are revising their sick leave policies to permit employees to stay home with them. Another advantage of this policy is that the worker will not have to lie about who is sick—the employee or a family member. A recent Conference Board survey of 521 large companies found that two-thirds of large companies offered sick leave for family members, although 59% of the sick leave was unpaid (Christensen, 1989).

Providing Information

Parents need help in finding child care services, and learning how much they cost, their hours, and the curriculum's appropriateness for their child. About 300 resource and referral agencies exist around the country to help parents shorten their search time and make them wiser consumers of the care they purchase (Friedman,

1986a). About 1,000 companies contract with these agencies to provide counseling and referrals to the employees. I.B.M. created a nationwide network of referral services which at least 35 other national corporations now use. Most employers who provide such services contribute funds to the R & R's for the development of new services. After four years of I.B.M. investment in this effort, about 10,000 new child care programs have been created each year, most of which were family day care homes.

Companies also provide information to employees through parenting seminars, caregiver fairs, support groups, handbooks, videos, libraries, and company newsletters. The employee assistance program (EAP) is expanding to include a wide range of family-supportive counseling to employees and their families.

Helping Parents Pay

Another real burden on working parents is the cost of the child care services they need, averaging $2,000 to $3,000 per year (Hofferth, 1989). Some firms contract with individual providers for a discount for their employees. Other companies subsidize child care costs at a program of the employee's choosing. Retail chains and fast food restaurants are the firms that offer this solution to their low-wage female employees because they are increasingly difficult to recruit.

The most popular child care option for companies is the Dependent Care Assistance Plan (DCAP) that is authorized under Section 129 of the Internal Revenue Code. This provision enables employees to use before-tax dollars to purchase dependent care expenses. DCAPs are the most popular form of child care support from the business community because they only cost companies a small administrative fee.

CORPORATE RESPONSES TO ELDER CARE

An estimated 200 employers have begun to respond to employees who provide care to an aging relative (Friedman, 1989). Elder care support is likely to flourish in the coming years as all sectors of society grapple with a rapidly aging society. In 1986, 30 million

Americans were over age 65, accounting for 12% of the population. By the year 2030, the number will double and senior citizens will comprise 20% of the population. The average 65-year-old can expect to live 17 years longer. However, while medical advances have enabled us to live longer, we will not necessarily live better (Friedman, 1986b).

About 75% of the aged lived with their children or nearby. Caring for elderly parents is not new; combining it with a career is. Between one-fifth and one-third of any workforce might have some caregiving responsibilities for an aging relative. A survey at The Travelers Companies found caregivers providing roughly 10 hours of care per week. About 10% provided 35 hours of care each week. A substantial portion—between one-third and one-half of caregivers—are responsible to an elderly relative living more than 50 miles away (Travelers, 1985).

Elder care responsibilities may involve transportation, housekeeping, bathing, personal care, shopping, cooking, and paperwork. Employees are forced to use company time for researching and conferring with doctors, finding health care, visiting nursing homes, and applying for Medicaid. In a survey conducted by the New York Business Group on Health, two-thirds of companies reported excessive telephone use by those caregivers, and half felt that these employees were less productive (Warshaw, 1986).

As a result of 20 years of the Older Americans Act, there is a network of services upon which companies can build, unlike the child care system. Most of the companies responding to elder care provide information to their employees about available services, the aging process, or company policy. Some information efforts are intended to reduce stress and make employees wiser consumers of the care they purchase. Some companies, such as Hallmark and Marriott Corporation, contract with a community-based organization or geriatric care manager to counsel employees about the services that would be most helpful. Several agencies now offer referral services to multi-site companies by contracting with referral specialists across the country. I.B.M., Arthur Anderson, American Express, and Johnson & Johnson have this type of nationwide service. Cross-country referrals can also be helpful to a single-site firm whose employees provide elder care support to relatives in other cities.

An expanded employee assistance program is an appropriate place to begin addressing elder care issues. Information can also be imparted through seminars at the workplace that address the aging process, the supply of services, and ways to handle family pressures. Support groups allow employees to share coping strategies where the company provides meeting space, and perhaps, time off to meet. "Caregiver fairs" provide an opportunity for community groups and geriatric specialists to distribute information about the costs and availability of services, thus shortening the search time for employees. Companies also create handbooks and videos that provide needed information.

Although companies are concerned about increasing benefit costs, there are several programs that can offset the cost of elder care services. Reimbursement accounts for dependent care include provisions for elder care. In order for an employee to use it for elder care expenses, however, the aging relative must live in the employee's home for eight hours a day and the employee must provide more than 50% of the elder's financial support. As a result of these conditions, few employees have been able to apply for this financial relief.

A company can subsidize directly a portion of elder care costs. Vouchers can be applied to adult day care centers or in-home health services. The real concern about costs is associated with long-term care. A growing number of companies such as John Hancock, Procter and Gamble, and American Express, offer long-term care insurance that covers the employee and their parents in time of need (Levin, 1988). Employees usually are expected to pay the full premium of these policies.

CORPORATE RESPONSES TO FLEXIBILITY

Employees with dependent care responsibilities need flexibility for the last minute emergencies and the planned-for changes in work scheduling. In a review of eight company needs assessments where employees were asked to rank the company responses that would be most beneficial to them, the breakdown shows an overwhelming preference for increased flexibility in work hours (Friedman, 1989). This might involve flextime, sick leave for family members, or part-time work with pro-rated benefits.

Flextime

In 1985, 12.3% of the workforce, or 9.1 million full-time wage and salary workers, were on flextime based on a 1988 Conference Board survey 50% of the 521 large companies responding offered flextime (Christensen, 1989). About half plan to increase flextime availability in the near future. In earlier years, flextime was not implemented to accommodate family needs. Companies were more likely to be concerned with tardiness, commuting, or morale. Yet, a growing body of literature suggests that flextime can address family needs.

While flextime will not reduce the total number of hours worked, it makes possible more conveniently arranged hours that may permit more time spent on activities outside work. In a 1981 study by the Office of Personal Management, where 325,000 employees were studied, flextime users spent more time with family, more time on household chores, and more time in children's school activities. The freedom to set their own work schedules enable employees to spend less money for babysitting services (Pierce, 1989). In a study at two Federal agencies where flextime users were compared to a control group, it was found that flextime users generally came to work earlier and gained increased family time in the evening (Winnett and Neale, 1985). The data strongly suggests that alternative work schedules may enhance the quality of family relationships.

Flextime has been shown to reduce negative work behaviors by reducing work-family conflict. One study, however, found that flextime creates less work-family stress, but not for mothers (Bohen & Viveros-Long, 1981). The authors conclude that, "The magnitude of the logistical, energy, and time demands on families with two employed parents or a single parent, cannot be dramatically altered by minor changes in daily work schedules." The flextime schedule under evaluation at this Federal agency allowed variations of one-half hour at either end of the day. The restricted program of fixed flextime would seem to do little to reduce the effects of work-family stress (Bohen & Viveros-Long, 1981).

Part-time Work

Reducing the number of hours worked each week is a common way in which employees with family needs balance their lives. In 1985, about one out of six workers, or 18 million people, worked less than 35 hours. About three-quarters of these part-time jobs were held by women (Christensen, 1987). Part-time workers rarely receive company benefits, such as health insurance, maternity leave, or pension coverage. Some companies that rely on part-time workers and that have difficulty recruiting and retaining them are beginning to consider pro-rating benefits for part-time workers and creating variations that allow for even greater flexibility. For instance, Shawmut Bank in Boston has developed "mothers' hours" that enable tellers to work from 9:00 a.m. to 3:00 p.m., with the summer months off. A survey by Catalyst indicated that women prefer part-time work as a transition following maternity leave and a growing number of companies now permit reduced hours for a period of time (Catalyst, 1983).

New Ways to Work, a national organization advocating alternative work schedules, has found job sharing to be a viable option for people with family needs. While many companies have one or two job sharing teams, very few encourage employees to pursue this option. It has been found to be enormously beneficial to employees whose work styles are complementary. Companies also report that they get far more than one full-time job accomplished with this arrangement (Olmsted and Smith, 1983).

Work at Home

Although frequently called telecommuting, the option of working at home need not involve a computer. A growing number of jobs can be accomplished out of the office, but they require a management that does not equate presence with performance. There must be a trust between the employee and the supervisor that the work can get done without supervision. According to telecommuting specialist Gil Gordon (1985), between 200 and 300 companies have eight to ten workers on some type of home-based arrangement.

Working parents who work at home admit that this option does not preclude the need for child care assistance. It is difficult to be productive with a two-year old tugging at one's sleeve. This arrangement, however, does provide employees with the most flexibility in the design of the work day. Work can go on in the evenings after the children are in bed.

CONCLUSION

There are many ways in which companies can support the family needs of workers. The future is full of ideas that deserve some experimentation by the business community as they make a contribution to the well-being of America's families. There are several patterns to the current employer experience that suggest future directions for corporate support to families.

No one option can solve all problems. Given the diversity of family needs, it is impossible for any one corporate initiative to address all employees' family concerns. As a result, most companies with a commitment to addressing family needs package a set of responses that typically include information, financial assistance, and time off. This multi-faceted approach requires integration—a strategic plan for work-family programming. A growing number of large companies, Aetna and I.B.M. among them, have created the position of "Manager of Dependent Care Programs." This makes clear to employees and managers where information about company policies and programs can be obtained. It also helps coordinate the various departments with responsibility for a particular family initiative.

The corporate culture must change. In some cases, there may be an explicit desire to change the culture to become more family supportive. This means that work-family issues will be "mainstreamed" throughout the organization. Part of changing the culture involves debunking several cultural myths that have persisted in the workplace. For instance, employees cannot "keep their personal problems at home" anymore. Management must get used to dealing with family problems. Many managers believe that if you "give them an inch, they take a mile." This kind of distrust will not lead to new programs or, if provided, will not result in the expected payback from employees. Finally, with such a diversity of need, it is not reasonable to think that "what you do for one, you must do for everyone." While equity means that everyone should be treated fairly, it does not necessarily mean that the exact same treatment should be given to all employees in all circumstances.

Since managers are the transmitters of culture, it is important that they understand the company's purpose in responding to family issues and develop a greater sensitivity to work-family problems. Very progressive companies in this emerging field, such as Johnson & Johnson, DuPont, and I.B.M., have developed management training programs to accomplish this goal.

Business cannot do it alone. The general pattern of corporate initiatives in child care and elder care suggests that companies are more likely to help employees find care or pay for care, than they are to provide the care directly. This is not unlike an earlier period when companies wanted to address the health needs of employees. Companies did not build hospitals; they helped their employees gain access to needed health services. Yet in order for referral or financing initiatives to be effective, there must be a system of services that employees can find or purchase. This is where government and the community play an important role.

The infrastructure of the service delivery system needs considerable repair if companies are to augment its capacity to serve their employees. This would involve start-up costs to develop new services, training programs and licensing reform to improve the quality of care, and referral programs to increase access to available care. Once in place, companies can build on a solid foundation of services. Government also has a role in serving those in greatest need who do not work for the kinds of employers currently providing family support.

Family-supportive programs are ripe for public-private partnerships. In former President Reagan's efforts to encourage such partnerships it was assumed that the less that government did, the more that business would do. However, current experience suggests that the more that government does, the more that business can do. As excited as one might get from the foray of business into the family arena, the limitations of their involvement must be acknowledged and the role of government pursued. Perhaps at the heat of the debate is the unresolved question of when a private choice becomes a public responsibility. Until we, as a society, accept a collective responsibility for the sound development of our next generation and the respect needed by the one that preceded us, we are unlikely to solve the larger economic and social problems that threaten our future.

The research community can play a significant role in moving the work-family agenda within business, government, and community. The gaps in research exist for many reasons related to the sensitivity of the subject, corporate naivete about social science research, and the cost of conducting methodologically sound research. The academic community has contributed to the lack of research because of the difficulty in conducting interdisciplinary research and the penchant for random samples which are more difficult to obtain in corporate settings. There is, however, a long list of interesting questions that may yet attract more of the academic and business community. Some ideas include the following:

- It is time to revisit theories about motivation and satisfaction at work by integrating a family focus. Classic management theory was conducted on men in the 1950's.
- There are virtually no analyses of family-supportive programs that have failed, nor do we know very much about the problems that arose when companies implemented their programs.
- We have limited knowledge of the effects on co-workers of work-family problems and solutions.
- Research is needed that compares various company options to determine which are more effective in solving certain problems.
- Very little is known about how men and women respond to different corporate initiatives.
- Due to recent welfare reform legislation requiring mothers to work, it is an important time to look at the work-family problems of lower income families and their reactions to various company supports.

- Research is needed on the effects of various programs on high performers compared to low performers.
- Work-family conflicts will change over the course of the life cycle. Research is needed that looks at different levels of commitment to work and family roles over time and where specific interventions work best.

These kinds of inquiries require that business become more family-friendly and research-friendly as well.

REFERENCES

Administration on Aging and Elder Services of the Merrimack Valley, Inc. (1987). *Elder Care Project for Dependent Elderly Relatives of Wang Employees.* Lowell, MA.

Axel, H. (1988). *Employment by family characteristics.* Unpublished memo from The Conference Board, New York, NY.

Baruch, G.K. & Barnet, R.D. (1981). Fathers' participation in the case of their preschool children. *Sex Roles, 7,* 1043-1055.

Berkeley Planning Associates (1988). *Small business options for child care.* Report to small Business Administration, Washington, DC.

Bohen, H. & Viveros-Long, A. (1981). *Balancing jobs and family life.* Philadelphia, PA: Temple University Press.

Burden, D.S. & Googins, B.K. (1987). *Balancing job and home life study.* Boston: Boston University School of Social Work.

Bureau of National Affairs (1986). *Work and family: A changing dynamic.* Washington, DC, BNA Special Report.

Catalyst (1983). *Maternity and parental leaves of absence.* New York, NY.

Christensen, K.E. (1985). *Impacts of computer-mediated home-based work on women and their families.* Paper commissioned by Office of Technology Assessment, U.S. Congress.

Christensen, K.E. (1987). Women and contingent work. *Social Policy, 17,* 15-18.

Christensen, K.E. (1989). *Flexible staffing and scheduling.* New York: The Conference Board.

Coolsen, P., Seligson, M., & Garbarino, J. (1986). *When school's out and nobody's home.* National Committee for the Prevention of Child Abuse, Chicago, IL.

Crouter, A.C. (1984). Spillover from family to work: The neglected side of the work-family interface. *Human Relations, 37,* 425-442.

Emlen, A. & Koren, P. (1984). *Hard to find and difficult to manage: The effects of child care on the workplace.* Oregon: Regional Research Institute for Human Services, Portland State University.

Enright, R.B. & Friss, L.R. (1986). *Employed caregivers of brain-impaired adults: An assessment of the dual roles.* San Francisco, CA: Family Survival Project.

Fernandez, J.P. (1986). *Child care and corporate productivity.* Lexington, MA: Lexington Books.

Freedman, A. (1989). *Human resources outlook 1989.* Research Bulletin No. 227. New York: The Conference Board.

Friedman, D. (1983). *Encouraging employer supports to working parents.* New York: Center for Public Advocacy Research.

Friedman, D. (1985). *Corporate financial assistance for child care.* New York: The Conference Board.

Friedman, D. (1986a). Child care for employees' kids. *Harvard Business Review, 64,* 28-34.

Friedman, D. (1986b). Elder care: The benefits of the 1990's? *Across the Board,* June.

Friedman, D. (1989). *Productivity effects of family problems and programs.* New York: The Conference Board (forthcoming).

Galinsky, E. (1988). *The impact of child care problems on parents on the job and at home.* Paper prepared for Child Care Action Campaign, New York, NY.

Galinsky, E. & Hughes, D. (1987). *The fortune magazine child care study.* New York: Bank Street College of Education. Unpublished paper.

Hofferth, S.L. (1989). *What is the demand for and supply of child care in the U.S.?* Washington, D.C. Urban Institute, Testimony presented before the House Committee on Education and Labor.

Johnston, W.B. & Packer, A.J. (1987). *Workforce 2000.* Indianapolis, IN: Hudson Institute.

Kamerman, S.B. & Kahn, A.J. (1987). *The responsive workplace: Employers and a changing labor force.* New York: Columbia University Press.

Kanter, R.M. (1977). *Work and family in the United States: A critical review and agenda for research and policy.* New York: Russell Sage Foundation.

Krug, D.N., Palmour, V.E., & Ballassai, M.C. (1972). *Evaluation of office of economic development child development center.* Rockville, MD: Westat, Inc.

Levin, R. (1988). *Long-term care.* Washington, DC: Washington Business Group on Health.

Marguart, J.M. (1988). *A pattern matching approach to link program theory and evaluation data: The care of employer-sponsored child care.* Ithaca, NY: Cornell University (Dissertation).

Milkovich, G.T. & Gomez, F.R. (1986). Day care and selected employee work behaviors. *Academy of Management Journal,* March.

Naisbitt, J. (1982). *Megatrends.* New York: Warner Books.

National Council of Jewish Women (1988). *Employer supports for child care.* New York: Center for the Child Report, August.

O'Connell, M. & Bloom, D. (1987). *Juggling jobs and babies: America's child care challenge.* Washington, DC: Population Reference Bureau, Inc.

Olmsted, B. & Smith, S. (1983). *The job sharing handbook*. New York: Penguin Books.

Pierce, J.L., Newstrom, J.W., Dunham, R.B., & Barber, A.E. (1989). *Alternative work schedules*. Boston, MA: Allyn and Bacon, Inc.

Pleck, J.H. (1989). *Family supportive employer policies and men's participation: A perspective*. Paper prepared for the Panel on Employer Policies and Working Families, National Research Council, Washington, DC.

Pleck, J.H., Staines, G.L., & Lang, L. (1980). Conflict between work and family life. *Monthly Labor Review*, March, 29-32.

Schwartz, F.N. (1989). Management women and the new facts of life. *Harvard Business Review*, *67*, 65-76.

Skelly, F.R. (1982). Changing values and their effect on employee attitudes, expectations and requirements. In Salisbury, D.L. (Ed.), *America in Transition: Implications for Employee Benefits*. Washington, DC: Employee Benefits Research Institute.

Stone, R., Cafferata, G.L., & Sangl, J. (1986). *Caregivers of the frail elderly: A national profile*. Washington, DC: U.S. Department of Human Services.

The Travelers Companies (1985). *The Travelers employee caregiver survey*. Hartford, CT.

Warshaw, L.J. & Staff (1986). *Employer support for employee caregivers*. New York: New York Business Group on Health.

Winnett, R.A. & Neale, M.S. (1985). Results of experimental study on flextime and family life. *Monthly Labor Review*, November, 29-32.

School and Family Connections: Theory, Research, and Implications for Integrating Sociologies of Education and Family

Joyce L. Epstein

All the years that children attend school, they also attend home. The simultaneous influence of schools and families on students is undeniable, but too often ignored in research and in practice. In research, social scientists who study one environment rarely give serious attention to another. Sociologists of the family rarely study how family practices affect student success in school, or how school practices affect family attitudes, interactions, and practices. Sociologists of education who study school and classroom organizations rarely examine how school practices affect home environments, or how family cultures, attitudes, and practices affect school practices and effects.

Most schools leave it up to families to decide whether and how to become involved with their children's schools. This means that some families are highly involved in their children's education and provide important guidance for their children, whereas other families are not involved much at all. Increasingly, schools are changing their laissez-faire practices concerning the family by designing and conducting programs to help more families become "knowledgeable partners" in their children's education. Legitimate and comprehensive school and family partnerships should alter the basic

This work was supported by a grant from the Office of Educational Research and Improvement (OERI) of the U.S. Department of Education. The opinions expressed in this publication do not necessarily reflect the position or policy of the OERI and no official endorsement should be inferred.

roles and behaviors of the average family and change the practices of the typical school.

Studying two environments with populations of parents, teachers, principals, and students is, of course, more difficult than studying one environment or one group. Measuring school and family processes, practices, and outcomes is harder than measuring simple categorical structures or events in one or both environments. But recent advances in studies of school and family connections show that this kind of research will be required in order to better understand families, schools, student achievement, and student development. It will also lead to more effective programs to improve family functioning, school effectiveness, and student success.

This paper reviews recent advances in this field and provides an overview of important issues that should be taken into account in new studies of families, schools, classrooms, and child and adolescent development and in related undergraduate and graduate courses. The first section presents a model of school and family connections that is an alternative to other theoretical approaches. Subsequent sections summarize research results, and discuss implications for new research and for integrating the sociologies of the family and education.

THEORETICAL ADVANCES IN SCHOOL AND FAMILY CONNECTIONS

The model proposed in this paper views the shared responsibilities of families and schools as a set of overlapping spheres of influence that alter the interactions of parents, teachers, students, and other members of the two institutions and affect student learning and development. (Epstein, 1987a; 1988a). This model recognizes that there are some practices that schools and families conduct separately, but that there are other practices that should be conducted as partners. Many students would be more successful if their schools and families provided them with consistent messages about the importance of education. More students would learn more if their schools and families combined all available resources to provide students with varied, intensive, and coordinated learning opportunities. Without this overlap of school and family, many students do not respond to school programs, fail courses, become truant, and drop out of school. With productive overlap, more students would know that their teachers and parents are working together to help them set and reach important goals. This view is in contrast to three alternative perspectives of family and school connections that emphasize the separateness, sequencing, or embeddedness of institutions.

An Emphasis on Separateness

One perspective on institutions and their relationships emphasizes the importance of their separate contributions to society. This view assumes, for example, that school bureaucracies and family organizations are most efficient and effective when their leaders maintain independent goals, standards, and activities (Parsons, 1959; Waller, 1932; Weber, 1947). Waller distinguished "school" and "not school" to try to understand how schools work as organizations. He discusses paths, channels, and crisscrossing of groups and subgroups who have relationships with schools, but the intent is to show how they might connect on occasion, not how they overlap in similar and shared responsibilities. Parsons emphasized the independence of school and family systems of discipline, rewards, and control, and the differences of teachers and mothers in their influence on students' personalities. Pictorially, this model could be drawn as a set of rectangles on an organizational chart that shows the clear boundaries of each institution. The shapes are connected by thin lines to indicate the potential for communication. Institutions that emphasize their separate goals and activities work together only when there are serious problems or trouble. For example, when schools and families are viewed as separate spheres of influence, teachers may never contact parents unless a student is in trouble with serious learning or behavior problems. Parents may never contact schools unless their children are unusually distressed or unhappy. Indeed, families that feel separate and different from the school may not contact teachers or administrators for fear that a child will be punished because of a parent's concerns or needs. Lightfoot (1978) described these relationships of schools and families as "worlds apart."

An Emphasis on Critical Stages and Sequencing

A critical stages perspective emphasizes that there is a recognized sequence in which parents and teachers contribute to child development and education. This approach is based on a belief that the early years of a child's life are critical for later success. Some believe that by the age of 5 or 6 years old, the child's personality and attitudes are well established and relatively fixed. Parents have responsibility for the first critical stage of learning to teach their children skills to prepare them for school; educators then assume the major responsibility for the education of school-aged children (Bloom, 1964; Freud, 1937; Kagan, 1980; Piaget and Inhelder, 1969). After the age of compulsory attendance or graduation from high school, young adults assume the major responsibility for their own education and training. Pictorially, this perspective might be drawn as a ladder or time line of influences on education and socialization, with the family, school, and individual as three successive "steps" to educational progress.

An Emphasis on Ecology and Embeddedness

An ecological perspective emphasizes the nested connections between individuals and their groups and organizations. This view is represented pictorially as a set of concentric circles of interaction and influence – an embedded system (Bronfenbrenner, 1979). As a result of this perspective, there has been increased attention to the multiple, expanding environments that influence individuals. However, the "concentric circles" model does not encourage questions about changing, developmental patterns or cumulative influences of multiple environments on students, parents, and educators across the school grades.

An Emphasis on Overlapping Spheres of Influence

A social organizational perspective of overlapping spheres of influence is offered in this paper as a basis for research on schools and families (Epstein, 1987a). The model also has been extended to include schools, families, community groups, and peer groups as the four major spheres of influence on student development (Epstein, 1988a). In this model, the key, proximate environments that educate and socialize children are shown pictorially as spheres that can, by design, overlap in their goals, resources, and practices. Within the external structure of overlapping spheres, the model recognizes an internal structure of interactions between and among the various members of school and family organizations in order to influence student learning and development.

The model includes three major "forces" that affect the content and extent of overlap. These are (a) time — to account for changes in the ages and grade levels of students and the influence of the historic period, (b) the philosophies, policies, and practices of the family, and (c) the philosophies, policies, and practices of the school. These forces determine how much and what kinds of "overlap" occur at any given time, and affect the interactions among the members of these institutions.

The overlapping spheres of influence model integrates and extends the work of Bronfenbrenner (1979), Leichter (1974), Litwak and Meyer (1974), and Seeley (1981) to account for several levels and layers of connections between institutions and individuals. For example, Litwak and Meyer emphasized the importance of connections and support between and among institutions and the importance of maintaining professional "distance" between institutions. They outlined a variety of social and educational connections between families and schools and considered the benefits that might result from such connections. They did not, however, focus attention on the overlap of family and school responsibilities to benefit children as students. When they introduced it, Litwak and Meyer's approach challenged the prevailing view of the importance of near-total separation of professional and parental roles for effective institutions.

Bronfenbrenner's ecological approach pushed the connections between social contexts further. He asserted that inter-setting or "mesosystem" connections are important for the individual, and he called for research on the effects of these connections. Bronfenbrenner hypothesized that personal development will be enhanced when exchanges between settings are "bi-directional, sustain and enhance mutual trust and goal consensus, and exhibit a balance of power." These are characteristics of true partnerships. Seeley, too, discussed the "shared responsibilities" for children of parents, teachers, and other members of the community. Leichter's phrase "families as educators" suggested that families can be viewed as partners in their children's learning and development. The theory of overlapping spheres of influence presented in this paper recognizes the interlocking histories of institutions that educate and socialize children, and the changing and accumulating skills of the many individuals in several institutions that affect children's learning and development.

When teachers and administrators stress separate or sequenced skills and contributions of teachers and parents, they emphasize the *specialization* of skills required by teachers for school training and by parents for home training. Teachers who have been advised to "stick to the basics" restrict their attention to the academic skills needed by students. They may diagnose students' needs with tests or other methods that emphasize the differences in approaches by schools and families. With specialization comes a *division of labor* that pulls the spheres of school and family influences and responsibilities apart, decreasing overlap and restricting interactions between parents and teachers.

In contrast, when teachers and parents emphasize their shared responsibilities, they support the *generalization* of skills required by teachers and by parents to produce educated and successful students. Teachers who are advised to "teach the whole child" increase their attention to the children's home life, and to the development of student self concept, aspirations, social skills, and development of talents—some of the traditional responsibilities of parents. When teachers ask parents to become partners in their children's education, they direct the parents' attention to their children's school life, and to the students' learning abilities and mastery of skills—some of the traditional responsibilities of teachers. Generalization reflects a *combination of labor* that pushes the spheres of family and school influence together, increasing overlap by increasing interactions between members of the school and family. This creates what we call more "school-like families" and "family-like schools" (Epstein, 1987a).

In summary, the different images of alternative perspectives of school and family connections—a bounded set, a series, concentric circles, and overlapping spheres—suggest that there are different patterns, purposes, and potentials for connections of families and schools. In order to understand how these alternative perspectives affect student development, research is needed that includes appropriate measures of school and family structures, characteristics, practices, interpersonal interactions, and outcomes for students, as well as outcomes for parents and teachers.

RESEARCH RESULTS AND DIRECTIONS

Research on family environments for nearly a quarter century shows that children have advantages when their parents support and encourage school activities (Coleman, Campbell, Hobson, McPartland, Mood, Weinfeld, & York, 1966; Clausen, 1966; Epstein and McPartland, 1979; Epstein, 1983; Heyns, 1978; Leichter, 1974; Marjoribanks, 1979; Mayeske, 1973; McDill & Rigsby, 1973; and others). This work revealed that there are typical or predictable patterns of higher involvement linked to higher family socioeconomic status and mother's education. Regardless of these variables, however, family practices are consistently important for student success. Some of the early studies were conducted at the secondary school level in surveys of middle school and high school students who reported about their families. Other studies were conducted in Head Start and other preschool, Follow-Through and other early elementary grades. The research suggests that students at all grade levels do better in their academic work and have more positive school attitudes if their parents are aware, knowledgeable, and encouraging about school.

The early research focused first on family structures and later on family behaviors that *varied naturally in the study samples*. Some researchers also measured school structure and processes, but there was no attempt to study the direct influence of individual teachers' practices on particular family behaviors in order to explain student success.

Over the past decade, research on school and family connections has progressed in two main directions. One line of research continues to focus on family social class, parent's education, and family practices to explain and discuss the natural variation of parent involvement among families. When parents are left on their own, the typical pattern continues to be more involvement by better educated parents and higher achievement of their children (Baker and Stevenson, 1986; Coleman, 1987; Entwisle, Alexander, Cadigan, and Pallas, 1986; Lareau, 1987). A recurring theme in this line of research is that less-educated parents cannot or do not want to become involved in their children's education. Little attention is given in this work to variations in teachers' practices to involve parents, or to the linkages of particular teachers' practices with the responses of the parents of the children in their classroom.

A second line of research focuses on whether school practices can change family behaviors and influence family environments in ways that help more students to succeed. This research prompts new questions about whether and how schools can successfully involve all parents in their children's education — especially those parents who are not likely to become involved on their own. And if parent involvement is increased, whether schools, families, and students benefit from that involvement. Some of these studies challenge the assumption that social class determines the effectiveness of family and school connections. They show that some poor and minority parents are involved in their children's education, and that some teachers successfully involve parents of even the most disadvantaged students in their children's education in important ways (Becker and Epstein, 1982; Clark, 1983; Davies, 1988; Epstein 1986; Scott-Jones, 1987). This research suggests that school policies, philosophies, and practices influence family environments and student learning and development.

Summary of Research Results on School and Family Connections

Studies over the past half dozen years of family and school connections in the elementary, middle, and high school grades are beginning to provide evidence of the effects of school and family overlap. Although many of the studies are small and use different research methods, the commonality of findings strengthens their credibility.

Effects on Parents

One goal of parent involvement — perhaps the most obvious one and the one most easy to produce in the short term — is to change parents' behavior. This includes improving parents' knowledge, parenting skills, parent-child interactions and relationships, and parent-teacher interactions and relationships. To study this topic, information must be obtained directly from parents about their understanding and practices concerning their children's education and schools, and from the schools about their practices to inform and involve parents. Reports about parents from teachers or students are measures of others' perceptions, which may differ from parents' reports about themselves. (c.f., Dauber and Epstein, 1989; Epstein and Dauber, 1988). From parents, we have learned many important things about school and family connections:

• Most parents want to know how to help their own child at home, and how to stay involved with their children's education. Despite a real decline in teachers' practices to involve parents in the upper grades, parents of children at all grade levels want the schools to keep them informed about their children's school programs and progress. Parents of children in the younger grades receive more help from teachers, but when middle grade and high school teachers involve parents, the parents respond. Over 90% of parents of elementary and middle grades students believe the school should tell them how to help at home (Epstein, 1986; Dauber and Epstein, 1989). This remains high — over 80% — for parents of high school students (Dornbusch and Ritter, 1988), and for parents of children in Catholic high schools (Bauch, 1988).

• Most parents help their children at home sometimes, but do not know if they are doing the right things, or doing things right. This is true for parents with all educational backgrounds, and especially those with little formal education. Less-educated parents report that they know *what* to do, but not *how* to translate the information into useful family practices to help manage and monitor the education of their early adolescents (Baker and Stevenson, 1986). Many low-income and less-educated parents of junior high or middle school students do not know what they should do for and with their children at that level of schooling. They report that they need to know more about school programs in order to help their children (Leitch and Tangri, 1988; Dauber and Epstein, 1989). Even in the early grades, some parents help their children with the best of intentions, but without information about *how to help*. Scott-Jones (1987) reported that low-income, minority parents of first grade students differed in the ways they help their children on their own, with some help of questionable value. New research is needed on how parents with different backgrounds respond to specific ideas and guidance from their children's teachers of how to help at home.

• Most parents cannot and do not participate at the school building (Bauch, 1988; Comer, 1980; Dauber and Epstein, 1989; Dornbusch and Ritter, 1988; Epstein, 1986; Leitch and Tangri, 1988). In our research, only 4% of the elementary school parents were active at the school building 25 days or more each year. Over 70% never volunteered in official ways, and over 60% worked full-or part-time during the school day (Epstein, 1986). Most parents who work or have other responsibilities cannot come to the school building during the school day for meetings or workshops (Espinoza, 1988). They could, however, use the information from workshops at other convenient times in other forms, such as tape recordings, video cassettes, newsletters, computerized messages, and other print and nonprint forms. The results from several studies also point to a clear need to more broadly define the term "volunteer" to include and to recognize the work that parents do at the school building during the school day, after school, on weekends, at home, or in the community to support school programs and student success. Research is needed on the effects on families and on schools of these different types of volunteer participation.

• Few parents participate directly in school decision-making as leaders or representatives of other parents as PTA leaders, as members of advisory committees, Chapter 1 committees or other activities (Bauch, 1988; Comer, 1980; Dornbusch and Ritter, 1988; Epstein, 1986; Leitch and Tangri, 1988).

Although the numbers of volunteers, leaders, and other participants at school could be increased with better recruitment, training, and deployment of parents, the vast number of parents want to be involved with their own child at home more frequently and more effectively. All or most parents in all types of schools and at all grade levels express the need for clear communications about their children's attendance, behavior, academic progress, the content of what their children are learning, and how to help their children at home.

• Parents whose children's teachers were "leaders" in the use of parent involvement were strongly influenced by the teachers' practices (Epstein, 1985, 1986). These parents were significantly more likely than other parents to report that they:

— received *many ideas* of how to help at home from the teachers;
— felt that they *should help* their children at home;
— *understood more* this year than in previous years about what their child was being taught in school, and
— *rated the teacher higher* in overall teaching ability and in interpersonal skills.

In urban schools, parents who reported that their children's teachers and schools had strong programs in particular types of involvement (e.g., at home or at school) were significantly more likely than other parents to be involved in exactly those types of activities. The evidence is clear that school practices affect family practices (Dauber and Epstein, 1989).

• Status variables are not the most important measures for understanding parent involvement. At all grade levels, the evidence suggests that school policies and teacher practices and family practices are more important than race, parent education, family size, marital status, and even grade level in determining whether parents continue to be part of their children's education (Becker and Epstein, 1982; Dauber and Epstein, 1989; Epstein, 1986; Epstein, in press b). Status variables may become increasingly important influences on parent involvement in the upper grades, especially in high school, because the schools do little to actively inform parents of appropriate family activities that support children's schooling (Dornbusch and Ritter, 1988; Bauch, 1988; Espinoza, 1988).

Parents respond in different ways to requests for involvement. For example, single mothers and mothers who work outside the home were less likely to come to the school building than other parents, but were as or more likely to spend time with their children at home to help them on school activities (Epstein, in press b). Research is needed on different approaches that meet the needs of families with different characteristics and constraints to help all parents become easily and productively involved. Unless researchers examine *both* family and school structure and practices, we will continue to receive contradictory and often false messages about the capabilities of single parents, poor or minority parents, and other hard-to-reach families.

Effects on Students

Another goal of parent involvement—the "bottom line" for many educators—is to increase student achievement and success in school. We define "achievement" broadly, including test scores, school work, the persistence of students in school, and the general development of attitudes and behaviors that characterize "successful students" (Epstein, 1988c). Research on effects of school and family connections on students has improved over the years from highly suggestive results to more focused, analytic studies.

• Gordon (1979), Gordon, Olmsted, Rubin, and True (1979), Rivlin and Timpane (1975), Sinclair (1980), Valentine and Stark (1979), and Zigler (1979) review early studies of Head Start and Follow-Through programs that suggest that there are generally positive effects of school and family connections on parents and on young children, but the measures of parent involvement in these studies were incomplete. Direct connections between teachers and parents were not measured. Others also have suggested that parents assisting their own children with learning activities at home (as opposed to the contact of a few parents in the school building) *should have* important consequences for student achievement and other outcomes such as school attendance, school adaptability, and classroom behavior (Comer, 1980; Gillum, 1977; Gotts, 1980; Rich, Van Dien, & Mattox, 1979). The measures in these studies are suggestive, lacking the rigor needed to demonstrate specific effects on particular students.

• Students benefit from parents' involvement at all grade levels. Rich and Jones (1977) present some early evidence suggesting that extra learning time at home produces gains in early elementary students' reading scores equivalent to those made by students under more expensive "pull-out" programs in schools. (Also see the annotated review by Henderson, 1987, of studies of student achievement by many researchers who looked at family influence.) Most of these studies, too, lack direct connections between particular school and family practices and individual student growth or change in achievement.

• Fifth grade students were surveyed for their reactions to teacher practices of parent involvement and their parents' help at home. Students whose teachers and parents used frequent parent involvement practices reported more positive attitudes toward school, more regular homework habits, more similarity between the school and their family, more familiarity between the teacher and their parents, and more homework on weekends (Epstein, 1982).

• In one study that directly connects teachers' practices, parent responses, and student achievement, students in grades 3 and 5 gained more in reading achievement test scores (but not math scores) from fall to spring of the school year if their teachers frequently involved parents in learning activities at home (Epstein, in press a). Most of the teachers' requests were for parent involvement in reading-related activities, indicating important subject-specific connections between parent involvement in reading activities with their children at home and their children's reading achievement test gains.

Based on the subject-specific connections of teachers' requests for parent involvement in reading, parents' responses of helping and encouraging their children in reading skills, and students' gains in reading, we have worked with teachers to develop a process called Teachers Involve Parents in Schoolwork (TIPS). The TIPS process is designed to assist teachers to increase parent involvement in math and science homework and discussions, encouragement, and enjoyment of these subjects at home (Epstein, 1987c). We hypothesize that parent involvement in specific subjects — such as math and science — will increase student skills and positive attitudes in those subjects, just as our early data suggests about reading. In addition, some specific results concerning math or science may occur. For example, mothers' involvement in TIPS math and science activities over many years of schooling may increase daughters' interest and attention in math and science, the number of courses students take in these subjects, and, perhaps in the long term, occupational orientations. Research is needed on the effects of the TIPS process and other subject-specific school and family connections on student achievements and attitudes.

Effects on Teachers

A third major goal of school and family connections is to help school administrators and teachers conduct more effective school programs. Several studies contribute to new knowledge of the effects of parent involvement on teaching practice:

• Teachers reported more positive feelings about teaching and about their school when there was more parent involvement at the school (Leitch and Tangri, 1988; Epstein and Dauber, 1988).

• Teachers who frequently involved parents in their children's education rated all parents—including less-educated parents and single parents—higher in helpfulness and follow- through than did other teachers. Teachers who were leaders in parent involvement did not make the stereotypic judgments about poor parents, less-educated parents, or single parents that were made by other teachers (Epstein, in press b). Working with parents, then, raised teachers' expectations and appreciation of parents as partners.

• Teachers in inner-city schools reported that they wanted all parents to perform over a dozen helpful activities at home in the elementary and middle grades. But, very few teachers had initiated practices to help parents understand how to conduct those activities with their children at different grade levels. Teachers tended to blame parents for their generally low level of involvement in the middle or junior high school grades (Leitch and Tangri, 1988; Epstein and Dauber, 1988). Yet, there were other teachers who successfully involved similar parents in their children's education as part of regular teaching practice.

• Teachers and parents disagree in their ideas of whether parents are involved and want to be involved with their children's education

(Dornbusch and Ritter, 1988; Epstein and Dauber, 1989; Leitch and Tangri, 1988). Teachers in urban, Chapter 1 schools said that most parents were not involved in their children's education and did not want to be. Parents in the same schools reported that they were involved with their children at home in a variety of ways, but that they needed more and better information from teachers about how to help at home (Dauber and Epstein, 1989). The discrepancies in parent and teacher reports need to be studied and resolved.

Five Types of Parent Involvement

The findings of our own and other studies suggest a typology of five major types of parent involvement that should be part of a comprehensive program for family and school connections in every school (Epstein, 1987b; Epstein, 1988b; Epstein and Scott-Jones, in press). These are:

TYPE 1. *The basic obligations of parents* refer to responsibilities of families for children's health and safety; parenting and child-rearing skills to prepare children for school; supervision, discipline, and guidance for children at each age level; and *positive home conditions* that support school learning and behavior appropriate for each grade level.

TYPE 2. *The basic obligations of schools* refer to the *communications from school-to-home* about school programs and children's progress, including the form and frequency of communications such as memos, notices, report cards, and conferences to inform all parents about school programs and their children's progress.

TYPE 3. *Parent involvement at school* refers to parent volunteers who assist teachers, administrators, and children in classrooms or in other areas of the school. It also refers to parents who come to school to support and watch student performances, sports, or other events.

TYPE 4. *Parent involvement in learning activities at home* refers to parent-initiated, child-initiated requests for help and, particularly, to ideas from teacher for parents to *moni-*

tor and assist their own children at home on learning
activities that are coordinated with the children's class-
work.

TYPE 5. *Parent involvement in governance and advocacy* refers
to parents in *decision-making* roles in the decision-
making PTA/PTO, Advisory Councils, or other committees or groups at the school, district, or state level.
It also refers to parent and community activists in independent advocacy groups that monitor the schools and
work for school improvement.

Schools vary in how much importance they place on each type of
involvement, how inclusive they are of all parents, how they organize activities, and whether and how they evaluate their effectiveness. Each of the five types has different goals; some occur in different locations at home, school, and in the community; each
includes scores of different practices; each requires different materials and procedures for successful implementation in practice; and
each requires different measures in research and evaluation.

The five types of parent involvement do not refer to unusual or
unfamiliar practices of schools. They include activities that a few
teachers in most schools conduct with a few parents, or that a few
parents in most schools conduct on their own. There are presently
pervasive weaknesses, however, in how most schools organize,
evaluate, and improve the five types of parent involvement so that
they become a regular part of the school organization and all teachers' practices. The following are some examples of new directions
that most schools need to take to structure school and family connections effectively for more families.

To assist parents to fulfill their basic obligations (TYPE 1), most
schools could improve how they help families find needed social
services; how the schools select topics and times for workshops on
parenting skills; organize video, tape, or print systems to summarize workshops for parents who could not attend; and conduct other
activities to provide parents with needed information about child
and adolescent development, and home conditions for learning at
each grade level.

To create more effective communications from school to home
(TYPE 2), most schools could improve the clarity and forms of the

memos, notices, and other communications they send to all families; experiment with innovative schedules, lengths, and content of parent-teacher conferences; explain report cards and how to help students improve their grades; use other strategies to inform parents of school programs and children's progress; and obtain useful information from parents to help the schools respond to the needs of individual children.

To increase the number of volunteers beyond a small clique of active parents (TYPE 3), most schools could improve how they welcome all parents to the school building; recruit and train volunteers so that they contribute productively to the school; schedule volunteers' hours so that more parents and others in the community can participate at convenient times; assign volunteers to assist teachers or administrators to strengthen and enrich school programs; assess the effectiveness of their efforts; and other ways of defining volunteers to enable more families to participate in activities that support the school and students at many times and places.

To assist parents in understanding and exercising their continuing role as educators (TYPE 4), most schools could improve the ways they give ideas and guidance to parents about how to help their children at home on learning activities and homework at each grade level in each school subject. Most schools could improve their procedures to guide parents in helping their children build the age-specific skills that build talents, social competencies, and other skills characteristic of successful students. This includes information on what skills children need to master in each grade, how to monitor students' work, and how to discuss schoolwork at home so that students will do their best in school.

To increase family and community leadership and participation in school improvement efforts (TYPE 5), most schools could do more to develop and use parents' leadership skills so that parents who are leaders communicate effectively with those they represent. This includes developing school-site management models that engage parent leaders in true partnerships in decision making with teachers, administrators, and other school staff on school improvement activities.

Research is needed on the design and implementation of different programs and practices of each type of involvement, and on the effects or different outcomes for students, parents, and teaching practice that result from specific programs and practices.

Extending The Research Agenda

Studies of teachers' practices of parent involvement are consistently reporting results that show that parents benefit in their roles as educators because of their connections with the schools. Students benefit in learning and in attitudes toward school. Teachers benefit in their understanding of families and in the ratings they receive from parents and from their principals for their efforts to involve parents. Although much has been learned about the nature, extent, and effects of practices that demonstrate school and family "overlap," much is still unknown. Research is needed on the effects of specific connections between and among institutions that share responsibilities for children across the grades. We do not yet know enough about the real limits or potential of parent involvement when highly effective practices are used regularly, frequently, and cumulatively by teachers and other educators. New research must raise questions about developmental patterns of involvement across the grades, and differentiated practices to involve families with different histories and needs (Epstein and Scott-Jones, in press).

Families are changing. The "traditional" family of two natural parents with mom working at home is now "untraditional" (Bureau of the Census, 1984). Most children live in other types of families — one-parent homes, reconstituted or blended families, joint-custody families, foster homes, extended families, relatives as guardians, and other variations. These arrangements cross economic lines and are not indicative of uncaring families. Many children come from families whose home language is not English, with rich but different family customs, and with parents who have little familiarity with U.S. schools.

Even within categories, families differ dramatically. For example, young, single, black, poor mothers have different histories, skills, and needs in their connections with their children's schools. A study of low-income black adolescent mothers in an urban area indicated that some women in their early twenties returned to school, often at the time their youngest child entered first grade

(Furstenberg, Brooks-Gunn, & Morgan, 1987). This important study examined how mothers and children progressed over time, but did not account for the practices of the different schools that the children attended, or how the schools' practices contributed to the patterns of success or failure of the children or the mothers.

It is also true that some young, single, black, poor mothers do not return to school. Some of these mothers had serious problems in school when they were students and are uncomfortable, even fearful, in school situations. Others just do not know how to help or how to make contact with their children's schools and teachers. We need to know more about the dynamics of school and family interactions that occur for important groups and subgroups of families.

In addition to single parents, there are many other groups of "hard-to-reach" families whose physical or social distance from the schools raise extra barriers to productive school and family overlap. These groups include: young parents, parents who work, parents of older children, older parents, less-educated parents, language minority parents, single parents, fathers, step-parents or parents in blended families, other adults with whom children live, parents of transfer or new students, parents of students who are adolescent parents, and others (Epstein and Scott-Jones, in press). These and other families have unique problems and needs. Yet, all families must understand the schools their children attend. All schools must understand the families that they serve. And, all schools and families must understand how they can influence each other to benefit the children that they share. A continuing research agenda needs to focus on questions of the effects on students of family and school programs that provide developmental and differentiated experiences for families of children at all grade levels and for the special needs of different families.

Children, parents, and teachers are changing—for better or for worse—as school and family connections are made across the school years. We have not paid enough attention to the simultaneous and cumulative influence of the two environments on each other and on the members in each setting. There is "a whole lot of changing going on," and we can no longer afford to focus attention narrowly on only one institution if we are to understand the dynamic, continuing affiliations of schools and families. The theoretical perspectives, research results, and research agenda discussed here have implications for linking schools and families in sociology of family courses, in sociology of education courses, and in social service practice.

IMPLICATIONS FOR LINKING SOCIOLOGIES OF EDUCATION AND FAMILY

Most family texts and courses ignore the school, and most education courses ignore the family. This is unfortunate, because many standard topics in these courses are directly linked to the issues raised in this paper. Overall, there are three broad issues that need to be added to family and education courses in order to incorporate new knowledge from the growing literature on school and family connections:

— Conditions and changes in families that affect parents' interactions with their children and with their children's schools, and how these aspects of family life affect student learning and development.
— Conditions and changes in families that affect school programs and practices, including the effects of parent involvement on teachers' and principals' attitudes and behaviors toward families and toward children.
— Conditions and changes in schools that affect parents' interactions with their children and with other family members.

These three general themes can be better understood by considering some specific topics in courses about the family and school:

• Discussions of the stages of family life, family development, child development, and how parents and children change across the years, should include attention to how these developmental patterns are affected by family interactions with other institutions, especially schools. The overlapping spheres of influence model and supporting research shows that parenting skills change as parents accumulate knowledge about their children and their schools. Family and child development cannot be fully understood without attention to the practices of the schools that children attend.

• Discussions of other prominent topics in family courses—e.g., divorce, children and divorce, remarriage, step-parenting, teenage parenthood, single-parent homes, working mothers, and dual-worker families—are incomplete without information about how these conditions of family life affect children as students and are affected by variations in school programs and, particularly, practices that connect schools and families. Discussions of families in society, families in context, and similar topics are enriched with information about the effects on family environments of their children's school environments, from preschool through post-secondary education.

• Discussions of prominent topics in sociology of education and other education courses—e.g., school and classroom organization and management, teacher effectiveness, principal leadership, student test performance, status attainment, desegregation and integration, school effects, the school as a social organization, and many others—are incomplete without information on how conditions of school life are affected by family culture, family strengths, needs, goals, and variations in practices of school and family connections. Those who study schools and student outcomes must understand the importance of measuring family processes, practices, and interactions in addition to family background and structures.

• Discussions of race, ethnicity, religion, income, and family structure should include coverage of what these characteristics mean as families begin and continue interactions with their children's schools. Because families are changing, courses about the family need to clarify how different family structures, cultures, values, and belief systems affect parents' relationships with teachers, principals, and other school staff.

• Discussions of gender roles, especially what mothers and fathers do in families, should include attention to mothers' and fathers' interactions and involvement with teachers and other authority figures who share responsibility for the socialization and education of children. Parents' interactions with their children about schoolwork also may be gender related.

• Discussions of fathers' roles need to include attention to patterns of fathers' interactions in the family, and in their children's education. New fathers' needs and their interactions with infants have been given some attention (Palm and Palkovitz, 1988; Lamb, 1981), but fathers' continuing responsibilities for their children's education, fathers' interactions with their children as students, and fathers' interactions with teachers and other school staff are also important. This includes fathers in two-parent and one-parent homes, as custodial and non-custodial parents, and in parent education programs. The types and levels of involvement of fathers and their investments in their children (Palm and Palkovitz, 1988) need to include attention to the interactions of fathers with other institutions that affect their children (McBride, 1989).

• Discussions of family stress and stress management (see, for example, McCubbin, Sussman, and Patterson, 1983) need to give attention to the stressors that occur for children and for parents at points of transitions, such as entry to preschool and elementary school, entry to middle school or high school, or other changes to new schools across the school years. Family stress and management of stress are affected by school policies and practices that involve or ignore parents.

• Discussions of social policies that concern families must include attention to concurrent policies that affect schools, the education of children, and family life that affects children's attendance and success in school (Haskins and Adams, 1983). Federal, state, and local policies concerning preschool programs, daycare, and other before- and after-school programs, high school and post-secondary education, family health and social services, parents' employment and employment benefits, and other policies have implications for successful partnerships between schools and families.

How would these and other topics change course coverage? Some researchers of the family acknowledge that *parent-child* interactions change across the grades (Newman and Newman, 1988), and that there are multiple influences on child development (Belsky, Lerner, and Spanier, 1984). It is also important, however, to understand how parent-child interactions change because of school levels and programs, and how parent-school interactions affect the children and the rest of the family.

Although *transitions* to parenthood (from non-parent status) have been given considerable attention (Skolnick and Skolnick, 1983; Leslie and Korman, 1985), little attention has been given to the effects of school programs and practices on *continuations* of parenthood across the years that children are in school. There are shifts in social relationships that occur during transitions to motherhood (Milardo, 1988) or parenthood (Palkovitz and Sussman, 1988). But there also are shifts in social relationships that continue across the years of early childhood, early adolescence, and later adolescence. Family researchers could contribute greatly to a better understanding of these topics.

Major and minor transitions and expected and unexpected transitions occur in families as children change grade levels and school levels. These have implications for school and family connections and student success in school. For example, parents separate, divorce, or remarry, families move, students select new schools or are forced to change schools for behavior or other reasons, teenagers have babies and become parents, and many others. Family transitions to new homes and schools may be more or less a problem for children, parents, and schools depending on whether schools have practices that are sensitive and responsive to new children and their families. One school in Illinois, for example, is operating a type of "welcome wagon for parent involvement" to see if new families in a highly mobile community can be better integrated into the life of their children's schools (Illinois State Board of Education, 1988). Similarly, children, parents, and schools may have few or many problems when parents separate or divorce, depending on whether or not schools have practices that accept and respond to single parents and children in one-parent homes. In all of the examples, the point is that the practices of children's schools must be considered in order to understand the effects of transitions on family members. Similarly, the practices of families must be considered in order to understand the effects of transitions on school programs and student success.

Teachers, administrators, and others in social service occupations are not presently prepared by the courses they take to understand or to implement inter-institutional connections with families. Undergraduate and graduate courses in sociology of the family, marriage and the family, and sociology of education could provide students with some background and understanding of the characteristics, strengths, and needs of families and the kinds of connections we have discussed. In many colleges and universities, sociology courses are the main (sometimes only) sources of information about contextual and environmental effects for students who intend to be teachers, social workers, family therapists, school administrators, school psychologists, and other related occupations (as well as those who will be parents) to understand important inter-institutional connections that will affect their clients, their children, and themselves.

All who are trained in sociology of the family, or as family therapists need to understand the schools as they relate to families. All who are trained in sociology of education, or as teachers, principals, other administrators, school psychologists, or school social workers need to understand families as they relate to schools. This includes family environments and ways that school policies and teacher practices affect parents, children, and relationships in families. This also includes school environments and the ways that family practices — not just family background — affect teachers, children, programs, and relationships in schools. Indeed, all who will be parents need to understand the roles and relationships of family members and their connections to the schools. We must actively integrate the sociologies of education and the family to understand schools and families as institutions and to understand the roles and relationships of the individuals that share responsibility for children.

REFERENCES

Baker, D. P. & Stevenson, D. L. (1986). Mothers' strategies for children's school achievement: Managing the transition to high school. *Sociology of Education*, *59*, 156-166.

Bauch, P. A. (1988). Is parent involvement different in private schools? *Educational Horizons*, *66*, 78-82.

Becker, H. J. & Epstein, J. L. (1982). Parent involvement: A study of teacher practices. *Elementary School Journal*, *83*, 85-102.

Belsky, J., Lerner, R. M., & Spanier, G. B. (1984). *The child in the family*. Reading, MA: Addison-Wesley Publishing.

Bloom, B. S. (1964). *Stability and change in human characteristics*. New York: Wiley.

Bronfenbrenner, U. (1979). *The ecology of human development*. Cambridge, MA: Harvard University Press.

Bureau of the Census (1984). *Statistical abstract of the United States, 1985.* Washington, D.C.: Government Printing Office.

Clark, R. (1983). Family life and school achievement. *Why poor black children succeed and fail.* Chicago: University of Chicago Press.

Clausen, J. A. (1966). Family structure, socialization and personality. In L. W. Hoffman and M. L. Hoffman (Eds.), *Review of Child Development Research, Volume 2,* pp. 1-53. New York: Russell Sage, New York.

Coleman, J. S. (1987). Families and schools. *Educational Researcher, 16,* 32-38.

Coleman, J. S., Campbell, E. Q., Hobson, C. J., McPartland, J. M., Mood, A., Weinfeld, F. D., & York, R. L. (1966). *Equality of educational opportunity.* Washington, D.C.: U.S. Government Printing Office.

Comer, J. P. (1980). *School power.* New York: Free Press.

Dauber, S. L. & Epstein, J. L. (1989). Parents' attitudes and practices of involvement in inner-city elementary and middle schools. Paper presented at the annual meetings of the American Educational Research Association, San Francisco, March.

Davies, D. (1988). Hard to reach parents in three countries: Perspectives on how schools relate to low-status families. Paper presented at the annual meetings of the American Educational Research Association, New Orleans, April.

Dornbusch, S. M. & Ritter, P. L. (1988). Parents of high school students: A neglected resource. *Educational Horizons, 66,* 75-77.

Entwisle, D. R., Alexander, K. A., Cadigan, D., & Pallas, A. (1986). The schooling process in first grade: Two samples a decade apart. *American Educational Research Journal, 23,* 587-613.

Epstein, J. L. (1982). Student reactions to teacher practices of parent involvement. Paper presented at the annual meeting of the American Educational Research Association. Parent Involvement Report P-21. Baltimore: The Johns Hopkins University Center for Research on Elementary and Middle Schools.

Epstein, J. L. (1983). Longitudinal effects of family-school-person interactions on student outcomes. In A. Kerckhoff (Ed.), *Research in sociology of education and socialization, vol. 4.* Greenwich CT: JAI Press.

Epstein, J. L. (1985). A question of merit: Principals' and parents' evaluations of teachers. *Educational Researcher, 14,* (7), 3-10.

Epstein, J. L. (1986). Parents' reactions to teacher practices of parent involvement. *The Elementary School Journal, 86,* 277-294.

Epstein, J. L. (1987a) Toward a theory of family-school connections: Teacher practices and parent involvement. In K. Hurrelmann, F. Kaufmann, and F. Losel (Eds.), *Social intervention: Potential and constraints.* New York/Berlin: Aldine/de Gruyter.

Epstein, J. L. (1987b). What principals should know about parent involvement. *Principal, 66,* 6-9.

Epstein, J. L. (1987c). Teacher Manual: Teachers Involve Parents in Schoolwork (TIPS). Parent Involvement Reports P-61. Baltimore: The Johns Hopkins University Center for Research on Elementary and Middle Schools.

Epstein, J. L. (1988a). Schools in the center: School, family, peer, and community connections for more effective middle grades schools and students. Paper prepared for the Carnegie Task Force on Education of Young Adolescents (Draft) June, 1988.

Epstein, J. L. (1988b). How do we improve programs in parent involvement? *Educational Horizons*, (Special Issue on Parents and Schools), *66*, (2), 58-59.

Epstein, J. L. (1988c). Effective schools or effective students? Dealing with diversity. In R. Haskins and D. MacRae (Eds.) *Policies for America's public schools: Teachers, equity, and indicators*. Norwood, NJ: Ablex.

Epstein, J. L. (in press a). Effects on student achievement of teacher practices of parent involvement. In S. Silvern (Ed.), *Literacy through family, community, and school interaction*. Greenwich CT: JAI Press.

Epstein, J. L. (in press b). Single parents and the schools: Effects of marital status on parent and teacher interactions. In M. Hallinan (Ed.), *Change in societal institutions*. New York: Plenum.

Epstein, J. L. & Dauber, S. L. (1988). Teacher attitudes and practices of parent involvement in inner-city elementary and middle schools. Paper presented at the American Sociological Association meeting, Atlanta.

Epstein, J. L. & Scott-Jones, D. (in press). School-family-community connections for accelerating student progress in the elementary and middle grades. Paper presented at the Stanford University Conference on Accelerated Education for At-Risk Students (November, 1988), to appear in the book of the papers prepared for that conference.

Epstein J. L. & McPartland, J. M. (1979). Authority structures. In H. Walberg (Ed.), *Educational environments and effects*. Berkeley: McCutcheon.

Espinoza, R. (1988). Working parents, employers, and schools. *Educational Horizons*, *66*, 63-65.

Freud, A. (1937). *The ego and mechanisms of defense*. London: Hogarth Press.

Furstenberg, F. F., Brooks-Gunn, J., & Morgan, S. P. (1987). *Adolescent mothers in later life*. Cambridge: University Press.

Gillum, R. M. (1977). The effects of parent involvement on student achievement in three Michigan performance contracting programs. Paper presented at the annual meetings of the AERA.

Gordon, I. J. (1979). The effects of parent involvement in schooling. In R. S. Brandt, (Ed.), *Partners: Parents and schools*, pp. 4-25. Alexandria, VA: Association for Supervision and Curriculum Development, 1979.

Gordon, I. J., Olmsted, P. P.,Rubin, R. I., & True, J. H. (1979). How has Follow-Through promoted parent involvement? *Young Children*, *34* (5), 49-53.

Gotts, E. (1980). Long-term effects of a home-oriented preschool program. *Childhood Education*, *56*, 228-234.

Haskins, R. & Adams, D. (Eds.) (1983). *Parent education and public policy*. Norwood, NJ: Ablex.

Henderson, A. (1987). *The evidence continues to grow: Parent involvement improves student achievement*. Columbia MD: National Committee for Citizens in Education.

Heyns, B. (1978). *Summer learning and the effects of schooling*. New York: Academic Press.

Illinois State Board of Education. (1988). West Elementary School Urban Education Partnership Grant Proposal. Chicago: Urban and Ethnic Education Unit.

Kagan, J. (1980). Perspectives on continuity. In O. G. Brim and J. Kagan, (Eds.), *Constancy and change in human development*, pp. 26-74. Cambridge: Harvard University Press.

Lamb, M. E. (1981). *The role of the father in child development*. New York: Wiley.

Lareau, A. (1987). Social class differences in family-school relationships: The importance of cultural capital. *Sociology of Education, 60*, 73-85.

Leichter, H. J. (1974). *The family as educator*. New York: Teachers College Press.

Leitch, M. L. & Tangri, S. S. (1988). Barriers to home-school collaboration. *Educational Horizons, 66*, 70-74.

Leslie, G. R. & Korman, S. K. (1985). *The family in social context*, (Sixth Edition). New York: Oxford University Press.

Lightfoot, S. L. (1978). *Worlds apart: Relationships between families and schools*. New York: Basic Books.

Litwak, E. & Meyer, H. J. (1974). *School, family and neighborhood: The theory and practice of school-community relations*. New York: Columbia University Press.

Marjoribanks, K. (1979). *Families and their learning environments: An empirical analysis*. London: Routledge and Kegan Paul.

Mayeske, G. W. (1973). *A study of the achievement of our nation's students*. Washington, D.C.: Government Printing Office.

McBride, B. (1989). Stress and fathers' parental competence: Implications for parent education. Paper presented at the annual meeting of the American Educational Research Association, San Francisco, March.

McCubbin, H. I., Sussman, M. B., & Patterson, J. M. (Eds.). (1983). *Social stress and the family: Advances and developments in family stress theory and research*. New York: Haworth Press.

McDill, E. L. & Rigsby, L. (1973). *Structure and process in secondary schools: The academic impact of educational climates*. Baltimore: The Johns Hopkins University Press.

Milardo, R. M. (1988). *Familes and social networks*. Newbury Park CA: Sage.

Newman, P. R. & Newman, B. M. (1988). Parenthood and adult development. In R. Palkovitz and M. B. Sussman (Eds.), *Transitions to parenthood*, pp. 313-337. New York: Haworth Press.

Palkovitz, R. & Sussman, M. B. (Eds.). (1988). *Transitions to parenthood*. New York: Haworth Press.

Palm, G. F. & Palkovitz, R. (1988). The challenge of working with new fathers: Implications for support providers. In R. Palkovitz and M. B. Sussman, *Transitions to Parenthood*, pp. 357-376. New York: Haworth Press.

Parsons, T. (1959). The school class as a social system: some of its functions in American society. *Harvard Educational Review, 29,* 297-318.

Piaget, J. & Inhelder B. (1969). *The psychology of the child.* New York: Basic Books.

Rich, D. & Jones, C. (1977). *A family affair: Education.* Washington, D.C.: The Home and School Institute.

Rich, D., Van Dien, J., & Mattox, B. (1979). Families as educators of their own children. In R. Brandt (Ed.), *Partners: Parents and schools,* pp. 26-40. Alexandria, VA: Association for Supervisors and Curriculum Development.

Rivlin, A. M. & Timpane, P. M. (1975). *Planned variation in education: Should we give up or try harder:* Washington, D.C.: The Brookings Institution.

Scott-Jones, D. (1987). Mother-as-teacher in the families of high-and low-achieving low-income black first-graders. *Journal of Negro Education, 56,* 21-34.

Seeley, D. S. (1981). *Education through partnership: Mediating structures and education.* Cambridge MA: Ballinger.

Sinclair, R. L. (Ed.) (1980). *A two-way street: Home-school cooperation in curriculum decision making.* Boston: Institute for Responsive Education.

Skolnick, A. S. & Skolnick, J. H. (1983). *Family in Transition* (Fourth Edition). Boston: Little, Brown, and Company.

Stallworth, J. T. & Williams, D. (1981). Parent involvement training in elementary teacher preparation. Paper presented at the annual meeting of the American Educational Research Association. Los Angeles.

Valentine, J. & Stark, E. (1979). The social context of parent involvement in Head Start. In E. Zigler & J. Valentine (Eds.), *Project Head Start: A legacy of the war on poverty (pp. 291-314).* New York: The Free Press.

Waller, W. (1932). *The sociology of teaching.* New York: Russell and Russell.

Weber, M. (1947). *The theory of social and economic organization* New York: Oxford University Press.

Zigler, E. (1979). Project Head Start: Success or failure? In E. Zigler & J. Valentine (Eds.), *Project Head Start: A legacy of the war on poverty,* pp. 495-507. New York: The Free Press.

Low-Income Families
and Public Welfare Organizations

Catherine S. Chilman

Families and welfare organizations are ecological systems. Families are variable, multigenerational systems, strongly affected by their own internal dynamics and by their interactions with the many environmental systems in which they are imbedded. Internally, family behaviors are outgrowths of the bio-social-psychological characteristics of each member and the nature of their family structures. Externally, family characteristics are a product of interactions with economic, social, political and physical systems of the larger society. These systems include, among others, educational, health, vocational, and public welfare organizations (Chilman, Nunnally, & Cox, 1988).

The same concepts apply to these organizations. They, too, are heavily affected by internal dynamics involving their historical backgrounds and their system and staff characteristics. These organizations also interact with the larger complex society of which they are a part. They are highly dependent on this society's ever-changing politics, economy, social values and goals, and resources.

The chief purpose of this essay is to increase understanding of recent trends in poverty among families and the probable causes and outcomes of this poverty. A closely allied purpose is to heighten awareness of problems in the major federal-state-local programs that have developed over the past half century to assist these families. This discussion, though overly brief, should demonstrate that both poor families and the organizations that are set up to serve them are intricate systems which are heavily affected by the increasingly complex larger social, economic, and political systems in which they are embedded. Finally, critically needed programs, policies, and evaluative studies are suggested with the hope that read-ers will be stimulated to give further consideration and informed support to the kinds of changes indicated.

THE NATURE OF HUMAN SERVICES ORGANIZATIONS

Public health and welfare organizations such as AFDC (Aid to Families with Dependent Children) are commonly referred to as bureaucracies. Recent theorizing and research about human service organizations, however, questions the prevalent characterization of these organizations as bureaucracies in the traditional sense. Weber (1947) saw bureaucracies as highly efficient formal organizations with clear allocations of tasks and powers. His ideal model was a tightly organized structure operating by legal and rational rules. Authority was organized through a clearly defined hierarchy of offices based on specific elaborated regulations and technical procedures.

The desirability and efficacy of such a model has been recently questioned (Sarri, 1987; Holland & Petchers, 1987). Contemporary concepts recognize that organizations are systems heavily influenced by irrational as well as rational aspects of human behavior and by external and internal politics (Hasenfeld & English, 1974). Human service organizations exist in a changing community environment. They have differing levels of financial support, changing legal requirements, newly emerging service technologies, shifting client characteristics and needs, and changing social service resources. To survive and obtain adequate funding, health and welfare organizations need highly competent administrators to deal with these many complex frequently, shifting, often competitive components (Hasenfeld, 1983). They also require an active, informed, socially-conscious electorate to push politically for adequate programs and funding.

Theory, practice wisdom, and research all point to the superiority of democratic over authoritarian modes of organizational structure and administration to address these diverse needs (Hasenfeld, 1983). Participation by staff at all levels of decision-making promotes employee morale, efficiency, and effectiveness. Involvement of clients in some aspects of policy-making is also an effective way of reducing client alienation and making services more relevant.

However, these recommendations rest on the assumption that the organization has an adequate and professionally trained staff; decision-making can be flexibly implemented; resources and regulations allow for client individuation and participation; and that the community will support these procedures. As will be seen in this paper, these conditions are often not present for public health and welfare organizations.

FAMILIES IN POVERTY

Trends

There are many definitions of poverty in this country (Zimmerman & Chilman, 1988). The commonly used, but frequently criticized, official definition of poverty which was established in 1963 is employed in this paper. Individuals and families with annual incomes below a certain level, determined primarily by food prices for a minimally adequate diet, are termed poor by this definition.

Although the poverty rate in the United States decreased from about 32% in 1949, to 20% in the early 1960s to about 9% in 1973, it rose to over 12% in 1982, falling slightly after that to about 11% in 1987. It was probably much higher during the Great Depression but exact data are unavailable. These changes in family poverty rates are largely a consequence of variations in economic conditions over the years, the incidence of female-headed families, and shifts in levels of governmental income maintenance (welfare) programs (Levy, 1987; Zimmerman & Chilman, 1988).

In 1986, almost one-fourth of the nation's children lived in families with incomes below the poverty line, a rise from 12% in 1973. This includes 18% of white children and almost half of black and Hispanic children under age six. Children in female-headed families are especially apt to be poor; this occurs in two-thirds of black and Hispanic families and one-fourth of white female-headed families (Garfinkel & McLanahan, 1986). Not only have rates of family poverty increased during the 1980s, but poor people have become poorer with their incomes falling further and further below the poverty line. On the average, there are not only more poor families, but more families have become extremely poor (Center on Budget and Policy Priorities, 1985).

In recent years there has also been an increase in the numbers of working poor families—those families with one or more members in the work force but whose earnings are so low that the family remains below the poverty line. For example, a parent working full-time during 1985, at the minimum wage, which had not increased from $3.35 per hour since 1979, would only earn about $7,000 a year, $5,000 short of the poverty line budget of $12,000 for a family of four. Even if two parents worked full-time this would hardly bring their families above the poverty line. Problems of the working poor have been exacerbated since 1981, when actions by the Reagan Administration reduced or eliminated their supplemental welfare assistance, including eligibility for Medicaid and Food Stamps.

The poverty rate for *young* families, those families with parents under age 30, has nearly doubled over the past 15 years (Children's Defense Fund and Center for Labor Market Studies of Northeastern University, 1988). Young families with children are seven times more likely to be poor than those without children. While full-time employment of each parent is the only escape route from poverty for many young couples, the costs of adequate substitute day care for their children is often beyond their reach.

At the other end of the age spectrum, the elderly, as a group, are better off financially today than in earlier times. This is primarily a result of the relatively generous Social Security (including Medicare) programs for the elderly and private work-related retirement pensions. The proportion of elderly in poverty has fallen from over one-third of the population in 1960, to about 11% in 1988 (Zimmerman & Chilman, 1988). Some of the aged have not been so fortunate as to be adequately covered by the above programs, but the great majority have adequate or more than adequate incomes.

Apparent Causes of Poverty

Problems in the economy are a major cause of poverty. There has been a gradual decrease in median real family income from 1973 to

1985 (Sawhill, 1988). As shown above, the decrease has particularly affected female headed, young and black, or Hispanic families.

The majority of the families who receive AFDC payments remain on welfare less than 3 years (O'Hare, 1987). Improvements in employment and helpful changes in family structure, such as the addition of a second wage earner, are the chief routes to their "escape from poverty"—at least from welfare dependency. However, the average length of time in poverty for children in female-headed families of all races combined was 7 years during the 1980s. For black children in female-headed families, it was 12 years (Zimmerman & Chilman, 1988).

One-third of poor families are headed by someone who is elderly or disabled; one-third are likely to remain poor only temporarily; and one-third are "hard core" poor—those who live in families with chronically low incomes despite being able-bodied (Sawhill, 1988). Some of this latter group are members of the "underclass." There are about 8 million of these people (about 3% of the total population) and their numbers are growing. Members of this underclass generally live in neighborhoods where there are high rates of welfare dependency, female-headed families, male joblessness, school dropouts, teenage unmarried parents, and chemical dependencies. This "underclass" population is described as being poorly educated, largely minority, and resident in the industrial cities of the midwest and northeast (Sawhill, 1988).

Sawhill, among others, holds that strong corrective measures are needed to prevent the continuation and growth of this permanently dependent group—members of the so-called "cycle of poverty." She calls for an empathetic but tough agenda to attack the three basic causes of their poverty: weak families, joblessness, and poor education (Sawhill, 1988). These concerns are addressed in the federal welfare reform bill of 1988. The bill's emphasis on education, employment, parental responsibility and income assistance is to be commended. However, it will probably be extremely difficult to implement, partly because of budget limitations plus the complex nature of federal, state and local human service organizations that are already in place, as discussed in the following section.

EXISTING PUBLIC PROGRAMS FOR POOR FAMILIES

There are a large number of federal-state-local programs for poor families. Aid to Families with Dependent Children (AFDC) is the most important program and the one that is commonly called "welfare." Other than AFDC, there are a number of programs for the elderly, with Social Security Retirement and Medicare being the most widely used, along with programs for the totally disabled, the insured unemployed, and Veterans. The costs of programs other than AFDC were over 250 billion federal dollars in 1980. In contrast, AFDC accounted for 12.5 billion and 35 billion was spend for aid to poor families through food stamps, Medicaid, and housing supplements. Thus, there is considerable error in the wide-spread belief that "welfare" (AFDC plus benefits in kind) is a huge part of the federal budget: it accounted for less than 1% of the total federal budget in 1985 (Chilman, 1988).

Aid to Families with Dependent Children
(AFDC)

AFDC, food stamps, Medicaid, and housing assistance is of crucial importance to poor families. AFDC (originally ADC), established in the landmark Social Security legislation of 1935, provided that the federal government would give grants to the states in order to administer income assistance programs for needy mothers and their children. Prior to this legislation, there had been little federal or state aid available for poor families, most of whom were dependent on the uncertain and meager largesse of private charities, local poor law officials or the county poor house (Trattner, 1984).

AFDC is an open-ended expenditure program. Congress must appropriate funding each year for whatever the program costs, rather than requiring expenditures to be kept within a previously budgeted amount. The federal government matches what states spend. The proportion of the match depends upon the per capita income of each state. Poorer states, therefore, receive a higher proportion of matching grants. Legislation requires that AFDC be available state-wide, administered efficiently through a single state agency with participatory state or local financing, and that confidentiality regarding the recipients be strictly observed (Carrera, 1987).

AFDC is federally administered through ten regional offices, but it is essentially state-run, thus resulting in a wide variety of benefits and procedures. The states determine their own standards of need and payment. These payments vary with the majority of recipients receiving allowances well below the poverty line and none above, except, as of 1986, for those who lived in the State of Alaska.

The very considerable powers that AFDC legislation leaves to the states reflects a pervasive problem in attempts to launch national programs. State jealousies regarding their own identities and powers, prejudices, and political prerogatives prevent a more rational, equitable nation-wide approach to numerous federal assistance and human services programs. Programs at state levels are also apt to be manipulated locally to meet community resources, citizen attitudes and values, and political arrangements. These conflicting power issues lead to a wide diversity in the way programs are administered along with huge, complex structures at each level of government. New legislation is frequently passed without repealing and eliminating old programs. This adds further complexity to welfare organizations. The hope is that new programs will correct defective old ones. Old programs, with their built-in special interest supporters (such as in the case of the Veteran's Administration or Railroad Retirement Plan) rarely cease to exist, resulting in a confusing, often conflicting or overlapping series of programs that sometime seem beyond comprehension or control.

AFDC laws and administrative guidelines have changed radically over the years. Not until 1956, did the federal government make it permissible to include unemployed fathers in the grants. Heretofore only mothers and children had been helped. However, only 28 states today (1989) include these fathers. Usually only a small proportion of fathers are aided, depending on whether they are deemed particularly worthy of assistance through having had a substantial connection with the labor force.

Also during the 1950s, the AFDC caseload grew rapidly. The country was growing richer and resources were more amply available for "the poor." The migration of needy blacks from the south to the north required expanded assistance programs. At the same time, the growing civil rights movement created pressures for help to these groups, and increasing rates of separation and divorce caused a rise in poor, female-headed households (Schorr, 1986).

Partly in response to these developments, 1962 amendments to the Social Security Act provided for a number of social services as a core part of the AFDC program. It was believed that highly trained social workers could move people out of poverty through treatment of their family and individual problems. People were viewed as dependent because of their personal attributes rather than because of the social and economic deficits of their environment. A number of scholars held that these families lived in a "culture of poverty," a culture with maladaptive (in middle class terms) values, attitudes and behaviors which originally arose from the poverty situation of unemployment and underemployment but which tended to keep the chronically poor in poverty from generation to generation in the so-called cycle of poverty (Burgess & Price, 1963; Chilman, 1966; Rainwater & Weinstein, 1960; Riessman, 1962).

Subsequently, this theory was severely criticized as "blaming the victim" for defects in larger societal systems, systems which were viewed by some as the basic causes of poverty (Ryan, 1967). Changes in theories about poverty, its causes and cures, and the emergence of the Civil Rights Movement, together played a central part in the launching of the so-called war against poverty in 1964. This program was administered by the Office of Economic Opportunity (OEO). Among other things, its programs sought to bypass complex organizational barriers that had developed in the administration of AFDC. It included such concepts as the right of poor people to welfare, the rights of applicants to know all welfare regulations, and to participate in policy-making (Piven & Cloward, 1977).

Analyses of large bodies of data regarding the outcomes of anti-poverty programs plus trends in the epidemiology of poverty leads, today, to the conclusion that in many cases the problem of poverty lies primarily in the economy; in fewer cases, it lies primarily in the person and family; and in others, the problems derive from a combination of economic and familial factors (Chilman, 1988).

However, this multiple causation view was not held in the personalistic concepts of the late 1950s and early 1960s, or in the societal concepts of the late 1960s and 1970s. For example, Congress failed to hold such a view in 1967 when it became irritated by the tendency of OEO to bypass local and state governmental bodies in launching their sometimes radical community action programs. It was also disillusioned with the social services people-changing approach of the 1963 amendments and appalled by the rising numbers of AFDC recipients. As a result, Congress passed new legislation in 1967, which provided for WIN, the so-called work incentive program, sometimes called the work "insensitive" program by welfare rights advocates. This program required that every AFDC recipient over age 16 register for "Manpower" services training or employment unless he/she was attending school or was exempted because of illness, the care of an incapacitated adult, or the care of a child under age 6. As it eventually turned out, resultant job training and placement programs were usually ineffective except in areas where numerous jobs were readily available because of a booming economy (Chilman, 1988).

The working poor were included in this 1967 legislation if their total income was below the poverty line. The first $30 per month of their income could be set aside for working expenses, as well as one-third of the earnings of other family members. This provision caused rapidly rising case loads and program expenses (Carrera, 1987).

After 1973, eligibility for AFDC was tightened and benefits lowered, chiefly because of a general squeeze on the economy as a consequence of rising inflation and unemployment. These conditions continued and the program tightening was furthered in 1981, by the Reagan Administration. This resulted in over a million eligible families of the working poor no longer receiving assistance from the program (Center on Budget and Policy Priorities, 1985). Reductions were also made in allowances for work expenses, eligibility for food stamps and Medicaid, and day care provisions. Incentives and resources for parents to seek and hold jobs were undermined even though pressures were increased for recipients to obtain employment.

In 1974, in an about face from the 1962 social service provisions, Congress passed legislation that completely separated eligibility determination and grant administration from a professional social work approach (Schorr, 1986). Social services for families were no longer available from public welfare agencies. Clerical workers were designated as staff personnel. Problems arose because inexperienced workers displaced experienced ones at the same time that clients were becoming more demanding. The atmosphere of welfare offices shifted from friendly or neutral to hostile. Staff members became reluctant to visit the homes of clients and guards were added to welfare offices. Also, during the 1970s and 1980s, public criticism of welfare led to even more requirements being put on welfare programs (Schorr, 1986). These included: the pursuit of absent fathers, referrals of mothers for family planning, and added requirements for assessing eligibility. These requirements were made without providing additional staff. Moreover, state public assistance manuals became so complex that few could keep track of the regulations.

Work incentive (WIN) provisions were so intricate and frequently ineffective that neither staff nor clients understood or believed in them. Thus, they had little motivation to participate in WIN and other work training programs (Chilman, 1988). The reluctance of clients was often heightened by the fact that WIN agencies were usually housed far from AFDC offices, causing transportation, child care, and related problems for WIN applicants.

During the 1970s, spurred by the federal government, states developed application forms that were long and difficult to read. Also, eligibility requirements called for birth certificates, pay stubs, rent receipts, dismissal notices, and doctor's statements: all documents that raised serious obstacles for many, probably most, applicants.

Today, the jobs of welfare department staff members have become overwhelming. They tend to use those rules that they understand and, as in many complex organizations, emphasize their own job security. This reactive behavior represents the extreme problems of a large, hierarchical, impersonal, rigidly controlled, underfinanced organization. There is much job dissatisfaction and high worker turnover in welfare agencies, leaving the job to inexperienced workers whose effectiveness is further undermined by many staff vacancies, a poorly motivated staff and severe administrative problems (Schorr, 1986).

Other Family Welfare Programs

Food stamps, Medicaid, and Housing Assistance are all closely associated with AFDC as family welfare programs. The food stamp program, administered by the U.S. Department of Agriculture, has nation-wide provisions for eligibility and benefits. In these respects it is unlike AFDC which is administered through the U.S. Department of Health and Human Services with state determination of eligibility and benefits. The food stamp program issues free vouchers to recipients for the purchase of food. This program has its problems since only about 60 percent of program eligibles obtain food stamps (Wells, 1987). This is mainly because the application is difficult to complete, it requires visits to the agency, and people are unaware of the program. Also, the use of food stamps is perceived by some individuals to be stigmatizing and embarrassing (Wells, 1987).

If AFDC and food stamp eligibility were linked, people would apply only once for both benefits. This would eliminate the need to complete the extensive forms of the two agencies. However, long-standing historical, staff, legislative, value and constituent differences between the two Departments (Health and Human Services for AFDC, Department of Agriculture for food stamps) create formidable barriers to apparently simple cooperation, let alone actual program merging.

Medicaid, Title XIX of the Social Security Act amendments of 1965, provides for the medical care of poor families. AFDC recipients are automatically eligible for its services, though these services vary from state to state. Somewhat like AFDC, Medicaid is a federal-state-local public assistance program which leaves up to the states about half of the funding and the determination of many of its components, including eligibility beyond that of AFDC recipients. Medicaid has a strong institutional bias, spending most of its funds on hospitals and nursing homes, primarily for the aged and disabled, rather than on ambulatory and community health services.

In the 1970s and early 1980s, costs became so high that numerous cutbacks occurred in terms of eligibility for Medicaid, the kinds of services covered, and the schedule of hospital and physician fees to be reimbursed by the government. These cutbacks were also stimulated by problems in the economy, a political backlash against welfare recipients, and, in all likelihood, less than enthusiastic program support by physicians because of low fees paid by Medicaid, the large amount of paper work involved, and the many problems often met in serving a very poor group of people. The result has been that by 1982, over half of poverty families were not covered by Medicaid programs and few by any other kind of health insurance (Chilman, 1988).

The housing problems of poor families is another societal issue which begs a solution. An increasing number of poor families have joined the swelling ranks of the homeless and many others are crowded into seriously inadequate housing where they pay exorbitant rents. The Reagan Administration provided a small number of needy families with housing vouchers to provide part-funding for housing in the private sector. The chief difficulty has been that these vouchers are far too limited to buy family housing chiefly because (a) there is an inadequate supply of homes and apartments, (b) inflation has caused an explosive rise in housing costs, and (c) most landlords do not want to rent to poor people, especially to poor people with children. Thus, a severe housing crisis has developed, especially for low-income families.

The housing programs have their own separate enabling legislation and budgets, and are run by a different federal Department (Housing and Urban Development) from those that control the AFDC and Medicaid and Food Stamp programs. These housing programs have their own set of special interest groups such as those found in the real estate and construction industries. The foregoing factors obstruct close, cooperative links with AFDC, Medicaid, or Food Stamp programs.

Child Care

Child day care is an important policy issue for all parents. But it is a particularly pressing matter for employed low income parents. The federal government has moved forward and backward in child care support since it first entered the field in the 1930s with the establishment of WPA-funded child care centers. This was largely an anti-Depression measure, which was phased out within a few years. However, centers were again established in the 1940s to provide care for those children whose mothers went to work in the war industries. But by the end of the 1940s, government funds for child care disappeared once again.

In the 1960s, there was a resurgence of the child care movement, spurred both by the War Against Poverty and the feminist movement. Programs during the 1960s resulted in a considerable range of projects, including the early childhood enrichment programs of Head Start and day care centers for employed parents, financed under Title XX of the Social Security Act.

The combined efforts of anti-poverty warriors, feminists, early childhood educators, and day care proponents from the child welfare field resulted in child day care legislation being passed by Congress in 1971. Unfortunately, this legislation was vetoed by President Nixon who stated that such programs would undermine the morality of the American home (Scarr & Weinberg, 1986)!

During the 1970s, Head Start, Title XX of the Social Security Act, and various other federally subsidized programs which provided child day care, remained. However, 1981 legislation markedly reduced this funding, except for Head Start, as part of the general conservative thrust that returned many government programs to the private sector. Attempts at federal support of adequate affordable child care were abandoned and the entire matter was returned to the states, many of which made little or no attempt to support substitute quality day care of children of working parents (Chilman, 1988).

SOME IMPLICATIONS FOR PROGRAMS AND POLICIES

First and foremost, today's public programs for assistance to poor families need massive increases in funding. No organizational or administrative changes by themselves can importantly improve severely underfunded programs, especially those that are required to meet basic survival needs of both children and adults. The recommendations that follow rest on the possibly fallacious assumption that program funding will be improved, at least to a moderate degree in the next decade. Such improvement would require, among other things, a rise in state and federal taxes: a politically frail proposition.

AFDC should be made a national rather than a federal-state program. At present, far too many aspects of AFDC are left to the differing politics, prejudices, and resources of the various states. A national system, rather like the present social security retirement system, would probably be far more efficient than one that has so many separate offices with differing regulations at federal, regional, state and local levels. A national program could also counter-balance the reactionary politics and lack of economic resources of some of the poorer, conservative states.

Arguments can be made against the national approach, however, including the possibility that a national program, subject to the turning tides of national politics might produce, on occasion, more miserly benefits than would otherwise be obtained in many of the more progressive states. Moveover, a national program may seem more remote to the populace, with less opportunity for involvement in its operation. This can breed local unconcern and distrust but it can also more readily insure objective, impartial program administration.

AFDC should not be a separate income maintenance program. Rather, it should be part of an over-arching general social security system that combines public assistance as one piece of the total social insurance (including retirement) package. In the United States, our separate assistance categories reflect unwarranted rejection of needy families as being less worthy than others, such as those, for example, whose long-term, successful, and, in many cases, fortunate connection with the work force assures them of retirement incomes and unemployment compensation. Our public programs for poor people tend to be inadequate and humiliating in contrast to those more generous, less intrusive retirement and Medicare sections of the social security act.

Administration of AFDC, Medicaid, Food Stamps, Housing, and other public programs for poor people could be vastly simplified by not investigating every individual application for assistance. Rather, people could apply for assistance on routine forms and mail them to the appropriate offices. Intensive administrative checks could be made with a sample of applicants and recipients in order to assess compliance with program requirements, much as is the current procedure of the Internal Revenue Service. Such a procedure should be both cost-effective and people-effective; i.e., less intrusive, time consuming, and humiliating than the current person-by-person intensive investigative methods (Schorr, 1986).

There should be one large national health insurance program which combines Medicaid and Medicare programs (health care for the insured elderly and disabled) (Sawhill, 1988). This program could be modeled after such apparently successful programs as those in Canada and the United Kingdom. Our present approach has numerous administrative and economic deficiencies, including a lack of financial support for health services for large numbers of people in and near poverty.

Every effort should be made to help adult members of low income families obtain and hold secure, well-paying jobs, especially if they do not have young children in the home. In order for this to be accomplished, several major requirements will need to be met (Chilman, 1988). Some of these include: (a) either a higher minimum wage or income supplements for "the working poor"; (b) readily available high quality, free or low cost child care centers that include after-school and vacation programs; (c) well paid flexitime or part-time work, especially for single parents of young children; (d) cheap low-cost transportation from home to work; (e) realistic job training for jobs that actually exist; (f) creation of jobs in the public sector when the private sector cannot employ all of those who are seeking work; (g) strong enforcement of equal education and employment rights of women and racial and ethnic minorities; and (h) AFDC regulations that provide possible supplements for people working at low wages so that they are in a better financial condition when they are employed than when they are welfare-dependent. This includes provision for low wage earners to be eligible for Medicaid, Food Stamps, child care, and housing allowances (when available).

Many "welfare reform" proponents recommend that welfare-dependent parents (especially single parents) of children under age six, be required to obtain employment outside the home. However, this overlooks the fact that parental caring for young children in their own home is crucially significant employment and that efforts to push parents into the work force and obtain substitute care for the very young can be damaging to both parents and children, as well as more costly to taxpayers than welfare assistance. Parents of young children should be given choices as to whether they will stay at home to care for their youngsters or seek employment outside the home.

Insofar as it is legislatively possible, the many programs that serve poor people should be housed in one or adjacent buildings to reduce travel time for applicants. Ideally, the numerous public services for families (whether indigent or not) should be administratively coordinated. Far-reaching changes are needed in most welfare departments to improve staff working conditions. This includes simplified administrative guide-lines and application forms, smaller case loads, fewer responsibilities per staff member, better staff training, and higher salaries.

A special unit of highly trained professionals could be established to work intensively with long-term, chronically poor families (Sawhill, 1988). Even with a highly competent staff and a democratic organization, however, successful outcomes of such interventions will depend on a multiplicity of factors including those in the environment, such as a lack of jobs, poor schools, and inadequate health services often found in areas with chronically depressed economies.

There have been several forms of direct services for families over the years. In the 1960s, there were community action and client participation projects which sought to counteract the sense of powerlessness, alienation, and distrust among poor people by involving them in decision-making and action for social change (Piven & Cloward, 1977). During the 1970s, family "strengthening" services such as family planning and child day care were available to some families under the Social Security Act Amendment (Title XX). In 1980, child welfare services were reorganized to provide intensive services to parents under the Adoption and Child Welfare Act. Direct family service programs may also be found in some of the Head Start and similar early childhood education projects that involve parents. However, despite these programs there has been little sustained and sufficiently funded government support for them and for other community and family direct services for the poverty population during the 1970s and 1980s (Wireman, 1987). Services funded by private foundations and privately financed human service agencies provide the relatively few other outreach interventions for poor families. These programs typically involve information and referral services, and advocacy to acquire needed services for families and their communities (Kruzich, 1988).

The recent rapidly escalating problem of drug abuse and allied family violence is recognized but not addressed here because there is severely limited knowledge about the scope, prevention, and treatment of this phenomenon.

Well-designed formal evaluations of programs working intensively with chronically poor families are needed. Prospective models and pilot projects are necessary in order to assess the many factors that should be involved in program changes and their probable outcomes (Weiss & Jacobs, 1987). Also, further study of the various health and welfare programs in other countries should provide insights as to possible applications in the United States (Kamerman & Kahn, 1981).

SUMMARY AND DISCUSSION

The rates of family poverty have shifted over the past 40 years or so, from about a third of the population in 1949 to 20% in the early 1960s to 9% in 1973 to 11% in 1989. From the long range view, remarkable progress has been made. This progress is largely a result of a number of changes in the economy as well as social legislation that has included expanded public welfare, health, and education programs. Although much progress has occurred, further advances are critically needed in the scope, funding and organization of these programs. It is important that all program and policy changes build on an understanding of both families and organizations as interacting ecological systems.

Poverty particularly affects children and youth, young families, female-headed families, blacks and Hispanics, and the so-called working poor: families whose wage earners are paid so little that, even with full-time employment, their incomes are below the poverty line.

Poverty is caused primarily by defects in our economic, social and political systems. Secondarily, it is a result of poverty-affected problems within families: physical or mental disabilities, family breakdown, drug or alcohol abuse, and the like. About one-third of poverty families (3% of the total population) constitute the "underclass" and tend to be poor from generation to generation. Their low-income life styles, a response to the poverty situation, include such attitudes as alienation, distrust and fatalism. These attitudes play into behaviors like early school leaving, delinquency, chemical abuse, teen-age pregnancy and the like. Such patterns, in turn, tend to perpetuate the poverty of these families.

Poverty is a particular problem in today's highly complex, technological, generally prosperous society. Children and youth who are members of chronically poor families live in a multiply disadvantaged situation. They are often the victims of poor housing, poor schools, poor health services, unemployment, disorganized neighborhoods, racism, and problem-ridden families. They have few opportunities for positive development. This is a severe problem for them now and in the future and for the future of our society, since about one-fourth of the nation's children live in poverty-stricken families.

Social legislation, originating with the Social Security Act of 1935, has been of prime importance in reducing poverty in our population. Over the years it has been amended so that today it provides various levels and kinds of benefits for dependent families with young children, the elderly, some of the unemployed, and the disabled. It also provides rather minimal health benefits for some of the poor (Medicaid) and more generous ones for the insured elderly (Medicare). Other assistance for poor families is variously available through Food Stamps, Veteran's benefits, and (to a slight degree) housing allowances. Crucial as these programs are, they have numerous problems today which include:

1. Severe underfunding, especially as a result of budget cuts during the Reagan years (1981-1989).
2. Multiplicity of uncoordinated programs in a number of different federal, state, and local departments.
3. Complexity of program regulations that have multiplied over

the years so that efficient, fair program administration has become almost impossible.

4. Sharp reductions in program staff, poorly trained staff, work overload, staff "burn out."

5. Basic programs such as AFDC (Aid to Families of Dependent Children) and Medicaid receive differing amounts of federal support in the different states. States, in turn, differ enormously among themselves in respect to the kinds and levels of benefits they provide. In virtually all states, benefits are so low that recipients have incomes far below the poverty line.

6. Unlike many other modern countries, the U.S. has a two-tier set of income maintenance programs: generous, relatively efficient ones for the economically more advantaged (Social Security retirement and Medicare) and miserly, ineffectively administered programs for the poor. Poor programs for the poor tend to increase and perpetuate poverty.

All of the above deficiencies create enormous problems for families who need health and welfare assistance.

These welfare and health programs have evolved over the years in response to shifts in the economic, social, and political systems in which they are embedded. In some decades, programs have been relatively generous and humane (the 1930s and the 1960s). In other years, regression has occurred (the 1940s and 1950s plus the 1970s and 1980s). These shifts have been in response to trends in the economy, demographic factors (such as the baby boom of the 1950s followed by the baby bust of the 1970s), social attitudes and behaviors (such as the extreme materialism and individualism of the 1980s), and political trends (such as the reactionary, cynical, antigovernment values of the 1980s).

It is time for another shift: one that revives the enlightened humanism of the 1930s and 1960s. Hopefully, this may occur. If so, knowledge gained from the past 50 plus years of social research and policy experience should help expand and improve such needed programs as national, rather than federal-state-local health and income maintenance programs; higher minimum wages or low-wage supplementation; national health insurance free or low-cost, high quality child-care centers; enhanced education and job-training, development and placement programs; subsidized low-income housing; radically improved program organization and administration and highly skilled, experimental, intensive family treatment services, especially, but not exclusively, for chronically poor families. The foregoing programs, especially the latter, require highly competent, ongoing evaluations to measure their effectiveness.

It is hoped that family scholars will lend their expertise to further consideration of the issues outlined here and give their support to the critically needed programs and policies that should reduce the severe problems faced by families who suffer the ravages of poverty, especially those families who are mired in poverty from generation to generation.

REFERENCES

Burgess, E. & Price, D. (1963). *An American dependency challenge*. (Available from American Public Welfare Association, 1313 E. 60th Street, Chicago, IL).

Carrera, J. (1987). Aid to families with dependent children. *Encyclopedia of social work* (Vol. I, pp. 126-132). Silver Spring, MD: National Association of Social Workers.

Center on Budget and Policy Priorities. (1985). *Smaller slices of the pie: The growing economic vulnerability of poor and moderate income Americans*. Washington, D.C.

Children's Defense Fund and Center for Labor Market Studies. (1988). *Vanishing dreams: The growing plight of America's young families*. Washington, D.C.: Northeastern University.

Chilman, C. (1966). *Growing up poor*. Washington, D.C.: U.S. Government Printing Office.

Chilman, C., Cox, F., & Nunnally, E. (1988). Introduction. *Families in trouble: Employment and economic problems* (Vol. I, pp. 107). Newbury Park, CA: Sage Publications.

Chilman C. (1988). Public policies and families in financial trouble. In C. Chilman, F. Cox, & E. Nunnally (Eds.), *Families in trouble: Employment and economic problems* (Vol. I, pp. 183-236). Newbury Park, CA: Sage Publications.

Garfinkel, I. & McLanahan, S. (1986). *Single mothers and their children*. Washington, D.C.: Urban Institute Press.

Hasenfeld, Y. (1983). *Human service organizations*. Englewood Cliffs, NJ: Prentice Hall.

Hasenfeld, Y. & English, R. (1974). *Human service organizations*. Ann Arbor, MI: University of Michigan Press.

Holland, F. & Petchers, M. (1987). Organizations: Content for social service delivery. *Encyclopedia of Social Work* (Vol II, pp. 205-215). Silver Spring, MD: National Association of Social Workers.

Kamerman, S. & Kahn, A. (1981). *Child care, family benefits, and working parents: A study in comparative policy* (pp. 116-132). New York: Columbia University Press.

Kruzich, J. (1988). Helping families with income problems. In C. Chilman, F. Cox, & E. Nunnally (Eds.), *Families in trouble: Employment and economic problems* (Vol I, pp. 125-136). Newbury Park, CA: Sage Publishers.

Levy, F. (1987). *Dollars and dreams*. New York: Russel Sage Foundation.

O'Hare, W.P. (1987). *America's welfare population: Who gets what?* Washington, D.C.: Population Reference Bureau.

Piven, F. & Cloward, R. (1977). *Regulating the poor: The functions of public welfare*. New York: Vintage.

Rainwater, L. & Weinstein, K. (1960). *And the poor get children*. Chicago: Quadrangle Books.

Riessman, F. (1962). *The culturally deprived child*. New York: Harper & Row.

Ryan, W. (1967). Savage discovery: The Moynihan Report. In L. Rainwater & W. Yancy (Eds.), *The Moynihan Report and the politics of controversy* (pp. 453-478). Cambridge, MA: MIT Press.

Sarri, R. (1987). Administration in social welfare. *Encyclopedia of social work* (Vol. I, pp. 27-40). Silver Spring, MD: National Association of Social Workers.

Sawhill, I. (1988). *Challenge to leadership: Economic and social issues of the next decade*. Washington, D.C.: Urban Institute Press.

Scarr, S., & Weinberg, R. (1986). The early childhood enterprise. *American Psychologist, 41*(10), 1140-1146.

Schorr, A. (1986). *Common decency*. New Haven, CT: Yale University Press.

Trattner, W. (1984). *From poor law to welfare state: A history of social welfare in America*. New York: Free Press.

Weber, M. (1947). *Theory of economic and social organization*. New York: Oxford University Press.

Weiss, H. & Jacobs, F. (Eds.). (1987). *Evaluating family programs*. New York: Aldine.

Wells, E. (1987). *The food stamp program*. Encyclopedia of social work (Vol. I, pp. 628-634). Silver Spring, MD: National Association of Social Workers.

Wireman, P. (1987). Citizen participation. *Encyclopedia of social work* (Vol.I, pp. 275-280). Silver Spring, MD: National Association of Social Workers.

Zimmerman, S. & Chilman, C. (1988). Poverty and families. In C. Chilman, F. Cox, & E. Nunnally (Eds.), *Families in trouble: Employment and economic problems* (vol. 1, pp. 107-124). Newbury Park, CA: Sage Publishers.

The Responsiveness
of Early Childhood Initiatives to Families:
Strategies and Limitations

Douglas R. Powell

In America today, there is widespread and unprecedented recognition of the need to provide programs that support families with young children. Two related factors are responsible for the growing interest in the development of child care services and parent-child programs that strengthen the family's capacity to provide optimal environments for young children. One is the dramatic change in the structural, cultural, and labor force characteristics of families. Images of the traditional Anglo nuclear family, upon which most child-serving institutions have been organized, are being replaced with the realities of diverse family functions, forms, and lifestyles. Equally responsible for the interest in families is an awareness that traditional sources of child-rearing information and social support in communities and extended families are increasingly less viable for growing numbers of parents at all economic strata. Within communities throughout the U.S., there has been an erosion of social capital that for generations has provided a rich system of supports for young children and their families (Coleman, 1987).

In response to these changes, a wide variety of early childhood initiatives is being pursued at federal, state, and local levels (see Powell, 1989a; Kagan, Powell, Weissbourd, & Zigler, 1987). Families are the focus of services for handicapped infants and toddlers in recent Federal legislation, efforts are underway to encourage public school programs to be more responsive to families, and states such as Minnesota and Missouri have expanded ambitious

149

educational programs aimed at young children and their parents. Moreover, in 1988 and 1989 there has been a plethora of bills at federal and state levels that seek to expand the availability of child care services.

The development and expansion of programs that support families with young children have been accompanied by considerable interest in efforts to strengthen the responsiveness of programs to family values and life conditions. While Americans have long cherished family freedom and authority in child-rearing matters, since the 1960s there have been additional sources of pressure on programs to accommodate diverse family characteristics and circumstances. In the late 1960s and 1970s, community-based early childhood programs aimed at politically disenfranchised populations encountered resistance from low-income parents to being "treated" by professionals with the assumption that economically disadvantaged families were deficient (Radin, 1985). New modes of program operations and responsiveness were needed. From efforts to provide early education programs for ethnic minority children came the realization that effective programs require more than simply extending existing service models. Programs also need to be culturally responsive to patterns of learning and interpersonal relations among children and parents of different backgrounds (Rogler, Malgady, Constantino, & Blumenthal, 1987; Tharp, 1989). In addition to these factors, attempts to replicate early childhood program models in diverse communities in the 1970s led to a recognition of the significant influence of the host community on program design and implementation, and of the fallacy of assuming that one program model can serve diverse populations (Halpern & Larner, 1988).

This paper identifies and assesses major strategies that have been pursued to strengthen the responsiveness of early childhood programs to the families and communities they seek to serve. For each of five major strategies, the paper (a) describes briefly the design of the strategy; (b) reviews research, if available, on the implementation and effects of the strategy; and (c) identifies issues, limitations and/or questions regarding uses of the strategy. The paper concludes with a discussion of three major limitations that need to be addressed if further advances are to be made in enhancing the responsiveness of programs for young children and their families.

STRATEGIES

This paper considers the following strategies of increasing program responsiveness to families: Initiating and sustaining program-family communication; providing opportunities for parental choice of early childhood programs; conducting systematic assessments of family needs to inform the design of program services; using indigenous community residents as program workers and employing collaborative staff roles to reduce the social distance between program and parents; and placing parents in program decision-making roles. The first three can be considered minimalist efforts in that they are the least intrusive on program operations, while the latter two strategies require a considerable amount of change and accommodation in the ways programs traditionally have provided services.

Enhancing Program-Family Communication

Early childhood practitioners and researchers long have issued calls for initiating and sustaining communication between parents and programs. The primary rationale is that program-family communication serves to reduce conflicts or discontinuities between families and early childhood programs, thereby improving the child's socialization experiences (for a detailed treatment of this topic, see Powell, 1989a). The assumption is that communication will lead to program and family accommodations that ease the child's transitions to and from the early childhood setting.

The National Association for the Education of Young Children, the leading early childhood practitioner group in the U.S., has generated standards of professional practice in early childhood programs which are used by the National Academy of Early Childhood Programs (NAECP) to accredit programs for young children. They call for parents to be well informed about and welcome as observers and contributors to the program. The standards specify that high quality early childhood programs, (a) information about program philosophy and operating procedures should be given to new and prospective families; (b) children and parents should be oriented to the center through such means as a pre-enrollment visit or parent meeting; (c) staff and parents should communicate regarding home and center child-rearing practices; (d) parents should be welcome as visitors in the center at all times; and (e) a communication system should be established to share day-to-day exchanges between parents and staff.

A recent review of the existing research on communication between parents and early childhood providers concluded that in general the quality of relations between parents and staff in center-based early childhood programs does not satisfy recommendations for appropriate program-family interconnections advanced by the NAECP standards (Powell, 1989a). A majority of parents and early childhood staff has been found to communicate in person on a weekly or more frequent basis, but the exchange typically occurs at drop-off and pick-up times when individuals may be preoccupied with other matters. Moreover, a prevalent staffing pattern at centers is for the core (decision-making) staff to be present during the morning and early afternoon hours, with aides on duty in the late afternoon when parents retrieve their children. In some cases the extent of overlap between the core and late afternoon staffs may be minimal, reducing the opportunity for staff to exchange information about children and families. In this typical staffing arrangement, then, parents are conversing with staff who are likely to have limited first-hand information about the child's day and who occupy low-status positions in the center decision-making structure.

In a large interview study in Detroit area child care centers, Powell (1978) found that the most frequently discussed topic was what the child's day is like at the center. Parent- and family-related topics were infrequently discussed. A majority of parents and staff believed that the center should not be kept informed of family activities on a routine basis. Overall, more parents (58%) than staff (25%) were pleased with the level of discussion surrounding parental expectations of the center.

Studies suggest that in general parents spend a limited amount of time on the center premises, thereby limiting their ability to monitor program operations. In one study in a university-based child care center committed to the concept of parent involvement, parents were found to spend on the average 7.4 minutes a day in the center (Zigler & Turner, 1982). Ten percent of the parents did not enter the center with their children in the morning, and another 10% of the children were typically brought to the center by someone other than a family member.

Data from several studies of parents suggest that relations between parents and early childhood providers may be stronger in
family day care than in center-based arrangements. Parents using
family day care have reported closer personal relationships with
caregivers than parents using child care centers (Pence & Goelman,
1987). One study found that center providers spent an average of
13.7 minutes per week with each parent while family day care providers spent 54.7 minutes per week with each parent (Hughes,
1985). The higher ratio of providers to children in centers may
translate into less available time for interaction with parents.

A crucial question is what staff do with information they receive
from parents. Unfortunately, little research information is available. In an exploratory study involving a variety of center-based
early childhood programs, Powell and Stremmel (1987) found that
overwhelmingly teachers indicated they used parent-provided information about a child to enhance interactions with the child. For
instance, if the teacher knew that an out-of-town relative was visiting and a child seemed particularly excited about this, the teacher
would talk with the child about the relative's visit. Parent-provided
information also was used by staff to generate inferences about the
causes of child behavior. "Knowing what's going on at home" was
reportedly useful to staff in better understanding child interests and
moods. A third use of information from parents was to monitor
parents' perceptions of the program, including judgments of the
staff. The absence of information from parents was troubling to
teachers; it was difficult for staff to determine whether parental si-
lence reflected a lack of interest in the program and/or the child, or
a lack of trust in the center staff.

Providing Opportunities for Parent Choice

The doctrine of parental rights is a basic American value that
gives parents the first and foremost responsibility for determining
the best interests of the child (Coons & Sugarman, 1978). The
widespread use of early childhood programs, especially full-day
child care, has been accompanied by concern that secondary institutions might replace families as the primary child-rearing system.
President Nixon's 1971 veto of the Comprehensive Child Development Bill reflected this concern, and Executive Order 12606 signed

by President Reagan in 1987 calls for executive departments and agencies to consider the impact of policies and regulations on the authority and rights of parents in the education, nurture, and supervision of their children.

The doctrine of parental rights has supported a view of the parent as a defacto guardian who selects a preschool setting that is compatible with family values (Fein, 1980). The doctrine is the crux of efforts to maximize parental choice and the range of early childhood programs available to parents. It is by virtue of parental delegation of their authority that early childhood staff have authority over children.

Concerns about the erosion of parent choice surfaced in the 1988 round of U.S. Congressional consideration of the Act for Better Child Care Services of 1988. In the final report on the bill from the House of Representatives, 10 members of Congress offered a dissenting view of the bill that indicated "government policy should preserve and promote a diverse child care system to ensure maximum freedom of choice in the care and rearing of children" (pp. 25- 26). The essence of their argument is found in the following statement:

> . . . supporters of the Act for Better Child Care Services apparently have more faith in the ability of government than they have in parents to make good decisions about child care. The primary mechanism to deliver assistance in their bill is for government bureaucrats to make grants to child care providers, rather than to offer assistance directly to parents. And the result of the Act for Better Child Care Services will be an increasingly uniform child care system, dictated by Federal standards, that relies on regulated, mostly center-based care provided by trained professionals as the only child care arrangement sanctioned by the government. (p. 26)

Parent choice arguments largely are philosophical in nature. There appear to be no empirical data on the relation between parental choice and program responsiveness. Research on parents' searches for child care can be interpreted as suggesting that parents view child rearing as a private family matter in that parents exhaust kin and friend networks in looking for child care arrangements before tapping more public or institutional resources (Powell & Eisenstadt, 1982). Presumably parental choice could increase the likelihood of value consistency between family and nonfamilial early childhood settings. Whether parent choice enhances the responsiveness of early childhood programs to individual concerns may depend in part on the extent to which programs compete for a limited pool of parent-clients.

The revolutionary legislation mandating educational services for handicapped children — the Education of All Handicapped Children Act of 1975 (Public Law 94-142) — specified a parental role in decisions about child testing and placement in special education programs, and the right to initiate due process hearings. Parents played a crucial political advocacy role in the passage of this legislation (Pizzo, 1987). However, the literature indicates that parents often are passive participants in the development of the Individualized Education Plan (IEP) (Brickerhoff & Vincent, 1986; Yoshida, Fenton, Kaufman, & Maxwell, 1978). Parental attendance and signatures are mandated in the formal decision-making meetings regarding the IEP, but there are claims that parents typically are excluded from meaningful participation in the evaluation process or in the pre-meeting conferences held to assemble the relevant information (Dokecki & Heflinger, 1989).

Some comprehensive parent-child programs offer a cafeteria approach that enables parents to determine their mode of participation by selecting from a range of options (e.g., classes on child development; parent-child activity sessions; drop-in center). This format is common in many family resource programs where family strengths rather than deficits are emphasized (Weissbourd, 1987).

Needs Assessments of Program Participants

Since the 1960s and 1970s, systematic assessments of individual and community needs have been promoted as a mechanism for providing information that can be used to design human and educational services that are responsive to the targeted population group (Witkin, 1984). In the past three decades, early childhood initiatives have experimented with a variety of needs assessment methods, including questionnaires or interviews involving potential program participants and formal procedures for assessing the needs of actual participants. As a recent example, consider Part H of P. L. 99-457 (Education of All Handicapped Persons Amendments of 1986) which calls for family needs to be assessed in a comprehensive and multidisciplinary manner. The Individualized Education Plan (IEP) of P.L. 94-142 has been renamed the Individualized Family Service Plan (IFSP), and is to delineate both family strengths and needs regarding the development of the child with a handicap.

It has been argued that needs assessments are especially crucial in the human service arena because the existing social science data base provides "a dearth of information resources about how to intervene strongly, successfully, and with a minimum of negative fallout" (Mindick, 1986, p. 111-112). It is difficult to tell from the existing literature how common it is for community-based early childhood initiatives to undertake a needs assessment as part of service design decisions, and what uses are made of needs assessment information where it exists. It appears that many interventions are launched with a meager understanding of the backgrounds of the populations to be served (Slaughter, 1988).

Reports on the uses of needs assessments in early childhood initiatives indicate there are at least four unresolved issues or problems. One issue is who should collect the needs assessment data. On the one hand, it has been argued that program workers should not gather information from actual or prospective participants regarding their needs and interests because program workers are "not disinterested parties" and hence may collect or edit information in a way that perpetuates existing organizational structures (Mindick, 1986, 1988). On the other hand, it has been suggested that program workers can provide unbiased information that may prove to be valuable in understanding the program's role in facilitating growth and change in the parent (Cochran, 1988a). Quantitative data on this issue appear to be lacking.

Second, the field needs to give further consideration to what information should be gathered. It is common in a needs assessment to ask participants to identify various areas of concern or need to presumably help make decisions about program content or information to be disseminated. Of equal importance in designing programs is information that would inform decisions about program methods or the manner in which the program is delivered. What program structures (e.g., home- versus group-based), styles (e.g., didactic versus open-ended discussion), and staff roles (e.g., expert versus facilitator) would be appealing to participants and compatible with their learning processes? It appears that most pre-program assessment tools have given little or no attention to areas pertaining to program methods.

A third problem regarding needs assessments is the potential to over-generalize the findings to a particular population group. For instance, efforts to match educational programs to different cultural groups have found that broad educational prescriptions for such populations as Afro-Americans or Native Americans or Latinos may be met with resentment from culture members who are dissimilar from these generalizations (Tharp, 1989). A recent study of immigrant Mexican and Mexican-American mothers of young children found significant acculturation differences regarding preferences for such program methods as staff roles, delivery format, and the involvement of extended family members (Powell, Zambrana, & Silva-Palacios, 1988). The task is to recognize within-group variations in generating a differentiated grid of matches between program design and population characteristics.

Fourth, a key issue is the extent to which participants are involved in interpreting and making decisions about needs assessment information. One approach is for program designers to function as "experts" in a unique position to determine what type of program content and methods are likely to be useful to prospective participants. An alternative approach is for staff and participants to collaboratively determine a plan of action. This latter strategy is inherent in an empowerment paradigm that provides an equal balance of power between professionals and parents, and has been pursued in such early childhood initiatives as the Syracuse Family Development Research Project (Lally, Mangione, & Honig, 1988) and the Family Matters program (Cochran, 1988b). Staff roles are discussed in the following section.

Altering Staff Roles and Personnel

For the past three decades, parent-child initiatives have experimented with different staffing patterns partly in an effort to enhance program responsiveness. Most of this activity has focused on staff roles and on the use of indigenous community residents as paraprofessional staff.

The social and political currents of the civil rights movement and Great Society programs of the 1960s largely are responsible for initiating a trend toward collaborative relations between parents and program staff. Arrangements where staff serve as facilitators of goals and activities determined jointly by parents and staff increasingly are deemed superior to staff roles that emphasize the expert status and dominance of the professional. Indicative of this shift is the growing emphasis on parental empowerment. (For a detailed treatment of this shift, see Powell, 1988c.)

The existing empirical literature provides little information about the extent to which collaborative or empowerment relationships are being realized in a genuine manner. One process study of a program adhering to the empowerment concept found initial awkwardness on the part of staff and parents in adjusting to the unusual staff role of facilitation versus direction (Mindick, 1986, 1988). Another major unknown is the feasibility and appropriateness of utilizing collaborative parent-professional relations with some populations. It has been suggested, for instance, that adolescent mothers want structure and firm direction from program staff (Musick & Barbera-Stein, 1988). Further research is needed to determine the conditions under which collaborative ties between program staff and parents are acceptable and useful to the population to be served (see Powell, 1988a).

The paraprofessional movement of the late 1960s and 1970s was partly in response to the notion that program workers who are indigenous to the host community could serve as catalysts for program responsiveness and change. The idea was that prospective and actual program participants would have an informal representative voice on the staff via workers with strong ties to the community being served. This strategy has been implemented in many community-based early childhood intervention programs in the past three decades. However, there are few reports of program experiences regarding the paraprofessional's role as a stimulus for program responsiveness (see Musick and Barbera-Stein, 1988; Halpern & Larner, 1988). In recent years rationales for using paraprofessionals in human service programs seem to have focused more on cost efficiency than on program responsiveness.

Placing Parents in Program Decision-Making Roles

In democratic societies and institutions, citizen participation typically is advanced for the purpose of assuring institutional responsiveness. Adherence to this notion long has been evident in community-based early childhood programs. In the parent cooperative movement which began in the 1920s, parents were centrally involved in making decisions about program philosophy and operations, including staff selection. Some early childhood programs established in recent years have made structural provisions for parental influence on program decisions. Each of Minnesota's community-based Early Childhood and Family Education Programs includes a parent advisory committee, for instance.

The spirit of citizen involvement was extended to early childhood programs serving low-income populations during the 1960s era of political and social unrest and War on Poverty initiatives. The Economic Opportunity Act of 1964 called for the "maximum feasible participation" of citizens in community action programs. Head Start was founded during this period, and initially engaged in a good deal of experimentation with the concept, ranging from traditional parent education meetings run by middle-class white professionals for low-income black parents, to the innovativeness of the Child Development Group of Mississippi where the Head Start program for a poor Black community was run totally by the people themselves (Greenberg, 1969).

In 1970 the national Head Start office issued performance standards that specified four areas of parent involvement in program operations, the first of which is participation in the process of making decisions about the nature and operation of the program. The standards continue to be in effect. They call for each local program to establish and operate a Head Start Policy Council, the composition of which is at least 50% parents of Head Start children presently enrolled in that delegate agency program plus representatives of the community. No Head Start staff member is to serve on the council in a voting capacity. All parents serving on the policy group must be elected by parents of Head Start children currently enrolled in the program. Among the more significant functions to be carried out by the policy council is the approval of the hiring and firing of the Head Start director and staff.

In keeping with the tradition of parental involvement in program decision-making, the National Black Child Development Institute (1987) recently issued a set of ten "safeguards" or guidelines for programs for four-year-olds in the public schools that emphasize parental roles in decision-making structures. The NBCDI plan calls for public school early childhood programs to involve parents in decisions about curriculum and program policy. The suggestions include an active parent role in evaluations of program operations, and a standing parent committee to work with teachers surrounding curriculum issues.

To what extent has parent participation in program decision-making been realized in early childhood efforts? What are the effects? Data on these questions are seriously limited. It appears that a high percentage of Head Start programs in fact provide the mandated parent involvement opportunities. Current and former Head Start parents have been found to comprise 89% of the centers' policy-making councils, for instance (Stubbs, 1980). However, a recent extensive review of Head Start literature concluded that the extent of parent involvement is uneven, with "a core of parents contributing a disproportionate share of time" (McKey, Condelli, Ganson, Barrett, McConkey, & Plantz, 1985, p. 17). In a study of 28 demonstration projects in the Handicapped Children's Early Education Program which were mandated to show evidence of parent participation, Hocutt and Wiegerink (1983) found that relatively few of the programs granted the parents genuine decision-making or policy-making responsibilities. The tendency was to relegate parents to the role of instructional helper.

Needed is research which illuminates the dynamics of parental involvement in program decisions where parental participation is mandated. What is the level of parent participation at decision-making sessions? To what extent are parents involved in formulating policies as opposed to voting on staff-generated plans? What steps are taken to meaningfully inform parents of their responsibilities and rights as program decision-makers?

While evidence is limited as to whether early childhood programs are more responsive to families when parents assume program decision-making roles, there are some data to suggest that parent participation in early childhood programs enables parents to make other institutions in their community more responsive to their needs. A ten-year follow-up study of the Yale Child Welfare Project found that program mothers were more likely to have initiated contact with their child's teacher in the past year compared to control group mothers who had a pattern of relating to the school in response to a teacher's request for contact (Seitz, Rosenbaum, & Apfel, 1985). One large study of Head Start found that in centers where parents were not highly involved, parents expressed less confidence in their ability to influence their local schools (Midco, 1972). One of the major problems with research on program participation is that many study designs do not enable a determination of causal relations; for instance, one study found that most parents who were involved in Head Start and subsequently in other community organizations were involved in community activities prior to their Head Start participation (Midco, 1972).

In full-day child care centers not governed by Head Start regulations, dated but nationally representative survey data indicate that in only a minority of centers parents were involved in program decision-making roles. In a 1976-77 study of approximately one out of six child care centers in the U.S., the National Day Care Study found that 33% of the centers indicated that parents were involved in reviewing center budgets and programs. At 22% of the centers, parents participated in staff selection. There were major differences between for-profit and non-profit centers. Three percent of the for-profit but 22% of the non-profit centers indicated that parents participated in staff selection. At 35% of the non-profit centers but only 12% of the profit centers, parents reportedly were involved in reviewing budgets and programs (Coelen, Glantz, & Calore, 1979).

Even though the early childhood field includes notable efforts to involve parents in decision-making roles, the concept has been marked by controversy and confusion. There is discomfort with the idea of lay control over decisions that are seen as largely within the province of professional judgment (Powell, 1988a). Historically, the early childhood field has viewed parents as clients in need of education rather than equal participants in an educational enterprise. Operationally this tradition has been found to create confusion in situations where programs desire parents to be involved in both program decision-making and parent-as-learner roles (Joffe, 1977). Placement of parents in *decision-making* roles assumes that parents have sufficient knowledge about child development to make informed program decisions, while placement of parents in *learner* roles assumes they need greater exposure to information about child development. It is interesting to note that a historical assessment of Head Start policies and practices regarding parent involvement indicates that the political organizing role originally envisioned for Head Start parents has diminished, and an emphasis on parent education has come to dominate the Head Start parent involvement component (Valentine & Stark, 1979).

NEEDED DIRECTIONS

Three areas in need of attention in future efforts to strengthen the responsiveness of early childhood initiatives can be discerned from the foregoing identification of problem areas within each strategy. These include program design and resources, conventional tenets of professionalism, and vague or limiting policy statements.

Program Design and Resources

Participants in a community-based early childhood program will not always match the staff's images of what children and parents need. Implicit or explicit adherence to a particular theoretical orientation can serve as a program blinder to individual behaviors or circumstances that are not within the purview of a given theoretical paradigm.

In a case study of a parent-child program based in a low-income neighborhood, Powell (1988b) identified the program's strong commitment to a peer discussion group format as a limit on program responsiveness to potential participants. Not all prospective participants were able or willing to accommodate the interpersonal and logistical demands of a small, long-term group. Home-based consultation was added to the program in response to this situation, but staff visits to the home were viewed as a vehicle for preparing and recruiting individuals to join a group and not as a full-fledge service delivery system in its own right. The case study also indicated that over time program workers found at least three distinct subgroups of residents in a neighborhood that initially was seen as relatively homogeneous. Moreover, the three subgroups seemed to adhere to value systems and perceptions of each other that inhibited integration of different subgroup members into one discussion group. For instance, there was a tendency for some prospective participants to respond to program descriptions in this manner: "Your program sounds great. The people who need you live over there" (Powell, 1988b, p. 131).

Decisions about a program's service domain also may function as a limit on program responsiveness. In the early childhood field, there has been a propensity to view the child, not the family, as the primary client of program services. The National Day Care Study, for instance, found that only a minority of centers provided such parent-related services as referral to community agencies (Coelen, Glantz, & Calore, 1979). Clearly this pattern conflicts with the view of child care as a family support system.

Resource availability is an obvious limit on program responsiveness. Most human service programs in the U.S. are underfunded and hence cannot provide the scope of services that different families may need. Even if unlimited resources were available, however, it is questionable whether programs can or should attempt to be all things to all people. As discussed below, members of the helping professions are unlikely to give up their notions of what clients need. Moreover, theoretical coherence in program design may enhance the efficacy of program services (see Weikart, Epstein, Schweinhart, & Bond, 1977). The problem is that in most communities there is an insufficient number of distinct programs from which families can choose, and for low-income families there may be few or no choices among early childhood programs.

There are two promising program designs that warrant further consideration in experimentation with program responsiveness. Cafeteria approaches to program delivery, discussed earlier in this paper in regard to comprehensive parent-child initiatives, are an alternative to services that offer a sole or narrow range of content and methods. While research on how parents use cafeteria programs is needed, it seems plausible that cafeteria programs are more responsive to family circumstances than narrow-band programs. Resource limitations no doubt constrain the scope of services available in most cafeteria programs. Perhaps more significantly, it is highly probable that there are ideological limits to the range of diversity that is allowed to flourish under the umbrella of a cafeteria program.

Home visiting programs, which enjoy a long history in the social service arena, also afford the option of a high degree of program responsiveness through the individualization of services by the home visitor. Key determinants of responsiveness in home visiting seem to be the level of flexibility in the curriculum or treatment plan and the resourcefulness of the home visitor in terms of available time to work with a family, and technical and interpersonal skills (Powell, 1989b). Unfortunately, process research on what happens during home visits is extremely limited. Research is needed to determine the conditions under which home visitors attend and respond to child and family circumstances.

Professionalism

Each of the five strategies for facilitating program responsiveness to families tampers with conventional images of professionalism. The most dramatic departure from the prevailing image of professional conduct is found in the move toward collaborative ties between parents and staff in early childhood programs. Efforts that focus on communication are the least disruptive of professional perogatives because they do not require the professional to consider the parent's wishes.

The professional culture that permeates many service agencies and training programs is a major deterrent to efforts to enhance the responsiveness of human service programs. In a review of the literature in medicine, psychiatry, psychology, and social work, Moroney (1980) found that professionals tended to view families as less than capable caregivers, and when families were included as part of the helping team it typically was in a role ancillary to the professional. He suggested that this perspective is shaped by the pathology-oriented medical model that dominates the socialization of professionals in training programs and the ethos of human service agencies.

Efforts to enhance the responsiveness of early childhood programs prompt questions about the autonomy and professional status of program staff. Professional groups generally strive for freedom from client control of services; early childhood workers prefer to work with parents who do not attempt to influence program activities (Powell & Stremmel, 1987). Further, most professional training programs in the early childhood field prepare individuals to work with children, not parents.

Program workers who wish to be responsive to families need to modify the traditional image of professionalism, especially the idea that work should be relatively free of lay interference (e.g., Tyler, Pargament, & Gatz, 1983). A major task is to define in clear terms the competencies and behaviors that are inherent in the collaborator or facilitator roles increasingly advocated for professionals in working with families. By what process do parents and program staff collaboratively move toward an agreement about the content and method of program services? At present, much of the program literature describing the desired realignment of parent-professional relations delineates what is inappropriate (e.g., dictate to parents) rather than what is appropriate practice (see Powell, 1988b). Yet there are difficult issues to be addressed. For instance, one of the external pressures on many early childhood programs is to provide a structured academic curriculum that employs the direct instruction methods (e.g., rote memorization) of a traditional classroom (Gallagher & Coche, 1987). Parents reportedly are a major source of pressure on some teachers for this approach, but most practitioners strongly believe that structured academic curricula represent a "hothousing" of children that robs them of their childhood (Sigel, 1987). How might a professional operating in a collaborative mode be responsive to parental wishes of this nature?

Policy Guidelines

Most policy statements regarding program responsiveness are vague and often do not provide details of implementation procedures. A case in point is the landmark Economic Opportunity Act of 1964, which provided the funds and philosophy for Head Start. The legislation defined a community action program as one ". . . which is developed, conducted and administered with the maximum feasible participation for the residents of the areas and members of the groups served . . ." (cited in Fein, 1980, p. 163). What does "maximum feasible participation" entail? Moynihan (1968) summarized the options succinctly: Were programs to "hire the poor, involve the poor, or be dominated by the poor?"

To this day, efforts to clarify the intended role of parents in Head Start continue to be problematic. A recent report of a task force on parent involvement in Head Start created by the Commissioner of the U.S. Administration for Children, Youth, and Families noted that there are variances between regional offices in the interpretation and enforcement of parent involvement policies and performance standards, resulting in some local grantees "carrying out improper procedures" (p. 12). The report also acknowledged "a history of local Head Start programs misinterpreting the parent involvement performance standards" (p. 15).

The Education of the Handicapped Act Amendments of 1986 (P.L. 99-457) provides another recent example of vague policy statements regarding family participation. As noted earlier, the family is to be a major target of intervention services, but the legislation leaves unanswered numerous questions about specific roles and implementation procedures (Dokecki & Heflinger, 1989). Missing, for instance, is a definition of parent involvement.

The challenges here are familiar to seasoned architects of public policy. Ambiguous policy statements are no doubt the result of disagreements that lead to compromises in policy language. Controversy easily can stem from conflicting ideological perspectives on the roles of professionals who work with families and young children. Ambiguous policies also can reflect ambivalent or limited support of a principle. Strategies of program responsiveness are particularly vulnerable in this regard because they can be used in a cosmetic manner to provide an aura of legitimization of program services in the public's eye, but in reality the practice can be mandated in sufficiently vague terms so as to permit maintenance of the status quo (see Beattie, 1985). In addition, individuals who formulate policy statements also struggle with the need to provide overall direction for needed practices but at the same time allow sufficient autonomy for responding to local circumstances.

CONCLUDING COMMENT

Community-based programs for young children and their families have made important strides in the past three decades of experimentation with strategies for improving program responsiveness to family and community conditions. In this regard, the cup is half full. Yet this paper's examination of program experiences indicates that the cup is also half empty. Existing research on the processes and effects of various strategies is limited in quantity, scope, and methodology, with a resultant dearth of empirical knowledge about the ways in which various strategies work and fail to work. Future progress depends on more than research, however. At the heart of efforts to improve the responsiveness of early childhood programs are issues of control and power. Advances in the field require movement on these difficult fronts as well.

REFERENCES

Beattie, N. (1985). *Professional parents*. London: Falmer Press.

Brickerhoff, J. L., & Vincent, L. J. (1986). Increasing parent decision-making at the individualized educational program meeting. *Journal of the Division for Early Childhood, 11*, 46-58.

Cochran, M. (1988a). Parental empowerment in family matters: Lessons learned from a research program. In D. R. Powell (Ed.), *Parent education as early childhood intervention* (pp. 23-50). Norwood, NJ: Ablex.

Cochran, M. (1988b). Generic issues in parent empowerment programs: A rejoinder to Mindick. In D. R. Powell (Ed.), *Parent education as early childhood intervention* (pp. 67-78). Norwood, NJ: Ablex.

Coelen, C., Glantz, F., & Calore, D. (1979). *Day care centers in the U.S.* Cambridge, MA: Abt Associates, Inc.

Coleman, J. S. (1987). Families and schools. *Educational Researcher, 16*, 32-38.

Commissioner's Task Force on Parent Involvement in Head Start (1987). Final

Report. Washington, D.C.: Head Start Bureau, U.S. Department of Health and Human Services.

Coons, J. E., & Sugarman, S. D. (1978). *Education by choice: The case for family control*. Berkeley, CA: The University of California Press.

Dokecki, P. R., & Heflinger, C. A. (1989). Strengthening families of young children with handicapping conditions: Mapping backward from the "street level." In J. J. Gallagher, P. L. Trohanis, & R. M. Clifford (Eds.), *Policy implementation and P.L. 99-457: Planning for young children with special needs* (pp. 59-84). Baltimore: Brookes Publishing.

Fein, G. G. (1980). The informed parent. In S. Kilmer (Ed.), *Advances in early education and day care* (pp. 155-185). Greenwich, CT: JAI Press.

Gallagher, J. M., & Coche, J. (1987). Hothousing: The clinical and educational concerns over pressuring young children. *Early Childhood Research Quarterly, 2*, 203-210.

Greenberg, P. (1969). *The devil has slippery shoes: A biased biography of the Child Development Group of Mississippi*. New York: Macmillan.

Halpern, R., & Larner, M. (1988). The design of family support programs in high-risk communities: Lessons from the Child Survival/Fair Start initiative. In D. R. Powell (Ed.), *Parent education as early childhood intervention* (pp. 181-207). Norwood, NJ: Ablex.

Hocutt, A., & Wiegerink, R. (1983). Perspectives on parent involvement in preschool programs for handicapped children. In R. Haskins & D. Adams (Eds.), *Parent education and public policy* (pp. 211-229). Norwood, NJ: Ablex.

Hughes, R. (1985). The informal help-giving of home and center childcare providers. *Family Relations, 34*, 359-366.

Joffe, C. E. (1977). *Friendly intruders: Childcare professionals and family life*. Berkeley, CA: University of California Press.

Kagan, S. L., Powell, D. R., Weissbourd, B., & Zigler, E. F. (1987). *America's family support programs: Perspectives and prospects*. New Haven, CT: Yale University Press.

Lally, J. R., Mangione, P. L., & Honig, A. S. (1988). The Syracuse University Family Development Research Program: Long-range impact of an early intervention with low-income children and their families. In D. R. Powell (Ed.), *Parent education as early childhood intervention* (pp. 79-104). Norwood, NJ: Ablex.

McKey, R. H., Condelli, L., Ganson, H., Barrett, B. J., McConkey, C., & Plantz, M. C. (1985). *The impact of Head Start on children, families and communities*. Washington, D.C.: CSR Inc. (DHHS Publication No. 85-31193).

Midco Educational Associates, Inc. (1972). Investigation of the effects of parent participation in Head Start. Final Technical Report. Denver, CO: Author.

Mindick, B. (1986). *Social engineering in family matters*. New York: Praeger.

Mindick, B. (1988). Lessons still to be learned in parent empowerment programs: A response to Cochran. In D. R. Powell (Ed.), *Parent education as early childhood intervention* (pp. 67-78). Norwood, NJ: Ablex.

Moroney, R. (1980). *Families, social services and social policy*. Washington, D.C.: U.S. Government Printing Office.

Moynihan, D. P. (1968). The crisis in welfare. *The Public Interest, 10,* 3-29.

Musick, J. S., & Barbera-Stein, L. (1988). The role of research in an innovative preventive initiative. In D. R. Powell (Ed.), *Parent education as early childhood intervention* (pp. 209-27). Norwood, NJ: Ablex.

National Academy of Early Childhood Programs (1984). *Accreditation criteria and procedures of the National Academy of Early Childhood Programs*. Washington, D.C.: National Association for the Education of Young Children.

National Black Child Development Institute (1987). *Safeguards: Guidelines for establishing programs for four-year-olds in the public schools*. Washington, D.C.: Author.

Nixon, R. (1971). Text of veto message of Comprehensive Child Development Act of 1971. *Congressional Record*, Dec. 10, pp. S21129-21130.

Pence, A. R., & Goelman, H. (1987). Silent partners: Parents of children in three types of day care. *Early Childhood Research Quarterly, 2,* 103-118.

Pizzo, P. (1987). Parent-to-parent support groups: Advocates for social change. In S. L. Kagan, D. R. Powell, B. Weissbourd, & E. F. Zigler (Eds.). *America's family support programs: Perspectives and prospects* (pp. 228-242). New Haven, CT: Yale University Press.

Powell, D. R. (1978). The interpersonal relationship between parents and caregivers in day care settings. *American Journal of Orthopsychiatry, 48,* 680-689.

Powell, D. R. (1988a). Challenges in the design and evaluation of parent-child intervention programs. In D. R. Powell (Ed.), *Parent education as early childhood intervention* (pp. 229-237). Norwood, NJ: Ablex.

Powell, D. R. (1988b). Client characteristics and the design of community-based intervention programs. In A. R. Pence (Ed.), *Ecological research with children and families: From concepts to methodology* (pp. 122-142). New York: Teachers College Press.

Powell, D. R. (1988c) Emerging directions in parent-child early intervention. In D. R. Powell (Ed.), *Parent education as early childhood intervention* (pp. 1-22). Norwood, NJ: Ablex.

Powell, D. R. (1989a). *Families and early childhood programs*. Washington, D.C.: National Association for the Education of Young Children.

Powell, D. R. (1989b). Models of home visiting. Report to the A. L. Mailman Foundation. West Lafayette, IN: Purdue University.

Powell, D. R., & Eisenstadt, J. W. (1982). Parents' searches for child care and the design of information services. *Children and Youth Services Review, 4,* 223-253.

Powell, D. R., & Stremmel, A. J. (1987). Managing relations with parents: Research notes on the teacher's role. In D. L. Peters & S. Kontos (Eds.), *Continuity and discontinuity in child care* (pp. 115-127). Norwood, NJ: Ablex.

Powell, D. R., Zambrana, R., & Silva-Palacios, V. (1988, October). Designing culturally responsive parent programs: A comparison of the preferences of low-income Mexican and Mexican-American parents. Paper presented at the biennial meeting of the Family Resource Coalition, Chicago.

Radin, N. (1985). Socioeducation groups. In M. Sundel, P. Glasser, R. Sarri, & R. Vinter (Eds.), *Individual change through small groups, 2nd ed.* (pp. 101-112). New York: Free Press.

Rogler, L. H., Malgady, R. G., Constantino, G., & Blumenthal, R. (1987). What do culturally sensitive mental health services mean? The case of Hispanics. *American Psychologist, 42,* 565-570.

Seitz, V., Rosenbaum, L. K., Apfel, N. (1985). Effects of family support intervention: A ten-year follow-up. *Child Development, 56,* 376-391.

Sigel, I. E. (1987). Does hothousing rob children of their childhood? *Early Childhood Research Quarterly, 2,* 211-225.

Slaughter, D. T. (1988). Programs for racially and ethnically diverse American families: Some critical issues. In H. B. Weiss & F. H. Jacobs (Eds.), *Evaluating family programs* (pp. 303-314). Hawthorne, NY: Aldine de Gruyter.

Stubbs, J. L. (1980). National Head Start Parent Involvement Study. Part I; Opportunities for parent involvement. United Research and Development Corporation.

Tharp, R. G. (1989). Psychocultural variables and constants: Effects on teaching and learning. *American Psychologist, 44,* 349-359.

Tyler, F. B., Pargament, K. I., & Gatz, M. (1983). The resource collaborator role: A model for interactions involving psychologists. *American Psychologist, 38,* 388-398.

Valentine, J., & Stark, E. (1979). The social context of parent involvement in Head Start. In E. Zigler, & J. Valentine (Eds.), *Project Head Start: A legacy of the War on Poverty* (pp. 291-313). New York: Free Press.

Weikart, D. P., Epstein, A. S., Schweinhart, L. J., & Bond, J. T. (1977). *The Ypsilanti Preschool Curriculum Demonstration Project: Preschool years and longitudinal results.* Ypsilanti, MI: High/Scope Press.

Weissbourd, B. (1987). A brief history of family support programs. In S. L. Kagan, D. R. Powell, B. Weissbourd, & E. F. Zigler (Eds.), *America's family support programs: Perspectives and prospects* (pp. 38-56). New Haven, CT: Yale University Press.

Witkin, B. R. (1984). *Assessing needs in educational and social programs.* San Francisco: Jossey-Bass.

Yoshida, R., Fenton, K. S., Kaufman, M. J., & Maxwell, J. P. (1978). Parent involvement in special education planning process. *Exceptional Children, 44,* 531-533.

Zigler, E. F., & Turner, P. (1982). Parents and day care workers: A failed partnership? In E. F. Zigler, & E. W. Gordon (Eds.), *Day care: Scientific and social policy issues* (pp. 174-182). New York: Free Press.

The Role of Formal and Informal Groups in Providing Help to Older People

Eugene Litwak
Peter Messeri
Merril Silverstein

There is currently a running debate between those who bemoan the waning of the family and those who see it as a foundation stone of modern society. Among the former, the large formal organization is viewed as a relentless competitor whose technical effectiveness and impersonal objective style has driven the family to the fringes of social life, a weak token of past eminence. Among latter, the justifications for family viability ranges from moral imperatives to supportive empirical studies. In this paper, a task specific theory is presented that synthesizes past theories, defines the unique contributions of families and formal organizations and argues they are interdependent (i.e., that they can best achieve their respective

The material for this paper was gathered under funds supplied by NSF grant SES 8800083 and NIA grant R01AG04577-01A1. However, the granting agencies are in no way responsible for the conclusions reached in this paper. Thanks are owed to Donald Unger for his help in editing the manuscript.

goals by closely coordinating with the other despite conflicting structures). These ideas are applied to the family and human service organizations in aging to show which activities families can best manage, which activities organizations must undertake, and how the two are optimally coordinated.

The early social theorist, as well as some contemporary ones, felt that the modern family would play a weak role in a modern industrial society (Gasset, 1932; Huizinger, 1936; Nisbet, 1969; Redfield, 1947; Stein, 1960; Tönnies, 1940). For all of these writers, the decline of the family was a matter of empirical fact or, as in the case of the humanistic psychology (Polsky & Duberman, 1979) a combination of empirical fact and moral imperatives. If this was in truth typical of modern industrial society, one would expect that older people would get very little help from their kin. The astonishing fact is that 90% of the older people who need help receive it from family and friends rather than formal institutions (Shanas, 1979; Kendig, 1983). Is this evidence that prior thinkers were wrong about the demise of the family, or does it represent residual effects of the past role of the family?

Max Weber (1947) provided a sophisticated theoretical rationale for the view that strong kinship systems could *not* survive in a modern industrial society. He assumed that most tasks benefited from technical knowledge, that is, knowledge based on specialized training and not everyday socialization. He further showed that in a modern moneyed economy, the monocratic bureaucracy was most able to deliver technical knowledge. It recruited people on the basis of technical skills, was committed to employees only as long as they could meet current technological standards of work, and motivated their staff through impersonal economic incentives which prevented the rise of favoritism that is destructive of the utilization of technical services. The family as a primary group was the very antithesis of the monocratic bureaucracy and therefore was the least able to optimize technical knowledge. It recruited people on the basis of birth and love instead of technical training, stressed long term ties that prevented the removal of technologically inefficient members, and motivated its members through an internalized commitment of love or duty which could easily lead to nepotism at work. As a consequence, the family provided minimal technical knowledge. It also had a structure that would directly conflict with that of the formal organization.

Weber advanced two theoretical reasons as to why primary groups were inconsistent with a modern society: (a) they were least likely to encourage technical knowledge which is optimal for most tasks, and (b) their structure conflicted with organizations that were optimal for technical knowledge. Primary groups such as the family would not survive even though there were some "family tasks" for which they were best suited, e.g., maintaining the kinship system. Implicit in the Weberian formulation was the basic theoretical principle that groups optimally manage tasks that have dimensions which matched their structure. He saw the key dimension of most tasks required technical knowledge and the key dimension of groups related to technical knowledge.

Since the 1940's, there has been an increasing crescendo of theories which have sought to deny Weber's thesis that family units will play negligible roles in society. These theoretical formulations were in part based on a wave of empirical works that suggested that primary groups were necessary for achieving most social goals. Parsons (1944) argued that there was one form of family structure, the isolated nuclear family, which must exist in a modern industrial world because the functions it performed, that is, early socialization of the child and adult tension management, were necessary for societal survival. Primary groups were better suited to managing these two tasks than formal organizations because these tasks required personal emotional commitments.[1]

Having answered the first part of Weber's thesis, Parsons had to now explain the second part: how could two organizations with antithetical structures exist in society at the same time? He argued that as long as contact between the two organizations could be reduced to a minimum they could exist without destructive conflict. This isolation could be arranged because the tasks of the primary groups could be isolated from those of the formal organizations. Structural changes in the family could also prevent close contact between members of the two systems. The structural change he proposed was to have the family linked to the world of work by one person, the husband (Parsons & Bales, 1955). That would be possible if the family system consisted only of the husband and wife and young children. It would mean the end of the large kinship system but not of the family. This modification of kinship structure not only isolated the family from the occupational world, but it also permitted the family to accommodate to the formal organization's need to distribute labor rationally and appoint individuals on merit. A large kinship system with many different members in the labor force would place a strong barrier to any individual moving geographically without the rest of the family members and it would be difficult, when one member moved, to find jobs for all the other members. It would also mean that every time one member of the kinship system was occupationally advanced, all other members in the labor force had to be advanced. Insofar as this assumption could not be met, the large kinship system would discourage differential mobility based on merit.

Parsons' eloquent formulations provided a theoretical answer to Weber's equally sophisticated analysis. Parsons also implicitly adopted the principle that groups are optimally able to manage those tasks which match their structure. For example, he argued that early socialization and tension management required internalized commitments of duty or affection and that primary groups, having this structural aspect, were best able to manage these tasks (Parsons & Bales, 1955). All other tasks required technical knowledge, formal organizations had the structure which recruits and promotes people on this basis, and consequently were optimal for these tasks.

Both Parsons' and Weber's formulations began to crumble before the empirical findings that kinship systems and other primary groups continued to play a major role in modern society. The first signal that something was empirically amiss came from the empirical findings by Sussman (1953), that middle class kinship groups, the prototype family in Parsons theoretical scheme, in fact exchanged services that significantly affected the life chances of their members. The empirical foundations for Parsons' formulations were also undermined by major studies that showed that primary-like groups promoted the effectiveness of formal organizations such as factories (Roethelsberger & Dickson, 1939), armies (Shils & Janowitz, 1948), mass media, politics, and consumer behavior (Katz & Lazarsfeld, 1955). More recent findings have shown that older people receive the majority of help from family and friends

(Shanas, 1979), that urban dwellers have strong informal friendship networks (Fischer, 1982), that primary groups significantly reduce mortality rates (House, Landis, & Umberson, 1988; Litwak & Messeri, 1989).

We believe that the attempts to theoretically account for the role of primary groups in a modern industrial society often faltered because both the structure of the groups and the nature of tasks were not simultaneously taken into account (Fischer, 1982; Granovetter, 1974; Katz & Lazarsfeld, 1955; Mayhew, 1968; House, Landis, & Umberson, 1988).

THEORIES EXPLAINING THE UNIQUE ROLE OF PRIMARY GROUPS AND FORMAL ORGANIZATIONS

Theories seeking to explain the unique role of primary groups in a modern society must systematically contrast the structure of formal organizations with primary groups as well as indicate the tasks for which each is optimally suited (Litwak, 1960a; Litwak, 1960b; Sussman, 1965; Sussman, 1977; Litwak & Meyer, 1966). This theoretical orientation is called a task specific theory (Cantor, 1979). The task specific theorist questioned Weber's (1947) major assumption that most tasks benefit from technical knowledge. For instance, in the field of health there are significant causes of death that can be reduced by people with no technical training but only the knowledge based on everyday socialization (Litwak & Messeri, 1989). For example, removing a cigarette from the hands of a sleeping individual requires no technical training. Similarly, it can be argued that the ordinary individual can be effective in dealing with causes of death where a companion is falling asleep at the wheel, is too drunk to drive, or who has forgotten to take their daily after dinner high blood pressure medication.

Granted that some tasks do not require technical knowledge, the question arises as to why it is that primary groups are better able to manage them than formal organizations. The theoretical answer lies in the comparative analysis of the structure of the formal organization and the primary group. Where technical knowledge is not required, the structure of the primary groups makes them less expensive than formal organizations because they do not have to pay for specialized training (Mayhew, 1968). They have faster and more flexible lines of communication because of their small size, lack of long ladders of hierarchy, and lack of a detailed division of labor. Furthermore, their internalized motivation assures that members will have incentives to act even without supervision. This is not true of the impersonal economic incentives required by formal organizations. In other words, when technical knowledge is *not* an issue, the structure of the primary group makes it cheaper, faster, more flexible, and assures more motivated individuals than the formal organization. However, as Weber (1947) so clearly documented, the structure of the formal organization makes it cheaper, faster, more flexible, and provides more motivated individuals when the task *requires* technical expertise. What the task specific theorist argues is that most tasks require *both* technical expertise and every-day socialization (Litwak & Figueria, 1968) and, therefore, it is necessary for both formal organizations and primary groups to work close together in most areas of life.

From a theoretical perspective, this formulation agrees with the implicit view of Weber's that the structure of the group must match the structure of the tasks in order for the group to optimally manage the task. It disagrees with his assumption that all tasks benefit from technical knowledge and therefore there is only one optimal organizational structure and only one dimension of task to be measured, that is, technical knowledge. Rather, task specific theory asserts that tasks vary in terms of the technical knowledge they require. The primary group structure matches the dimensions of tasks that do not require technical knowledge while the formal organization matches tasks that require technical knowledge.

Such a formulation would account for the empirical evidence which shows informal social supports operating in most areas of life alongside formal organizations. It provides the theoretical rationale for the findings that the bulk of household services required by older persons who need help are provided by informal social support groups rather than formal organizational ones (Shanas, 1979; Kendig, 1983). It also permits one to incorporate the work of prior writers with only slight modifications. Mayhew (1968) and Granovetter (1974) viewed that primary groups existed because they were "cheaper." This makes complete sense if they account specifically for managing non-technical tasks. Katz and Lazarfeld (1955) viewed that primary groups provided instrumental help in uncertain situations. This makes sense if it is understood that uncertain situations stands for tasks where technical knowledge and services cannot be brought to bear in time to make a difference. The medical sociologists (House, Landis, & Umberson, 1988) view that social supports provide instrumental and emotional help. This is consistent with the task specific theory if this finding is modified to state "for tasks which do not require technical services." Similarly, Fischer (1982) reports that networks are essential for all human activities. His analysis could be modified to recognize the differences between networks that describe formal organizations from those that describe primary groups. For instance, the primary group networks he was studying were essential for tasks which required non-technical services.

TASK SPECIFIC THEORY
AND ORGANIZATIONAL CONTINGENCY THEORY

Task specific theories which simply contrast formal organizations and primary groups, and examine tasks in terms of the degree of technical and non-technical knowledge they require, could be as easily explained by an expanded organizational contingency theory (Litwak & Messeri, 1989).[2] The limitation of an expanded organizational contingency theory, however, was that it saw only two dimensions of tasks as being crucial, that is technical knowledge and the degree of uncertainty. What task specific theory emphasizes is that groups can optimally manage those tasks which match their structures and that tasks can be specified by precisely the same set of dimensions that are used to describe groups, that is, size, type of motivation, length of commitment, communality of life style, and the degree to which they require a division of labor.

The full sociological richness of the task specific theory can be appreciated if it is applied to primary groups with different structures, i.e., the marital dyad, friendship, neighborhood, and the kinship system. Technical knowledge will not play a key role in such an analysis since none of the primary groups have structures that emphasize technical knowledge. Primary groups in a modern industrial society, however, can have very significant structural differences on other dimensions (Litwak, 1985). For instance, kinship members can be separated by distance and not necessarily share common life styles while still retaining long term commitments. Neighbors, by contrast, have immediate proximity but do not necessarily have long term commitments or common life styles. Friends can stress common life styles but they are often not immediately proximate and they may or may not have longterm commitments. The marital unit may have immediate proximity, longterm commitment, and common life style, but it has a small size. The task specific theory predicts that these structural differences will mean that each group can optimally manage different tasks (Litwak, 1985). This requires that each task is classified by the same dimensions used to differentiate the structures.

Kinship systems, marital dyads, and neighbors typically differ in terms of proximity and length of commitment. It is therefore necessary to classify tasks in terms of the degree of proximity they require and the length of commitment. Providing daily food, cleaning the house, helping bedridden individuals with personal grooming, cannot be managed over distance, while the telephone permits individuals to provide emotional succor, advice, and information without face-to-face contact. In a similar fashion, some tasks require long term continuous commitment while other tasks do not require long term commitment. Unless older persons feel that the individual who controls their income has a long term commitment, they would be reluctant to give that control since the current mismanagement by the individual can seriously affect their future. By contrast, some tasks do not require that individuals assume future responsibility. The neighbor who calls the fire department because an older person's house is on fire does not need to have a future or past link to the older person in order to be effective.

The idea of a systematic classification of tasks in terms of dimensions of the group is not commonly undertaken by the modern primary group theorist. Generally when tasks are classified it is in terms of some pragmatic goals, in terms of some abstract theme thought to universally represent all tasks, or on the assumption that all tasks share the same set of dimensions. Consequently, it is often impossible to say which primary group can optimally manage which task.

Rix and Romashko (1980), seeking to show who will help older people in need, focused on immediate household needs such as providing food, cleaning the house, and help in personal grooming. The tasks they selected have underlying dimensions which require (1) long term commitment, (2) close proximity, and (3) do not benefit from a division of labor so can be managed most flexibly by two-person households. Their findings that spouses play a key role in helping older people is not surprising given the nature of tasks they selected. If they had selected tasks which require proximity, but combined with limited time commitments and larger size groups, they would have concluded that neighbors were key. Neighbors are the basic elements of buddy networks which check on the elderly daily, are most likely to hear calls for help in an emergency, lend small household goods, etc. By contrast, if questions were asked about services which required long term commitment and large size but not proximity, Rix and Romashko would have found that kinship plays the key role. For instance, if they asked older people who is most likely to come to their home for a week to help out with daily household activities while they are recovering from an acute illness, the answer is likely to be a member of the kinship system. In short, work such as Rix and Romashko (1980), which suggests that one type of primary group is more important than another, are really saying that some types of tasks are more important than others without explicitly evaluating them.

In summary, the task specific theory argues that tasks can be described by the same set of dimensions that characterize the structure of the groups. To know which group can optimally manage which task or which group can optimally substitute for another (Litwak, 1985), the structure of the group should be matched with the structure of the task. Litwak (1985) points out that if individuals want to optimize all of their tasks, they should have the entire range of primary groups.

There have been several alternative formulations on the diverse roles of primary groups. Cantor (1979) has argued for a "hierarchical" theory in which older people give first preference to kin and only go to a task specific formulation if kin are not available. This theoretical framework does not conflict with the task specific formulation, since Cantor is talking about individual preferences while task specific theory is referring to effectiveness. For instance, a single older person living alone might prefer that kin come to their aid if they have an accident and cannot reach the phone, but unless the kin are neighbors within shouting distance they cannot provide this service. Cantor's framework does raise the important issue of how individuals do choose their helpers. Are people inclined to choose their helper in terms of their effectiveness or their preferences. Alternatively, do their preferences for a given primary group cause them to reshape their lives so as to insure that a particular primary group will be available? The latter course of action is encouraged by traditional kinship structures such as the Amish (Huntington, 1981) and ultra orthodox Jewish groups (Schwartz, 1985).

The older person's age and degree of frailty must be taken into account when considering the relationship between effectiveness and preference. The task specific theorist argues that among the very old who are sick and single, the only primary group that is structurally able to manage the daily household tasks are kin (i.e., children, or younger close relatives) who live very close by. The empirical evidence indicates that older people understand this point and move closer to their children when such situations arise (Litwak, 1985; Litwak & Longino, 1987; Silverstein, Litwak, & Messeri, 1989) if they are middle class. If they are working class and already live close by, they simply remain close. Consequently, for the very old single persons who are ill and for those who value traditional kinship structures, the task specific and the hierarchical theory would have overlapping predictions.

Many primary group investigators (Babchuk, 1965; Adams, 1971) had an implicit theory that primary groups can substitute for each other, although not perfectly. Task specific theory does not rule out substitution of one group for another as suggested by Noelker and Bass (1989). It simply argues that the new group will be less effective unless it alters its structure to be the same as the old one. Task specific theory goes even further in suggesting which of the several alternative primary groups can best substitute for the one which has been shattered, i.e., the one whose structure most closely matches the task at issue. For a widower, tasks which require proximity, such as emergency first aid, but not necessarily long term commitment, can best be managed by neighbors. The sociability functions of a spouse are best supplied by friends. Kin can best manage those aspects of the marital household that require long term commitments, but not necessarily immediate proximity, such as taking care of monthly bills, or doing small household repairs (Litwak, 1985). It is only for some very specific activities that functions are completely lost because no alternative group can match the precise structure of these tasks. This can most clearly be seen in nursing home care, where the primary group that is most able to help older residents is their children. The structure of that relationship does not permit hourly contact each day and, consequently, it cannot manage tasks which require continuous contact, such as maintaining surveillance over the residents' personal possessions in daily use.

THEORY EXPLAINING HOW GROUPS WITH STRUCTURAL CONFLICT CAN EXIST SIMULTANEOUSLY

How does this task specific formulation deal with the problem of structural conflict between formal organizations and primary groups? It advances a proposition that modern industrial society will be in a state of perpetual conflict between formal organizations and primary groups. There are two underlying conditions which make such a continuing state of conflict possible: (a) where conflict is moderate, groups can exist side by side indefinitely; and (b) organizations can simultaneously have major conflicts in one area of life while seriously interdependent in another. Task specific theory argues that primary groups and formal organizations are seriously interdependent because most goals require both technical knowledge and everyday knowledge. Good health, for example, requires strong primary group enforcers of health behaviors as well as having doctors and hospitals available to deal with accidents, heart attacks, and cancers (House, Landis, & Umberson, 1988; Litwak & Messeri, 1989). The fact that structural conflict takes place within a context of mutual need moderates the severity of the clash. A moderate state of continuous conflict will always characterize modern urban society as long as most goals in our society have both technical and non-technical aspects.

Rules for adjudication of non-resolvable conflicts are different from those which are used for resolvable conflicts. Any adjudication must insure the survivability of both groups, that is, mergers or removal of groups are not alternatives. In the case of primary groups and formal organizations, the adjudication process starts with the assumption that there are two kinds of costs. First, the cost of having formal organizations and primary groups too far apart runs the risk that the non-technical and technical aspects of the tasks will not be coordinated. For instance, older people who are not in close contact with their doctors might not discover that they have high blood pressure. The second type of cost is having people so close that the norms of the formal organizations destroy the primary group or the latter destroys the former. For instance, older people who become overly concerned with their health and the value of doctors may become hypochondriacal and overuse medical resources to the point where it prevents its use for people who are in greater need. It can also lead to over-medication. These types of costs have diametrically opposed solutions. To avoid the first error, it is necessary to bring formal organizations and primary groups in closer contact; to avoid the second error, it is necessary to keep them apart.

This conflict is mediated through a "balance theory of coordination" (Litwak & Meyer, 1966; Litwak, Meyer & Hollister, 1977; Sussman, 1977). When the primary groups and the community are too close, the organizations use linkages that open up distance. When they are too far apart, they use linkages that close the distance. The two groups are considered at a balance point when they are at a mid-point in social distance; that is, close enough to communicate, but not so close that they should destroy each other. For instance, if a doctor has an older patient who is hypochondriacal, balance theory would predict optimal ties would result from his use of passive linkages that restrict contact, i.e., by sending information on diets through the mail, speak on the telephone, discourage office visits except for regular examinations or clear cut emergencies, and suggest the patient seek help from a completely different professional such as a psychotherapist. By contrast, for patients who are resistant to health promotion, the theory would argue that the doctor should take the initiative in making the contact; that is, establish outreach clinics in their neighborhood, send health educators to their homes, address their voluntary associations such as churches, or hire indigenous workers to make the patient less fearful (Strauss, 1974). Key issues raised by the balance theory of linkages between formal organizations and primary groups are virtually unexplored.

SOME PROGRAMMATIC CONSEQUENCES OF THE TASK SPECIFIC THEORY

The theoretical assertion that formal organizations can optimally manage technical tasks and that informal ones can optimally manage non-technical ones has particular relevance to the efforts of human service organizations in delivering help to older persons. These formal organizations are generally trying to take over tasks which were originally managed by primary groups. For instance, nursing homes provide daily meals and personal grooming to chronically disabled. Meals on wheels programs and home care agencies similarly provide household services for disabled older persons. The task specific theory states that formal organizations are slower, costlier, do not motivate people well, and lack the flexibility when dealing with household tasks (i.e.,tasks requiring only everyday socialization).

From this flow three generic principles; (a) formal organizations representing human service delivery will never be able to manage tasks to the full expectation of the society no matter how good the staff or sophisticated the organizational design, (b) human service agencies will need to work very closely with the remnants of the older persons primary group networks to optimize their services, and (c) this will produce very special problems of balancing the needs of the formal organizations and the primary groups. We shall illustrate these principles with several institutions delivering human services to older people.

The formal organization attempting to manage tasks which do not suit its structure can either transform the task so as to take greater advantage of its structure, perform the task at a low level of effectiveness, or simply abandon the attempt to manage the task at all. For instance, the nursing home is able to duplicate individual household services by transforming the services into standardized events. If one resident would like to get up at 8 a.m., while another at 7 a.m., and a third at 9 a.m., that is not possible. If a woman resident can no longer comb her hair then standardization is achieved by cutting the hair short so it does not have to be combed, or drawing it back and binding it with a rubber band. Where activities cannot be routinized they are often dropped, e.g., brushing teeth.

There are in-between activities which are not easily supervised and, consequently, staff have an option as to how much they want to do. Providing water on request for bedridden patients, or the frequency with which staff moves bedridden patients to prevent bed sores are examples. The extent to which staff members perform these activities in ways that are comfortable to the patients depends on the internalized motivation of the staff. Unlike primary groups, the staff of formal organizations are chiefly motivated by economic incentives. When they must perform services which are not easily supervised, there is a greater probability that they will do that which is easiest for them.[3]

Despite these structural limitations the formal organization is often the optimal choice because the burden of 24 hour continuous care overwhelms typical primary groups. These defects of the formal organizations, however, offer compelling incentives for the older person's remaining primary groups to provide supplemental corrective services. Children of residents can bring weekly food treats to supplement the standardized meals, they can bring bedspreads and pictures to supplement the standardized room furniture, they can provide emotional succor to supplement the nursing home care, and provide for weekly grooming. Evidence indicates that this is precisely what goes on for many nursing home residents (Litwak, 1985; Dobrof, 1976).

The theoretical framework, however, also cautions that heavy involvement of children in the nursing home creates a risk of structural conflict. Children, guided by the particularistic family norms, put pressure on the staff to take care of their parent without thinking of the formal organization's universalistic criteria that residents should be taken care of in terms of their needs. The very internalized motivation which guarantees that the children will seek to meet the non-standardized needs of their parent can also lead to violation of formal organizational norms of equity.

Clearly, what is needed are the balance principles suggested above. Those children who are so demanding that they violate the universalism of the nursing home staff could be encouraged to spend less time in the nursing home, while children whose parents suffer because they do not visit at all could be encouraged to come in. The questions arises as to how this balance principle operates in practice. At this historical moment, the nursing homes and the families of the residents are at an imbalance. The staff of the nursing home is organized either through nursing home associations or staff unions. The children of nursing home residents have only the beginnings of an organization. Without an organizational base, the children of a nursing home resident run some serious risk in protesting actions of the staff. The nursing home administrator can simply tell the resident parent of the protesting children to leave. Alternatively, the children may be afraid to protest too much out of concern that the staff will punish their parents when they are not around. To manage this problem, children have become aware of advocacy groups and incipient forms of such organizations are spontaneously springing up.

The need for some client protection is also recognized in state laws requiring residents' councils, family councils, and ombudsmen. Such laws do not, however, amply recognize that residents in nursing homes are too physically disabled and in too dependent a position to form advocacy groups on their own behalf. These laws also fail to recognize that family councils organized by the nursing home administrators are not structurally consistent with the notion of legitimate conflicts between the nursing home staff and resident primary groups. Such laws see only the areas of cooperation between nursing homes and family groups. Task specific theory prevents such oversights. It suggests that family and friends of nursing home residents must have an autonomous organization which can operate in partial states of conflict as well as under conditions of cooperation, much like union and management relations in industry.

The laws which create ombudsmen do not recognize what it takes to monitor non-technical tasks, and consequently, are seriously under-funded. One ombudsman may be asked to represent many nursing homes. Given the fact that abuse often takes place in areas not easily observed, it is clear that an ombudsman cannot be the one to continuously monitor patients. This often requires a relative with a one-to-one relationship. Unless the law provides for an organizational structure that brings these relatives together with the ombudsman, the ombudsman can only deal with (a) easily observed gross uniform violations, or (b) with violations brought to their attention by especially energetic relatives.

Some gerontologists argue that nursing homes should be abandoned because of the humiliation that nursing home routinization forces upon residents. They suggest that society make use of human service agencies that more nearly approximate primary group structures, that is home services such as home care agencies. Task specific theory would suggest that this simply changes the dimension stressed, but not the magnitude of the problem. In nursing homes, the most obvious problems are those of routinization and linkages to residents' primary groups while problems associated with staff motivation are fewer in number. By contrast, the problem of motivation is central for home care agencies and the problems of routinization and agency community linkages are fewer in number.

Home care agencies offer an organizational solution which more closely approximates the primary group in structure. They have one caretaker to one resident. As a result, the caretaker does not have to standardize tasks as much as do those in nursing homes. They can more easily cook meals to the residents' specifications and help the patients take baths at times more convenient to them. There are still some elements of standardization, that is, the homemaker is only available at fixed hours on certain days. What becomes more visible in this structural setting is the inability of the homemaker to match the family's internalized commitment. Moreover, by virtue of trying to emulate the primary group's ability to provide unique services, there is no easy way for the home care worker to be closely watched by their agency's supervisors.

A reasonable solution to this dilemma is to make use of the older person's existing primary group structures to supplement home-makers services (Noelker & Bass, 1989). If the older person has a child who could come in once or twice a week and keep in daily telephone contact with the homemaker, it could considerably re-duce the likelihood that abuse would occur. The child is more likely, than an agency supervisor, to know if possessions are miss-ing and to be aware if the home care worker is consistently coming late.

The problems of balance that face nursing homes also face home-maker services. Because homemakers are so highly decentralized, however, the problems may not become apparent. Difficulties would arise in situations where the child felt the homemaker was incompetent and the agency felt because of the shortages it could not provide an alternative. In short, task specific theory suggests that home care services are optimally suited to residents who are sufficiently intact so that they can energetically represent them-selves to the agency supervisor or, alternatively, have kin who can supplement agency supervision. They have some problems of stan-dardization (e.g., the homemaker can only come on certain days and certain hours) but, compared to a nursing home, standardiza-tion is far less of a problem. Home services do, however, have major problems of motivation due to the inability to supervise. The task specific principles hold for any formal organization seeking to substitute for primary groups services.[4]

WHEN PRIMARY GROUP SUPPORT IS NOT AVAILABLE

It is comparatively rare to find older people who have no kin or friends with long term commitments. The treatment of this group is, however, important. Some suggest that volunteers can be used to help older people bereft of children, relatives, and friends. Task specific theory proposes that typical voluntary organizations ("Gray Ladies," Lions' Clubs) do not have the structure to manage some of the most crucial household services required by very dis-abled older persons. What characterizes these organizations is a very small central core manned by especially dedicated volunteers or paid professionals, and a very large membership who have more limited commitments. The majority of members see occupational and family duties as taking precedence over voluntary associational activities and cannot, generally, undertake any long term activities that require substantial daily commitments. For instance, the typical volunteer cannot undertake to provide daily meals to a homebound person for a period of one year, cannot guarantee to visit given residents weekly and keep sufficiently close supervision so that they can keep track of missing possessions, and if they notice bed sores, bodily bruises or abuse, cannot engage the staff in a form of advocacy which could lead to very stressful interpersonal relations, as well as running the risk of having the home request that the resident be removed.

The application of task specific theory to typical voluntary associations, however, highlights their key structural features and consequently, the nature of tasks which they can optimally manage. Structural features of this type of voluntary organization suggest it can manage long term tasks if the task does not require the same individual to provide the service. The large size and centralized structure of this kind of voluntary association permits it to assure an older person that someone will be available to provide daily services, even though the voluntary association cannot guarantee it will be the same person each time. For instance, it can guarantee that people will be available to make sandwiches on a daily basis, that a driver can take them to a weekly occupational therapy treatment, or that they will have individuals available to write letters for them. Having such a set of principles clearly in mind should be invaluable to policy makers and to program developers. More generally, this theory makes it very clear why typical voluntary associations are not adequate substitutes for those who are bereft of any primary groups.

A second solution is to move toward the use of professionals or professionals in combination with ordinary citizens. The professional is assumed to have much more internalized commitment than the typical home care worker. Consequently, they should be able to manage primary group tasks with less risk of abuse. The chief barrier to their use is the cost and the low status of home care work. Therefore, what is envisioned is the professional supervising home care workers, but with a somewhat different model than is currently used. The professional would have to establish a relationship with the older person that would be sufficiently intensive to undertake a role similar to that of a relative, e.g., be able to provide emotional support for daily hassles, to distinguish between crankiness and real complaints, to drop in on the older person several times a week, and to supplement the day care worker with household and leisure time activities.

CONCLUSION AND SUMMARY

The task specific theory compels investigators to focus on both the structure of the task and the structure of the group. It is this focus that makes it clear that formal organizations cannot optimally manage tasks which are typically handled by primary groups. Therefore, if formal organizations must be used because primary groups no longer have sufficient resources, it is possible to specify which problems will arise from which type of formal organization. For example, nursing homes have major problems in loss of services produced by standardization, and minor problems arising form losses produced by lack of staff motivation. Conversely, home care agencies have major problems that arise from lack of motivation, and minor problems arising from standardization. Task specific theory also shows why in both nursing home and home care service, the older person's remaining primary group can optimize services by providing supplemental help. This theory makes clear that coordinating the primary group and formal organizations has special problems because their structures are in conflict even while their goals are complementary. It suggests the general nature of linkages that are likely to moderate the conflict.

This theoretical orientation provides a research agenda for social science researchers seeking to improve services for the elderly. To provide scientific justification for this framework, the initial research made use of a few tasks for which there would be face validity and typical primary groups (Litwak, 1985). For this theory to be of value to service providers, it is now necessary for researchers to engage in a difficult empirical job of measuring the dimensions of the entire range of services that older people require as they move from states of health to disability. It is no longer permissible for investigators seeking to differentiate between home care agencies and primary group help to ask very general questions such as "who helps you with meals; who helps you get in and out of bed; who cleans your house; who helps with your medication? etc." It is now necessary to find out if the service is provided in a standardized way, or if it is designed to meet the idiosyncratic needs of the older person. To differentiate between kin help and neighbor help it is no longer permissible to ask, "who provides you with help when you are sick?" It is necessary to ask, "who provides you with emergency help if you fall down and cannot reach the phone; and who provides you with longer term care, such as daily meals?" This is not simply an admonishment to researchers, but it is a statement to funding agencies. To provide practitioners with useful information, they must be prepared to fund research that is far more elaborate than the typical study design of the past. It is also necessary to research and identify the dimensions of the full range of primary groups that confront practitioners, not simply the typical one (e.g., traditional kin as well as modified extended structures, incomplete families as well as complete ones, etc). A major research effort is also required to identify the various linkages used to adjust social distance in different substantive areas (e.g., nursing homes, home care agencies, senior citizen centers, etc.) and to understand the conditions under which they operate to produce a balanced or unbalanced tie. In short, task specific theory opens up a rich research vein for those seeking to optimize services to the elderly. It awaits both empirical and theoretical mining from those researchers seeking to help the elderly.

NOTES

1. The assumption being that both of these functions required a loving interpersonal relationship which formal organizations could not entertain because they would introduce nepotism. Parsons did not recognize the wider implications of his analysis, that most tasks had some part which did not require technical knowledge. Parsons saw tension management and early socialization as becoming highly professional tasks which would be managed by the family. The term professional obscured the extent to which he felt this knowledge was founded on everyday socialization or required training through formal organizations.

2. The organizational contingency theorists simply argue that tasks which

have much uncertainty are best managed by the formal organizations which have some of the key qualities of primary groups, e.g., some internalized commitments, longer commitments to their members, peer ties, and use of committee meetings. By contrast, where tasks have fewer contingencies they are best managed by the monocratic organizations as specified by Weber (Litwak, 1961; Perrow, 1967; Thompson, 1967). The underlying assumption in all of the analysis was that all tasks require a certain modicum of technical knowledge and, therefore, all tasks required some degree of formal organizational resources. The expanded contingency theorists (Litwak & Figueira, 1968; Litwak & Messeri, 1989) simply pointed out that tasks could also vary in terms of their technical knowledge as illustrated above. Where tasks have both uncertainty and require only everyday knowledge, the primary group has the structure that optimally matches the tasks.

3. Nursing homes are very sensitive to the need to hire staff with internalized motivation, but this is very difficult to assess. Also, the pay for nursing home aides is sufficiently low that the people in these professions often have large family burdens of their own which makes it difficult for them to provide altruistic care to others. Especially when this altruism means extra work for them.

4. The task specific principle holds for any formal organizations seeking to substitute for primary group services. For instance, "meals on wheels" programs must standardize the time they provide meals as well as the range of choices open to consumers. They cannot deliver hot meals and cannot provide the more idiosyncratic services associated with primary groups' delivery of meals, that is, insure that the individuals have eaten the meals, that the individual is alright physically, and cannot provide emotional succor and information during meal times as family members might. Consequently, it would be argued that "meals on wheels" provides the most satisfactory services where the individuals have some primary group support that checks up on them daily and can provide special group support and can provide special food treats. Where such primary group social support is not available, "meals on wheels" programs will be less successful.

REFERENCES

Adams, B.N. (1971). Isolation, function, and beyond: American kinship in the 1960's. In C.B. Broderick (Ed.), *A decade of family research in action* (pp. 163-186). Minneapolis: National Council on Family Relations.

Babchuk, N. (1965). Primary friends and kin: A study of the associations of middle class couples. *Social Forces, 43*, 483-493.

Cantor, M.H. (1979). Neighbors and friends: An overlooked resource in the informal support system. *Research on Aging, 1*, 434-463.

Dobrof, R. *The case of the aged: A shared function*. Unpublished doctoral dissertation, Columbia University, School of Social Work. New York, 1976.

Fischer, C.S. (1982). *To dwell among friends: Personal networks in town and city*. Chicago: University of Chicago Press.

Gasset, J.O. (1932). *The revolt of the masses*. New York: W.W. Norton & Co.

Granovetter, M. (1974). *Getting a job: A study of contacts and careers*. Cambridge, MA: Harvard University Press.

House, J.S., Landis, K.R., & Umberson, D. (1988). Social relationships and health. *Science, 241*, 540-545.

Huizinger, J. (1936). *In the shadow of tomorrow*. New York: W.W. Norton & Co.

Huntington, G.E. (1981). The Amish family. In C.H. Mindel & R.W. Habenstein (Eds.), *Ethnic families in America: Patterns and variations* (2nd Ed.) (pp. 295-325). New York: Elsevier.

Katz, E. & Lazarsfeld, P.F. (1955). *Personal influence*. Glencoe, IL: Free Press.

Kendig, H. (1983). Blood ties and gender roles: Adult children who care for aged parents. In *Proceedings of the Australian Family Research Conference: Family Support Networks* (Vol. 5). Melbourne, Australia: Institute of Family Studies.

Litwak, E. (1960a). Occupational mobility and extended family cohesion. *American Sociological Review, 25*, 9-21.

Litwak, E. (1960b). Geographic mobility and extended family cohesion. *American Sociological Review, 25*, 385-394.

Litwak, E. (1961). Models of bureaucracy which permit conflict. *American Journal of Sociology, 67*, 177-184.

Litwak, E. (1985). *Helping the elderly: The complementary roles of informal networks and formal systems*. New York: The Guilford Press.

Litwak, E. & Figueira, J. (1968). Technological innovation and theoretical functions of primary groups and bureaucratic structures. *American Journal of Sociology, 73*, 468-481.

Litwak, E. & Longino, C. (1987). Migration patterns among the elderly: A developmental perspective. *Gerontologist, 25*, 385-394.

Litwak, E. & Messeri, P. (1989). Organizational theory, social supports, and mortality rates: A theoretical convergence. *American Sociological Review, 54*, 49-66.

Litwak, E. & Meyer, H. (1966). A balance theory of coordination between bureaucratic organizations and community primary groups. *Administrative Science Quarterly, 11*, 31-58.

Litwak, E., Meyer, H., & Hollister, C.D. (1977). The role of linkage mechanisms between bureaucracies and families: Education and health as empirical cases in point. In R.J. Liebert & A.W. Imershine (Eds.), *Power paradigms and community research* (pp. 121-152). Beverly Hills: Sage.

Mayhew, L. (1968). Ascription in modern society. *Sociological Inquiry, 38*, 105-120.

Nisbet, R. (1969). *Community and power* (2nd Ed.). New York: Oxford University Press.

Noelker, L.S. & Bass, D.M. (1989). Home care for elderly persons: Linkages between formal and informal caregivers. *Journals of Gerontology, 44*, S63-S70.

Parsons, T. (1944). The social structure of the family. In R. Anshen (Ed.), *The family: Its function and destiny* (pp. 173-201). New York: Harper & Row.

Parsons, T. & Bales, R.F. (1955). *Family, socialization and interaction process.* New York: Free Press of Glencoe.

Perrow, C. (1967). A framework for the comparative analysis of complex organizations. *American Sociological Review, 32,* 194-208.

Polsky, H. & Duberman, L. (1979). The changing American family: From traditional to companionship to existential. In H. Polsky (Ed.), *Social system, culture, and role theory: Applications in the helping professions.* Lexington, MA: Ginn Custom Publishing.

Redfield, R. (1947). Folk society. *American Journal of Sociology, 52,* 293-308.

Rix, S.E. & Romashko, T. (1980). *With a little help from my friends.* Final report to Administration on Aging, U.S. Department of Health, Education, and Welfare, AOA Grant No. 90A-1320. Washington, D.C.: Department of Health, Education, and Welfare.

Roethlisberger, F.J. & Dickson, W.J. (1939). *Management and the worker.* Cambridge, MA: Harvard University Press.

Schwartz, S. *A society unto themselves: A theoretical and empirical examination of woman's proclivity for depression.* Unpublished doctoral dissertation, Columbia University. New York, 1985.

Shanas, E. (1979). The family as a support system in old age. *Gerontologist, 19,* 169-174.

Shils, E.A. & Janowitz, M. (1948). Cohesion and disintegration in the Wehrmacht in World War II. *Public Opinion Quarterly, 12,* 280-315.

Silverstein, M., Litwak, E., & Messeri, P. (1989). The effects of health and social class on the geographic dispersion of older people and their helpers. Unpublished manuscript.

Stein, M. (1960). *Eclipse of community.* New York: Harper & Row.

Strauss, A.L. (1974). Medical ghettos. In S. Huber & H.T. Chalfant (Eds.), *The sociology of American poverty* (pp. 234-246). Cambridge, MA: Schenkman.

Sussman, M.B. (1953). The help pattern in the middle class family. *American Sociological Review, 18,* 22-28.

Sussman, M.B. (1965). Relationship of adult children with their parents in the United States. In E. Shanas & G. Strieb (Eds.), *Social structure and the family: Generational relations* (pp. 62-93). Englewood Cliffs, NJ: Prentice Hall.

Sussman, M.B. (1977). Family, bureaucracy, and the elderly individual: An organizational linkage perspective. In E. Shanas & M.B. Sussman (Eds.), *Family, bureaucracy, and the elderly* (pp. 2-20). Durham, NC: Duke University Press.

Thompson, J.D. (1967). *Organizations in action.* New York: McGraw-Hill.

Tönnies, F. (1940). C.P. Loomis (Trans.), *Fundamental concepts of sociology.* New York: American Book Company.

Weber, M. (1947). *The theory of social economic organization.* In A.M. Henderson & T. Parsons, (Eds. & Trans.). New York: Oxford University Press.

The Place of Kinfolk in Personal Community Networks

Barry Wellman

COMMUNITIES AS NETWORKS

Family sociologists have usually treated kinship networks as discrete systems in Western (post)industrial societies. While separate treatment is useful for studying such matters as inheritance and ceremonial obligations, it wrenches out of context an assessment of how ties with kin fit into everyday lives. My purpose in this paper is to assess the place of kinship ties in *personal community networks: intimate* and *active* ties with friends, neighbors, and workmates as well as with kin.

Social network analysis helps researchers to compare kin with kith. In a tradition started by Bott (1957), network analysts look at

This paper integrates and develops work in Wellman (1982, 1984, 1988, forthcoming; Wellman and Berkowitz 1988; Wellman, Carrington and Hall 1988; Wellman and Wortley (1989a, 1989b). It is dedicated to Sabrina Meyrowitz Cutaia and Frieda Tuechler. A longer version of this paper, with much more extensive citations, is available as a Research Paper from the Centre for Urban and Community Studies, University of Toronto, Toronto, Canada M5S 1A1. The author wishes to thank the following for their intellectual support: J.A. Barnes, Bonnie Erickson, Vicente Espinoza, Bernard Farber, Claude Fischer, Nancy Howell, Renate Kalve, Catharine Mazeika, John Mogey, June Shinagawa, Susan Sim, Richard Stren, David Tindall, Donald Unger, Craig Urquhart, Bev Wellman, Peter Wilmott, and Scot Wortley. The author also thanks the following for their material support: The National Health Development and National Welfare Grants programs of Health and Welfare Canada, the Social Science and Humanities Research Council of Canada (general, population aging, and the human context of science and technology research programs), and the University of Toronto's Centre for Urban and Community Studies, Programme in Gerontology, McLuhan Programme in Culture and Technology.

how a person (or household) at the center of a network deals with the members of her/his egocentric universe. The network approach treats a community as a set of relationships stretching beyond the household—without *a priori* limitation on where network members live and how they are related to the person at the center of the network. It allows analysts to compare the characteristics of different kinds of community ties. It liberates analysts from looking only at communities which resemble traditional solidarities of neighbors and kinfolk.

Network analysts start with a set of all active or intimate relationships and only then ask if the *members* of such networks are kith or kin. They then ask about the *personal characteristics* of the members of their networks (e.g., gender, social class), the characteristics of the *ties* themselves (e.g., frequency of contact, kinship role), and ties among network members (Wellman, 1982, 1988). Most analyses are concerned with:

- *composition* (e.g., the percent who are kin, live near-by, or are working-class);
- *structure* (e.g., density of interconnections among network members),
- *contents* (e.g., the supportiveness of network members).

Thus the network approach provides a useful means for seeing how kin fit into personal community networks:

- How prominent are kin in personal community networks in terms of numbers and proportions?
- Do kin form separate clusters within personal community networks? Are their relations densely-knit and tightly-bounded? Or have kin become just a convenient recruiting area for friendships?
- Do kin differ from kith in the roles they play in such networks? Is kinship and friendship *fungible* in the economists' sense of substitutable resources? In particular, does the companionship and social support they provide differ in quality, quantity and reliability?
- How do kinship relations fit into the ways in which personal community networks help people and households deal with

problems and opportunities of reproduction and production? Do they provide collective relations that support and control kinfolk, or do they provide resources upon which kin can draw selectively and voluntarily?

I concentrate on describing that mythical category: *people in general*. Where necessary, I use as a baseline the networks of white, northern-European ethnicity, employed, once-married, North American, 40-year old (sub)urban women and men with a child in primary school. Although such persons make up a smaller share of the population than conservative mythologists would have us believe (Berger & Berger, 1983), nevertheless they remain a modal category of North Americans.

I focus on the *size, connectivity, contact and supportiveness* of network ties, acknowledging, but not emphasizing the ambivalence, stress and costs that most relationships experience. Fortunately, the studies of most scholars are comparable enough to permit me to interweave them into one integrated account. Nevertheless, I inevitably gloss over fascinating information about differences between subgroups (e.g., social classes, ethnicities, age strata, women/men, married/not married). Where the published findings are thin, I supplement them with material prepared specially for this paper from the first and second Toronto (East York) studies (Wellman, 1979, 1982; Wellman, Carrington & Hall, 1988; Wellman & Wortley, 1989a, 1989b).

ARE SISTERS AND COUSINS RECKONED BY THE DOZENS?

How Many Kin?

Fuzzy Sets: Personal community networks have even fuzzier boundaries than kinship networks. Because there are no gates (or gatekeepers) to divide members from non-members, analysts must develop a sharp picture from fuzzy reality. Defining personal communities entails the usual kinship dilemmas about including affines, relations continuing after divorces and deaths, and unrecognized kin. In addition, friends, neighbors and workmates come and go, their definition and importance varying by the hour, day and year. There is the "Bob and Carol and Ted and Alice problem" (Mazursky, 1969): Ties to a married couple can function as one relation or two. Indeed, there is no such thing as *the network*: analysts must specify inclusion criteria. For example, our research group studies only those co-workers who are seen socially outside of work.

Available and Actual Ties

The broadest possible personal community network of direct relations contains all those whom a person can currently deal with on an informal basis. Yet one rarely acquires relations through random encounters in cafes or on the streets. Rather, social and physical *foci* — such as kinship groups, churches, workplaces or neighborhood streetcorners — bring people together under auspices conducive for interaction (Feld, 1982).

I estimate that about *16,000* adults are potentially available for interaction with married 40-year olds who have a child attending primary school (Table 1; the rationale is in Wellman forthcoming). These comprise an estimated *2,700* ties directly available through foci (and a few random encounters), and an estimated *13,000+* relationships available through being friends (and kin) of existing friends (and kin). Most potentially-available ties never form (Column B of Table 1). Analysts have estimated that most people have between 250 and 1,000 actual ties with adults, with my own estimate being *400* (Boissevain, 1974; Pool & Kochen, 1978; Greenbaum, 1982; Killworth, Bernard & McCarty, 1984).

Weak ties of acquaintanceship far outnumber stronger ties of intimacy, support, companionship or routine contact. Table 1 shows an estimated average of 20 stronger, active ties (5% of all actual ties) and 380 weaker ties. These weak ties integrate social systems and speed the diffusion of information. Indeed, a person's many weak ties are more useful for this purpose than his/her smaller number of strong ties. Strong ties link people who travel in the same social circles and hence, learn similar things. Weak ties link people to networks whose members travel in different social circles and hence, hear new things (Granovetter, 1973, 1982).

What are the number and proportion of kin in such broadly-de-

TABLE 1: NUMBER & PERCENT OF KIN TIES IN AVERAGE NETWORKS

TYPE OF TIES	# OF TIES A	% OF ABOVE B	# OF KIN TIES C	% OF ABOVE D	% KIN OF ALL TIES E
POTENTIALLY AVAILABLE	16,000	--	55	--	0.3
DIRECTLY AVAILABLE	2,700	17	55	100	2
ACTUAL	400	15	35 (30-45)	63	9
ACTIVE	20 (14-23)	5	6 (6-10)	17	30
INTIMATE	5 (5-7)	25	3 (2-4)	50	50
INTERACTOR	10 (3-15)	50	4 (5-7)	67	40
CONFIDANT	2	40	1-2	50	50

199

fined networks? Firth, Hubert and Forge (1969) report that on the average Londoners recognize the existence of 55 living, adult kin — a category similar to Table 1's potentially (and directly) available kin. Most of these kin tend to be actual — and not just potential — members of broadly-defined networks. People tend to know an average of 35 kin including at least one parent (or adult child) and at least one sibling. This set of kin are about 63% of those available for interaction (Column D of Table 1; see Adams, 1968; Firth, Hubert, & Forge, 1969; Lüschen, 1972). This set excludes household members but includes in-laws and spouses of consanguines.

Thus kin make up about 2% of all ties directly available for membership in a personal community network and about 9% of all ties actually present in such a network (Column E of Table 1). Should we lament the irrelevance of kinship because kin make up *only* 10% of these networks? Or should we celebrate that kin make up *as much as* 10% of these networks? After all, the 90 or so available kin are such a tiny number when compared with the 2,700 potential network members directly available through foci and the 10,000 indirectly available? The second, more positive attitude is in better keeping with the increasing importance of kinship as definitions of network members tighten from all ties to intimate ties (Table 1).

Active Ties

Just as most kinship studies consider only those kin who have more than trivial relations (Firth, Hubert, & Forge, 1969; Farber, 1981), community network studies look only at small subsets of personal networks. Researchers have identified a range of 14-23 persons who are significant in one's life because of repeated sociable contact, supportiveness, or feelings of connectedness (Table 1).[1] This score of *active* ties provides people with most of their interpersonal support and companionship (Erickson, Radkewycz & Nosanchuk, 1988).

Kin are substantially represented in most active networks, making up at least 30% of the active ties compared with less than 10% of all ties and 2% of all potentially-available ties (Table 1). Thus a much higher percentage of kin than kith are actively involved in network relations. However, preferences for active involvement are bimodal, with most networks containing either few or many kin (Reiss & Oliveri, 1983; Wellman, Carrington, & Hall, 1988).

Not all types of kin are equally represented. Most active kin relations come from the small number of available *immediate kin* (parents, adult children, siblings, including in-laws). By contrast, only a small minority of available *extended kin* (aunts, cousins, grandparents, etc.) are active network members.

Some studies suggest that certain social characteristics foster networks that contain a higher number and proportion of kin:

— Married people who acquire a set of in-laws along with their spouse (Heiskanen, 1969; Wellman et al., 1988).
— Women actively involved in maintaining networks who bear a triple load of paid work, domestic work and community networking (Adams, 1968; Firth, Hubert, & Forge, 1969; Lee, 1980; Hammer, Gutwirth & Phillips, 1982; Wellman, 1985; Rosenthal, 1985).
— Residents of rural areas, perhaps lacking the opportunities of urbanites to make friendships based on shared interests (Mirande, 1970; Fischer, 1982b).
— Members of the working-class more reliant on kin for domestic support and less involved with workmates after hours (Adams, 1968; Bell, 1968; Fried, 1973; Willmott, 1987).

Interactors, Intimates and Confidants

Most network studies have looked at even smaller subsets of network members: either frequently-seen *interactors* or socially-close intimates. Only to some extent are the same persons both intimates and frequent interactors (Wellman, Carrington, & Hall, 1988; Milardo, 1989). Many of the 10 or so frequent interactors are neighbors or workmates who rarely are intimates (Walker, 1977; Kazak & Wilcox, 1984). However, the few immediate kin who frequently interact usually are intimate.

Most network studies identify about 25% of the active ties — 4-7 ties — as distinctively close and supportive *intimates*. Intimate networks tend to contain equal numbers of kin and friends. Most intimate kin are *immediate kin*: usually equal numbers of parents (or adult children, depending on age) and siblings. Although there is conflicting evidence about whether immediate kin tend to be a person's closest intimate, several studies report that an immediate kin is usually the socially-closest member of a network.[2] Extended kin rarely are intimates. For example, they make up only 6% of all intimates in the second Toronto study (Wellman, Carrington, & Hall, 1988).

A few studies have looked only at the tiny set of socially-close *confidants*: the 1-3 network members to whom people pour out their hearts. While most intimate and active network members provide only specialized kinds of support, confidants help in many ways. The largest and most reliable study of confidants — the 1985 General Social Survey — found that less than one-half of all confidants outside of households are kin.

Summary

Most kin who are potentially available do become actual members of personal community networks. The stronger the relationship used to define a network, the higher the proportion of network members who are kin. Indeed, most immediate kin — and some extended kin — have strong ties in these networks as active and even intimate members. Immediate kin tend to be intimates and even confidants. Extended kin tend to be (non-intimate) active network members or have even weaker ties.

Kinship Connections

Structure

Networks of similar density may have different patterns of integration and fragmentation within them. For example, two structurally different networks may have the same density. But one of these networks might contain a *cluster* of densely-connected kin plus several disconnected *isolates*. By contrast, the connectivity of the other network might be evenly distributed with all members having one-third of all possible ties.

In practice, the density of active and intimate networks ranges between 0.3 and 0.5. Only about one-third to one-half of the possible direct links between active or intimate network members actually exist.³ Thus most potential ties between network members have not actually become active ties. These network members may be connected but at lower levels of intensity. For example, while most of a person's intimates are not intimate with each other, many have weaker ties with one another.

Kinship Clusters

A set of kin form both a distinct social network and a part of a broader personal community network. The nature of this kinship system affects the structure and operations of personal community networks. Because kinship is an inherently-connected system, the kin who are active or intimate members of personal community networks are usually linked with each other (Firth, Hubert, & Forge, 1969; Johnson & Bond, 1974). At least one *kinkeeping* person — usually a mother or daughter — converts normative obligation into high centrality by taking upon herself the task of maintaining ties among kin. As Walker points out, "Family, like community, serves as a euphemism for women" (1986, p. 7; see also Bahr 1976; Rosenthal, 1985). The result of this kinkeeping is that two-thirds of active kin in the Toronto study — compared with only one-quarter of active non-kin — usually get together in group contexts such as dinners, holidays or picnics.*⁴ By contrast to kinship, most friendship ties meet more privately as relations between individuals or couples.

The interconnections of kinship both constrain and promote interactions. The constraints come from the limited number of kin available to be network members. Yet normative feelings of obligations encourage people to interact with kin, especially with immediate kin (Farber, 1981). At the same time, kinship connectivity fosters contact — and even frequent contact — with many persons whom they otherwise would not meet. For example, the first Toronto study finds that while three-fifths of all possible intimate links between kin actually exist, only one-fifth of all possible links between friends actually exist (Wellman et al., 1988). The upshot is that kin predominate in high-density networks while friends predominate in low-density networks (see also Shulman, 1972; Kazak & Wilcox, 1984; Oliver, 1984).

It is not that most people dislike their active kin. The Torontonians report disliking only 8% of their active immediate kin and 4% of their active extended kin. It is just that active friends are much more likely to want to interact voluntarily (84%) than are active extended kin (13%) or immediate kin (44%). It is these voluntary relations whom they are more likely to ask to go out to the movies or go partying.*

Marriage brings more kin into networks but lowers the density of connections in these networks (Lüschen, 1972; Gordon & Downing, 1978; Wellman et al., 1988). Because marriage increases network size, the number of additional ties would have to increase geometrically to maintain an equivalent density. Yet except for parents-in-law, there is little contact between in-laws (Farber, 1981). Similarly, although many of one spouse's friends become friends of the other spouse, only some of one spouse's friends become friends of the other spouse's friends (Kazak & Wilcox, 1984; Willmott, 1987). Furthermore, the number of friends may actually shrink after marriage, as spouses withdraw inwards to contemplate each other and their children (Johnson & Leslie, 1982).

Kin (and in-laws) form one or two distinct clusters in personal community networks. One consequence is that those people who have networks heavily composed of kin—such as homemakers without paid work—may have more densely-knit networks than other people (Hammer, Gutwirth, & Phillips, 1982; Wellman, 1985). Kin rarely have direct ties with their kinfolk's friends. (They are indirectly connected through their mutual ties to the focal person at the center of the network.) For example, only 7% of all possible intimate ties between Torontonians' kin and friends actually exist (Wellman et al., 1988).

This connectivity means that kin have the densely-knit relations useful for coordinating and controlling action. For example, they are quicker to mobilize to care for sick relations. At the same time, high density often leads to *inbreeding* of information and opinions. Thus kin are less open than friends to getting new information about health care, and they are more reluctant to send sick persons to doctors and hospitals (Salloway & Dillon, 1973).

Summary

Kin are usually the most densely-connected members of active and intimate networks. Thus they have a unique structural basis for coordinated action: be it supportive, sociable or controlling. The relative lack of ties between in-laws makes the networks of married persons more sparsely-knit than the networks of most unmarried persons. Kinship ties, while densely-knit, do not have tight boundaries. Their connectivity provides a more coordinated basis to connect network members to other social circles.

OVER THE RIVER AND THROUGH THE WOODS

Proximity

A key message of post-World War II research has been that kinship ties endure over long distances. Densely-knit structures and normative obligations encourage active kinship ties to maintain contact despite separation. Moreover, kinship ties — even formerly latent ones — often help migrants to obtain jobs, houses, spouses and local lore (e.g., Tilly & Brown, 1967; Anderson, 1974; Grieco, 1987). Community analysts have generalized this message from kinship relations to all community ties. They contend that phones, cars and planes enable relationships to be active and intimate over long distances (Wellman & Leighton, 1979).

Active and Intimate Ties

Active ties are dispersed ties. About three-quarters of active ties in Toronto (and San Francisco) extend beyond the neighborhood, one-third extend beyond the metropolitan area, and one-fifth stretch over 100 miles (Wellman, Carrington, & Hall, 1988; see also Fischer, 1982b).

Strong, intimate ties are even less likely to be local. For example, about seven-eighths of the intimate ties of Torontonians extend beyond the neighborhood, while one-quarter extend beyond the metropolitan area (Wellman, 1979; Wellman, Carrington, & Hall,

1988). Because of this dispersion and scant public transit, North Americans must rely on cars, planes and phones to maintain active and intimate ties. Yet even poorer persons, with less access to cars and planes, have many long-distance ties. For example, about half of the intimates of Black Los Angeleños live outside of their neighborhoods and over 10% live outside of the metropolitan area (Oliver, 1986).

Kinship Ties

Kinship relations reflect these broad tendencies. Most active and intimate kinship ties extend beyond the neighborhood but remain in the same metropolitan area. However, kinship ties withstand separation better than friendship ties. The norms and structures that link kin — especially immediate kin — help them to be active and intimate network members even at a distance. For example, about one-half of the active kin of the residents of the San Francisco Bay area live more than one hour's drive away while less than one-quarter of their active friends live that far apart (Fischer, 1982b). Indeed, these Californians have more long-distance kinship ties (2.9) than friendship ties (2.5) in their active networks, even though kinfolk make up only 34% of these networks. The second Toronto study shows similar findings, with more than half of active kinfolk living more than 30 miles [50 kilometers] away as compared with one-third of their active friends living so far apart.*

To be sure, distance reduces contact. Few kin now live near enough to make daily visits. For example, Torontonians have frequent contact (3x/week or more) with only one kin by telephone or in person. The biggest decline in contact occurs when the tie extends beyond the metropolitan area, more than about one hour's drive, or 30 miles (Wellman, 1979; Wellman, Carrington, & Hall, 1988). However, relations with kin are less sensitive to long distances than are relations with friends (e.g., Fischer, 1982a; Willmott, 1986; Oliver, 1986).

For example, the second Toronto study reports that 26% of active friends living more than 30 miles away are seen at least monthly, compared with 55% of active immediate kin and 46% of active extended kin. The telephone compensates for distance, especially for immediate kin. Seventy-two percent of the intimate immediate kin living outside of metropolitan Toronto talk on the telephone at least monthly, compared with 56% of extended kin and 50% of friends (Wellman et al., 1989).

In sum, despite the dispersion of kin, most people have an important minority of active and intimate kin living nearby. About one-quarter of active kin — including one or two intimate relatives — tend to live in the same neighborhood. As these are usually immediate kin, they are often quite supportive (cf. Fischer, 1982a, 1982b; Willmott, 1986, 1987; Gaunt, 1988). However, most local ties are with neighbors and not kin, and it is neighbors and friends who provide most support and companionship.

The other pattern is one in which many kin — extended as well as immediate — live nearby, visit often, and rely heavily on each other for support. Such clusters of kin occur among those who have poor linguistic or financial resources for dealing with bureaucratic institutions.[5] Willmott (1986) suggests that this pattern is more apt to occur in neighborhoods with a stable population, room for kin to settle nearby, and jobs available locally. It is especially likely to occur in neighborhoods with many poor residents who speak a different language or who are less-mobile manual workers.

Contact

Kinship scholars have been more interested in documenting the abundance of contact with kin than in comparing contact with kin to contact with friends. They have shown that almost all people are in at least weekly contact — in person or by telephone — with one intimate, immediate kin, and that most people also have weekly contact with one other intimate or active kin. At the other extreme, people are in contact less than once per month with about one-third of their active kin. Such contact is usually only for ritual occasions arranged by kinkeepers, such as birthdays, Christmas, and family get-togethers.

Frequency of contact with kin is a function of *kinship closeness* (immediate vs. extended kin), *social closeness* (intimate, active, latent), and *spatial closeness* (same neighborhood, metropolitan area). Immediate kin have more contact than extended kin. In part, this is because immediate kin are more apt to have active or intimate relations. However, at each level of intimacy, immediate kin are in more contact than extended kin (Pitrou, 1977; Fischer, 1982b; Leigh, 1982; Wellman & Wortley, 1989a). The same normative and structural factors which help most ties with immediate kin to be active despite distance fosters frequent contact among these kin. Hence contact with immediate kin diminishes less with increasing distance than does contact with extended kin (Adams, 1968; Klatzky, 1971; Leigh, 1982; Gaunt, 1988).

Many geographically distant ties are latent. They become briefly active during rare visits, but they only become really active when migration brings proximity and transient dependency. Hence migrants are likely to activate a few of their many weaker ties with extended kin, but they do not otherwise retain such people in their active networks.

An active kinship tie is apt to be in more frequent contact than an active friendship tie. For example, Americans have "recently" contacted one-third of their active kin but only one-quarter of their active friends (Tsai & Sigelman, 1982; see also Shulman's Canadian data 1972). Contact patterns are also different for immediate and extended kin. The second Toronto study reports in-person contact at least once per week with one-quarter of their active friends and immediate kin but with only 4% of their active extended kin. *Intimate* immediate kin also are more apt to have more weekly in-person contact: 37% compared with 20% for intimate extended kin and 26% for intimate friends.*

Despite the frequency of contact with immediate kin, most people have more friendship ties than kinship ties. Thus Londoners routinely meet a mean of 3.1 friends socially but only 2.6 kin (Willmott, 1987). Moreover, three-quarters of the active relations whom Torontonians contact at least three times per week are neither kin nor friends—but neighbors and coworkers (Wellman, Carrington, & Hall, 1988). Such routinely-seen ties often are not intimate or voluntary. The Toronto women who stay home to do childcare deal with similarly-occupied neighbors as if they were coworkers with whom they have been thrown together on the job (Wellman, 1985).

Summary

Few kin or friends live in the same neighborhood, but many live elsewhere in the same metropolitan area. Kinship ties are better able to remain active and intimate over greater distances than friendship ties. One result is that a higher proportion of kin than friends do not live in the same metropolitan area. Although network members who live far apart usually have lower rates of contact, contact with kin diminishes less over distance than does contact with friends.

There is much more contact with immediate kin than with extended kin at the same levels of activity or intimacy. Although immediate kin usually are in more contact than friends, extended kin usually have the least contact. Contact between immediate kin is the least affected by distance. Kinship structures keep kin in contact even at a distance, but only immediate kin usually maintain frequent contact.

To be sure, some people — usually from ethnic minorities or low socioeconomic circumstances — have large clusters of kin near at hand for companionship and support. Yet the more common pattern is to maintain intensive relations with a small set of immediate kin: densely-connected, but residentially-dispersed. Together with approximately equal numbers of friends — also residentially dispersed but less densely-connected than immediate kin — these ties make up the core of personal community networks. More latent relations with extended kin remain in place, to be activated for specialized needs, family get-togethers, or on migration.

BROTHERS' KEEPERS

Different network members provide different kinds of supportive resources. Just as general stores have given way to specialized boutiques, people must search their assortment of ties to find specific kinds of support.[6] For example, the second Toronto study found that different active network members often supply emotional aid, small services, large services, financial aid, companionship, and job/ housing information. Most network members provide 0-2 of these 6 kinds of support. About 60% of the members provide some kind of emotional aid, small service or companionship. However, only 10-

16% provide some kind of large service, financial aid or information. Less than half of the network members provide both emotional aid and small services (Wellman & Wortley, 1989b; see also Fischer, 1982b).

Density and Amity

As is the situation for contact, the densely-knit relations of immediate kin facilitate their mutual supportiveness. Interconnected ties aid the communication of needs and desires, and foster awareness of the material and immaterial resources that kin may have available to satisfy them. Densely-knit structures help kin to coordinate their supportive efforts to be more effective and to minimize individual burdens. For example, adult children often take turns giving care to ailing parents (Soldo, Wolf, & Agree, 1986). At the same time, densely-knit ties help kin to persuade shirkers to be supportive.

Cultural norms of *amity* encourage the provision of support to kin without an expectation of strict reciprocity. Such norms idealize family welfare, encourage kin to share resources, urge them to give other kin privileged access to these resources, and cherish long term reciprocity.[7] As Schneider argues, "The bond of kinship . . . is not contingent or conditional, and [supportive] performance is presumed to follow automatically if the bond 'exists'" (1984, pp. 165-66).

This view of kinship contrasts with contemporary depiction of friendship ties as sparsely-knit, voluntary relations requiring constant maintenance and reciprocal aid.[8] Pitt-Rivers argues that friendship "is but the exploitation of an implicit right to reciprocity. The paradox of friendship lies in this: though the favors of friends must be free, they must still be reciprocated if the moral status quo is to be maintained" (1973, p. 97).

Yet some active kinship ties are not supportive. Is support from kin as dependent on intimacy as is support from friends? Analysts have suggested that the mutual *concern* of parents and adult children and the mutual *interest* of siblings may lead to different kinds of supportive relations (Adams, 1968; Fischer, 1982b). They have lesser expectations for supportive relations with extended kin: grandparents, uncles, aunts, and cousins (Farber, 1981; Coombs,

1980; Cheal, 1988). Are immediate kin more apt to be supportive than extended kin just as immediate kin are more apt to be in frequent contact?

Unfortunately, there have been few comparisons of support from different types of kith and kin. However, several studies have argued the continuing importance of kinship by showing that most (immediate) kin are supportive. Although such studies do not present detailed comparisons of kin and kith, they do suggest that kin and kith differ in the quality and quantity of support they provide.[9]

Our research group used hierarchical cluster analysis to see if kin enact distinct supportive roles in personal community networks (Wellman & Wortley, 1989a). We compared the tendency of 20 different kinship and non-kinship roles to provide emotional aid, services, companionship, financial aid, and job/housing information. We found that that kin differ from kith in the patterns of support. Moreover, there are three distinct types of kinship roles: *parent-adult child, sibling* and *extended kin*, as well as roles of *friendship, neighbor* and *workmate*. Affines behave like consanguines. Because much support effectively goes to the household rather than to the focal person, kin often feel they are supporting their own blood relatives.

Parents and Adult Children

Relationships between parents and adult children have been celebrated for their combined supportiveness and destructiveness from Abraham (c1500 BCE) to Woody Allen (1989). While noting the strains in these ties, my interest is in the high level of supportive resources they convey. The bond between parent and adult child is the most supportive of all intimate and active ties, providing high levels of both material and emotional support. Such ties are so broadly supportive that weaker, but still active, relations are usually almost as supportive as intimate relations (Hoyt & Babchuk, 1983; Cheal, 1988; Wellman & Wortley, 1989a). Mother-daughter ties are especially supportive, building upon shared concerns about (grand)children and domestic tranquillity. The coming of grandchildren may well transform lifetime mother-daughter conflicts to cooperative efforts by domestic co-workers (Wood, Traupmann & Hay, 1984; Binns & Mars, 1984; Fischer, 1985; Willmott, 1987). Indeed, these strong bonds are the foundation of informal care for the elderly (Connidis, 1989; Crohan & Antonucci, 1989).

Parents and adult children are each others' pre-eminent sources of informal financial aid to buy a house, take a trip, or provide care for illness and infirmity (Sussman & Burchinal, 1962; Fischer, 1982b; Wellman & Wortley, 1989a). They are the most likely of all ties to give each other gifts, emotional support, child care, care for family illness, and help with major home maintenance (Table 2).[10] For example, 84% of the active parent/child relationships in the second Toronto study provide some kind of emotional aid and 39% provide some major services. By contrast, the percentages for all active ties are 62% and 16% respectively (Wellman & Wortley, 1989b). Moreover, parents do not reduce their support when many adult children compete for their attention (Aldous & Klein, 1983).

Parents and adult children usually support each other but often do not enjoy each other. They are not likely to choose each other as sociable companions (Wellman & Wortley, 1989a). Mothers and daughters often expect much support from each other, take its provision for granted, but complain when it is not given. Fathers and sons, who expect less, have fewer strains in their relationships.[11]

Siblings

Sisters and brothers give each other much support, but not as much as do parents and adult children. Unlike parent/child relations, there is much variation in the supportiveness of siblings: Intimate siblings exchange much more support than siblings with weaker ties. When there are more than two brothers and sisters, only some may form supportive bonds (Johnson, 1982; Cheal, 1988; Wellman & Wortley, 1989a).

Siblings, tending to be of similar ages, have shared similar histories and have similar concerns. Their similar current situations resemble those of friends, but their ties are overlain by longer histories, commitment to norms of amity, and common kinship structures. Indeed, the sibling role was more similar to friendship in our cluster analysis than it was to the parent, adult child or extended kin roles. The sociable relations of siblings are more similar to friendship than to relations between other kin. Siblings are as likely as friends to do things together and to provide emotional support, more likely to provide large services and help around the household, but less likely to discuss ideas or help each other outside of their households (Table 2).[12] Siblings (and siblings in-law) make up about one-fifth of the active network members who provide emotional aid, financial aid, services, or companionship (Wellman & Wortley, 1989a). Because the Torontonians have more siblings than parents (or adult children), siblings provide them with more emotional and material aid even though each sibling is less likely to be supportive than each parent.

Extended Kin

Extended kin have roles that are distinct from other kin and from friends. Even those few extended kin who have active relationships are less likely than other active network members to exchange social support. They are about one-half as likely as active immediate kin to provide each kind of support (Table 2). For example, 29% of these extended kin provide minor emotional aid as compared with about 60% of the immediate kin (Wellman & Wortley, 1989a). The combination of low numbers of active ties, weaker relations, and low likelihood of support means that extended kin are a negligible source of aid for most routine, chronic or acute problems.

The exceptions are in those situations such as migration or finding jobs where weak ties have a comparative advantage because of social and spatial dispersion. Although extended kin rarely are active or supportive, their ties are strong enough and connected enough to convey news. They are useful conduits of information, although the small number of kinship ties provides less news than do the larger number of acquaintances (Lin and Dumin, 1986).

Kith

Most of the active and intimate network members with whom people socialize are *friends* and not kin. "We typically have a good time with friends but turn to relatives in a crisis" (Fischer, 1982b, p. 132). Friends make up nearly half of most active and intimate

TABLE 2: PERCENTAGE OF ACTIVE NETWORK MEMBERS PROVIDING SPECIFIC KINDS OF SUPPORT

ROLE:	PARENT/ CHILD	SIBLING	EXTENDED KIN	FRIEND	NEIGHBOR	ORGANI- ZATIONAL
Emotional Aid						
Family Problems Advice	61	47	19	43	35	30
Minor Emotional Aid	68	50	29	59	39	38
Major Emotional Aid	58	43	27	34	23	15
Small Services						
Minor Services	58	28	24	48	55	23
Lending Items	65	39	7	34	60	15
Minor Household Services	68	41	10	33	48	10
Organizational Aid	19	7	2	6	13	18
Large Services						
Major Household Service	39	15	0	9	20	0
Major Services	19	12	2	6	6	0

Financial Aid

Small Loans	52	12	2	10	9	13
Large Loans	13	4	0	0	4	10
Housing Loans	29	3	2	0	0	0

Companionship

Doing Things Together	37	37	17	43	51	33
Discussing Ideas	34	32	25	61	60	50
Orgainzational Participation	3	11	5	17	30	33

Information

Job Information	6	5	0	6	7	18
Job Contact	0	4	0	4	7	13
Housing Information	6	5	0	6	3	3

Source: Second Toronto Study (Wellman 1982)

215

networks and usually form nearly half of the ties providing each kind of (non-financial) support (Fischer, 1982b; Willmott, 1987; Wellman & Wortley, 1989b). Although most friends provide somewhat less variety and quantity of support than do parents and adult children, they are as likely as siblings to provide support and much more likely to do so than extended kin (see Table 2). Moreover, many of those people who do not have active kinship ties have one or two intimate friends who act like immediate kin by reliably providing a wide range of social support.*

Many friendship ties are discrete, voluntary relationships that function outside of groups. Hence when friends are not helpful, the relationship often ends for lack of group support. Knowing this, many Torontonians report that they carefully limit the claims they make on friends (and some kin) for aid. It is not that friends are unsupportive when asked, but that people often do not feel confident that they can *ask* their friends for aid.*

By contrast, *neighboring* ties are often less voluntary, especially when they are between women staying home to do domestic care (Wellman, 1985). Proximity makes active neighbors a principal source of routine companionship and aid for children, homes and spouses (Table 2; see also Warren, 1981; Willmott, 1987; Wellman & Wortley, 1989b). However, quick access by car and phone means that the metropolitan area, and not the neighborhood, is often the effective limit on supplying goods and services.

Summary

To say that kin are supportive and friends are sociable is as much an oversimplification as to say that there is no difference in the content of relations between kin and friends. Kinship significantly affects the nature of ties, but it does so interactively with the strength of a tie, the shared interests of the network members, and their physical access to each other.

At one extreme, parents and children reliably exchange a broad range of support. Their relationship transcends intimacy, different stages in the life course, and physical access. At the other extreme, extended kin are rarely supportive, even if active or living nearby. In between are siblings whose conditionally companionate and supportive relations more closely resemble friends in their dependency on shared intimacy and in their life situations.

W(H)ITHER KIN IN NETWORKS?

The Prominence of Kin

Contemporary Westerners wander freeways and shopping malls surrounded by strangers. The few known faces they encounter rarely are kin. The people whose company they keep rarely are kin — in the neighborhood, at work, or at play.

No wonder that scholars have had to work so hard to assert the persistence and importance of kinship. Yet the closer one looks at personal community networks, the more prominent are kin. Out of their hundreds of relations, people form active ties with almost all of their immediate kin and some of their extended kin. These ties — often dispersed and invisible make up a large minority of active ties and about half of intimate ties. They loom even larger as reliable, flexible, longterm sources of support.

The prominence of kin in these networks is greater than current size and contact figures suggest. Because kin usually have known each other at least twice as long as friends, they have had many more person-years of contact. Because kin are densely-connected with each other, conversations between two kin often refer to other kin. By contrast, friends are more often apt to engage in separate duets.

The Uniqueness of Kin

The importance of kinship suggests its uniqueness. Why would active and intimate networks have so many kin if they were just like friends? To be sure, quasi-legal norms maintain kinship as systems. Rules and customs emphasize kinship rights to share housing, obtain inheritances, sponsor immigrants and receive confidential information from bureaucracies. Yet the differences separating kin from kith are neither neat nor simple. Not only do kin differ from friends and neighbors in structure and deed, different types of kin differ from each other. There are no inclusive rules of amity requiring all kin to be supportive, and there are many friends whose ties transcend marketplace reciprocity. *Parents and adult children* are remarkably supportive but often do not enjoy each other's company. *Extended kin* have little content to their relations even when active; they are bound together only by structure. *Sibling* ties are almost as supportive as parent/child relations and almost as sociable as friendships. *Friendship* ties are the most variable — the term is a residual grab-bag for relations which are *non*-kin, *non*-neighbor, and *non*-workmate — yet intimate friends often provide the broad, reliable support characteristic of immediate kin.

Underlying this diversity is the structural connectivity and normative amity of the kinship system. (It would be nice to know if it were the structure or the norms that were doing the job.) It is what keeps extended kin in personal communities, and it is what keeps parents and children supportive even when they do not enjoy each others' company. Friends must reaffirm their ties continually, while neighbors are apt to move away or break relations over petty disputes. By contrast, kinship ties are relatively reliable without needing direct, one-on-one reciprocity. Immediate kin are reliably there for support, and extended kin are reliably available for acquaintanceship, news and adaptive life-changes. Kin are not necessarily expected to reciprocate directly as long as they remain members in good standing of the kinship network. In their distinctive ways, both immediate and extended kin help people and households to reduce interpersonal uncertainties in making their way through stressful, problematic worlds. As Lyn Lofland has pointed out (1973), we live in "a world of strangers." Yet it is just such circumstances that makes so outstanding the contact, connectivity and supportive reliability of immediate kin.

Community Saved or Liberated?

For a time, community analysts thought that all communities were densely-knit, broadly-supportive, local solidarities helping people to endure the ravages of the (post)industrial Revolution. Such a *Community Saved* model — epitomized by Young and Willmott (1957) and Gans (1962) celebrated the vitality of kinship (and neighboring). As a counterpoise, network analysts have emphasized the diverse, ramified, sparsely-knit nature of most personal communities (e.g., Wellman and Leighton, 1979; Fischer, 1982b). In their view, communities are not merely havens from large-scale social forces but active arrangements by which people and households reproduce. Their *Community Liberated* model has had the virtues of emphasizing the *social* (and not spatial) basis of community and of showing how networks actively help people to engage with the outside world.

Yet communities are more apt to have mixed compositions and structures than to be purely Saved or Liberated. Within them, kin form a key core cluster efficiently structured for communicating needs and coordinating support. This Saved cluster provides a haven from the demands of the outside world and many of the interpersonal bandages for domestic sores. Complementing this involuted group are strong and weak ties with friends, stretching outwards to connect a focal person to the diverse resources of other groups. These Liberated ties provide companionship in many arenas as well as entry points to new arenas (see also Parsons, 1951; Wolf, 1966; Litwak and Szelenyi, 1969). To the extent to which both types of ties and structures are useful and complementary, then both are integral parts of a single personal community network.

Towards a Political Economy of Personal Community Networks

This paper has reviewed *supportive relations with kin and kith* as one of three basic ways by which most people obtain resources. The other two are *market exchanges* and access to *institutional resources* as citizenship rights, organizational benefits or charitable acts.

The uses of these three mechanisms differs substantially between social systems. In the Third World, personal community networks structure important relations of *production* as there are neither the structures nor the capital to support extensive market economies. In those Third World countries where employment is unstable and there are no retirement funds, secure survival is an urgent need. The socially-controlled reliability of kinship relations become crucial in such situations of competition for scarce survival resources. People develop broadly-based ties, expanding them from purely social relationships to key sources of material resources. Marginal groups rely on these ties as a basic survival strategy. Middle-class groups develop informal networks and formal relationships to support upward mobility. In all classes, such networks strongly channel access to such *reproductive* resources distributed by Third World institutions as schools, hospitals, and make-work jobs (Lomnitz, 1977; Roberts, 1978; Bandyopadhyay and van Eschen, 1981).

In the Second World, personal community networks help people maneuver through bureaucratic obstacles to institutional benefits and provide informal arrangements for production. Among other things, they provide the ties necessary to obtain the resources for getting a job done (Burawoy, 1985; Walder, 1986). Such networks are even more crucial for reproduction in such bureaucracy-laden societies by providing informal alternatives to rigid institutional procedures (Grossman, 1989). For example, groups of Hungarian kith and kin take turns building houses for each other (Sik, 1988). The only way to obtain a telephone in many such countries is to use informal connections; official queues remain dormant window-dressing.

By contrast, personal community networks in more comfortable western, First World milieus are principally relations of *reproduction*. The main difference is in the insecurity households in each world wish to diminish. This, in turn, affects the type of resources they mobilize through their networks. The low importance of the economic and political aspects of social support distinguishes the networks of most First Worlders from those social systems which are less economically or politically secure. They rely on market exchanges for almost all of their production and much of their consumption. Despite some variation, their institutional benefits such as schooling and medical care are available as citizenship rights. Hence they do not pay as much attention as do Second World residents to having network members with skills for fixing things and bureaucracies. Nor do they have the survival needs of Third World residents to blend domestic with employment relations in both the informal and formal sectors.

Hence the networks of First Worlders are built around companionship, soothing domestic stresses, and reliable, flexible, low-cost domestic services. These are not trivial pursuits as few people want to place themselves at the mercy of markets and institutions to deal with such needs. Although analysts are just starting to calculate the costs and benefits of community network relations, these networks clearly contribute important and central resources that enable people to go about their daily lives, handle chronic stresses, and cope with acute crises.

Our review suggests that First Worlders prefer to use personal community networks to meet many needs because they have more control over the workings of network relationships than they do over purchases or beneficences obtained from bureaucracies. They do not yearn to be self-reliant individualists — doing or purchasing all — or dependents of institutions (compare Gans, 1988). Yet their dispersed, fragmented networks require constant maintenance. The study of personal community networks should recognize how different types of relationships divide the labor of providing supportive resources. Reliable relations with immediate kin provide secure stocks of services, emotional aid, and finanical aid within these networks. At the same time, friends provide sociable pleasure, diverse resources, and access to social circles beyond the existing community.

NOTES

1. Studies include: Fischer (reported in 1982a, 1982b); Riley and Cochran (1985); Willmott (1986; 1987); Wellman, Carrington, and Hall (1988); Wellman and Wortley (1989a, 1989b); Milardo (1989).

2. Shulman (1972); Wellman (1979); Johnson and Leslie (1982); Hoyt and Babchuk (1983); Wellman, Carrington, and Hall (1988); see Burt (1986), Oliver (1986) for conflicting results.

3. *Confidants*: 0.41 (calculated from Laumann 1973, Table 6.1). *Intimates*: 0.33 (Wellman 1979) and 0.44 (Fischer 1982b); *active* network members 0.33 (Wellman, Carrington, and Hall 1988). These density statistics do not include always-present ties between respondents and network members.

4. Data calculated expressly for this paper are indicated with an asterisk:*.

5. American Blacks (Oliver 1986); poor white Londoners (Young and Willmott 1957; Willmott 1986); Italian-Americans (Whyte 1943; Gans 1962; Fried 1973; Johnson 1982); Italian-Canadians (Calzavara 1983), and Portuguese-Canadians (Anderson 1974).

6. Litwak (1985); Tardy (1985); Gottlieb (1985); Lin, Dean, and Ensel (1986); House, Umberson and Landis (1988).

7. E.g., Mogey (1977); Farber (1981); Willmott (1987); Cheal (1988).

8. E.g., Litwak and Szelenyi (1969); Allan (1979); Perlman and Gehr (1987); Duck (1983); Argyle and Henderson (1984); Blumstein and Kollock (1988); Berscheid, Snyder and Omoto (1989).

9. E.g., Warren (1981); Young, Giles & Plantz (1982); O'Connell (1984); Essock-Vitale & McGuire (1985); Gerstel (1988).

10. Johnson (1977); Mogey (1977); Pitrou (1977); Horwitz (1978); Unger & Powell (1980); Riley & Cochran (1985); Willmott (1987); Cheal (1988); Radoeva (1988); Wellman & Wortley (1989a).

11. Rosenblatt, Johnson & Anderson (1981); Marshall, Rosenthal & Daciuk (1987).

12. Wellman & Wortley (1989a); see also McLanahan, Wedemeyer & Adelberg (1981); Johnson (1982); Farber & Smith (1985).

REFERENCES

Adams B. (1968). *Kinship in an urban setting*. Chicago: Markham.

Aldous, J. & Klein, D. (1983). Sentiment and size: Models of intergenerational relationships in later life. Paper presented to the annual meeting of the American Sociological Association.

Allan, G. (1979). *A sociology of friendship and kinship*. London: Allen & Unwin.

Allen, W. (1989). *Oedipus Wrecks*. Part 3 of *New York Stories*.

Anderson, G. (1974). *Networks of contact: The Portuguese in Toronto*. Waterloo, Ont.: Wilfrid Laurier University Press.

Argyle, M. & Henderson, M. (1984). The rules of friendship. *Journal of Social and Personal Relationships, 1,* 209-35.

Bahr, H. (1976). The kinship role. In F. I. Nye (Ed.), *Role Structure and Analysis of the Family*, pp. 61-79. Beverly Hills, CA: Sage.

Bandyopadhyay, S. & van Eschen, D. (1981). *An extended summary of the conditions of rural progress in India*. Calcutta: Indian Statistical Institute.

Bell, C. (1968) *Middle class families*. London: Routledge and Kegan Paul.

Berger, B. & Berger, P. (1983). *The war over the family*. Garden City, NY: Doubleday Anchor.

Berscheid, E., Snyder, M., & Omoto, A. (1989). Issues in studying close relationships. In C. Hendrick (Ed.), *Close Relationships*, pp. 63-91. Newbury Park, CA: Sage.

Binns, D. & Mars, G. (1984) Family, community and unemployment. *Sociological Review, 32,* 662-95.

Blumstein, P. & Kollock, P. (1988). Personal relationships. *Annual Review of Sociology, 14,* 467-90.

Boissevain, J. (1974). *Friends of friends: Networks, manipulators, and coalitions*. Oxford: Blackwell.

Bott, E. (1957). *Family and social network*. London: Tavistock.

Burawoy, M. (1985). *The politics of production*. London: Verso.

Burt, R. (1986). Strangers, friends and happiness. New York: Center for the Social Sciences, Columbia University. Preprint P110.

Calzavara, L. M. (1983). Social networks and access to jobs: A study of five ethnic groups in Toronto. Centre for Urban and Community Studies, University of Toronto. Research Paper No. 145.

Cheal, D. (1988). *The gift economy*. London: Routledge.

Connidis, I. (1989). *Family ties and aging*. Toronto: Butterworths.

Coombs, G. (1980). Variant usage in American kinship: The nomenclator effect. In L. Cordell & S. Beckerman (Eds.), *The versatility of kinship*. London: Academic Press.

Crohan, S. & Antonucci, T. (1989). Friends as a source of social support in old age. In R. Adams & R. Blieszner (Eds.). *Older adult friendship*, pp. 129-46. Newbury Park, CA: Sage.

Duck, S. (1983). *Friends for life*. Brighton, England: Harvester.

Erickson, B., Radkewycz, A., & Nosanchuk, T. A. (1988). Helping hands. Toronto: Centre for Urban and Community Studies, University of Toronto.

Essock-Vitale, S. & McGuire, M. (1985). Women's lives viewed from an evolutionary perspective. II. Patterns of helping. *Ethology and Sociobiology, 6,* 155-73.

Farber, B. (1981). *Conceptions of kinship*. New York: Elsevier North Holland.

Farber, B. & Smith, K. (1985). Ties with children and siblings among residents of sun city. Paper presented to the annual meeting of the American Sociological Association, Washington, August.

Feld, S. (1982). Social structural determinants of similarity among associates. *American Sociological Review, 47,* 797-801.

Firth, R., Hubert, J., & Forge, A. (1969). *Families and their relatives*. London: Routledge & Kegan Paul.

Fischer, C. (1982a). The dispersion of kinship ties in modern society. *Journal of Family History, 7,* 353-75.

Fischer, C. (1982b). *To dwell among friends*. Berkeley: University of California Press.

Fischer, C. (1985). Studying technology and social life. In M. Castells (Ed.), *High technology, space, and society*, pp. 284-301. Beverly Hills, CA: Sage.

Fried, M. (1973). *The world of the urban working class*. Cambridge, MA: Harvard University Press.

Fried, M. & Gleicher, P. (1961). Some sources of satisfaction in an urban slum. *Journal of the American Institute of Planners, 27* (4).

Gans, H. (1962). *The Urban Villagers*. New York: Free Press.

Gans, H. (1988). *Middle American Individualism*. New York: Free Press.

Gaunt, L. N. (1988). The family circle: Challenge for planning. Paper presented to HPUI conference, Amsterdam.

Gerstel, N. (1988). Divorce and kin ties: The importance of gender. *Journal of Marriage and the Family, 50,* 209-19.

Gordon, M. & Downing, H. (1978). A multivariate test of the Bott hypothesis in an urban Irish setting. *Journal of Marriage and the Family, 40,* 585-93.

Gottlieb, B. (1985). Social support and the study of personal relationships. *Journal of Social and Personal Relationships*, 2, 351-75.

Granovetter, M. (1973). The strength of weak ties. *American Journal of Sociology*, 78, 1360-80.

Granovetter, M. (1982). The strength of weak ties: A network theory revisited. In P. Marsden & N. Lin (Eds.), *Social structure and network analysis*, pp. 105-130. Beverly Hills, CA: Sage.

Greenbaum, S. (1982). Bridging ties at the neighborhood level. *Social Networks*, 4, 367-84.

Grieco, M. (1987). *Keeping it in the family: Social networks and employment chance.* London: Tavistock.

Grossman, G. (1989). Informal personal incomes and outlays of the Soviet Union. In A. Portes, M. Castells, & L. Benton (Eds.), *The Informal economy*, pp. 150-70. Baltimore: Johns Hopkins University Press.

Hammer, M., Gutwirth, L. & Phillips, S. (1982). Parenthood and social networks. *Social Science and Medicine*, 16, 2091-2100.

Heiskanen, V. S. (1969). Community structure and kinship ties: Extended family relations in three Finnish communes. *International Journal of Comparative Sociology*, 10, 251-62.

Horwitz, A. (1978). Family, kin, and friend networks in psychiatric help-seeking. *Social Science and Medicine*, 12, 297-304.

House, J., Landis, K., & Umberson, D. (1988). Social relationships and health. *Science*, 241 (July 29), 540-45.

Hoyt, D. & Babchuk, N. (1983). Adult kinship networks: The selective formation of intimate ties with kin. *Social Forces*, 62, 84-101.

Johnson, A. & Bond, G. (1974). Kinship, friendship, and exchange in two communities: A comparative analysis of norms and behavior. *Journal of Anthropological Research*, 30, 55-68.

Johnson, C. L. (1982). Sibling solidarity: Its origin and functioning in Italian-American families. *Journal of Marriage and the Family*, 44, 155-67.

Johnson, L. C. (1977). *Who Cares?* Toronto: Social Planning Council of Metropolitan Toronto.

Johnson, M. & Leslie, L. (1982). Couple involvement and network structure: A test of the dyadic withdrawal hypothesis. *Social Psychology Quarterly*, 45, 34-43.

Kazak, A., & Wilcox, B. (1984). The structure and function of social support networks in families with handicapped children. *American Journal of Community Psychology*, 12, 645-61.

Killworth, P., Bernard, H. R., & McCarty, C. (1984). Measuring patterns of acquaintanceship. *Current Anthropology*, 25, 381-97.

Klatzky, S. (1971). *Patterns of contact with relatives.* Washington: American Sociological Association.

Laumann, E. (1973). *Bonds of pluralism: The forms and substance of urban social networks.* New York: Wiley.

Lee, G. (1980). Kinship in the seventies: A decade review of research and theory. *Journal of Marriage and the Family, 42,* 923-34.

Leigh, G. (1982). Kinship interaction over the family life span. *Journal of Marriage and the Family, 44,* 197-208.

Lin, N., Dean, A., & Ensel, W. (1986). *Social support, life events and depression.* Orlando FL: Academic Press.

Lin, N. & Dumin, M. (1986). Access to occupations through social ties. *Social Networks, 8,* 365-86.

Litwak, E. (1985). *Helping the elderly: The complementary roles of informal networks and formal systems.* New York: Guildford Press.

Litwak, E. & Szelenyi, I. (1969). Primary group structures and their functions. *American Sociological Review, 34,* 465-81.

Lofland, L. (1973). *A World of strangers.* New York: Basic.

Lomnitz, L. A. (1977). *Networks and marginality: Life in a Mexican shantytown.* Translated by Cinna Lomnitz. New York: Academic Press.

Lüschen, G. (1972). Family interaction with kin and the function of ritual. *Journal of Comparative Family Studies, 3,* 84-98.

Lüschen, G., Staikof, Z., Heiskanen, V. S., & Ward, C. (1972). *Social Compass, 19,* 519-36.

Marshall, V., Rosenthal, C., & Daciuk, J. (1987). Older parents' expectations for filial support. *Social Justice Review, 1,* 405-23.

Mazursky, P. (1969). *Bob and Carol and Ted and Alice.* Burbank, CA: Columbia Pictures.

McLanahan, S., Wedemeyer, N., & Adelberg, T. (1981). Network structure, social support and psychological well-being in the single-parent family. *Journal of Marriage and the Family, 43,* 601-612.

Milardo, R. (1989). Theoretical and methodological issues in the identification of the social networks of spouses. *Journal of Marriage and the Family, 51,* 165-74.

Mirande, A. (1970). Extended kinship ties, friendship relations, and community size. *Rural Sociology, 35,* 261-66.

Mogey, J. (1977). Content of relations with relatives. In J. Cuisnier & M. Segalen (Eds.), *The Family Life Cycle in European Societies,* pp. 413-29. Paris: Mouton.

O'Connell, L. (1984). An exploration of exchange in three relationships: Kinship, friendship and the marketplace. *Journal of Social and Personal Relationships, 1,* 333-45.

Oliver, M. (1984). The urban black community as network. Working paper. Los Angeles: Department of Sociology. University of California.

Oliver, M. (1986, May). Beyond the neighborhood: The spatial distribution of social ties in three urban black communities. Paper presented at the "Minorities in the Post-Industrial City" Conference, University of California-Los Angeles.

Parsons, T. (1951). *The social system.* Glencoe, IL: Free Press.

Perlman, D. & Fehr, B. (1987). The development of intimate relationships. In D.

Perlman & S. Duck (Eds.), *Intimate Relationships*, pp. 13-42. Newbury Park, CA: Sage.

Pitrou, A. (1977). Le soutien familial dans la soci t urbaine. *"Revue Française de Sociologie, 18,* 47-84.

Pitt-Rivers, J. (1973). The kith and the kin. In J. Goody (Ed.), *The Character of Kinship,* pp. 89-105. Cambridge: Cambridge University Press.

Pool, I. & Kochen, M. (1978). Contacts and influence. *Social Networks, 1,* 5-51.

Radoeva, D. (1988). Old Bulgarians: Value Aspects of their Attitude towards Children as a Part of the Family. Paper presented to the "Kinship and Aging" conference, Balatonzmardi, Hungary, April.

Reiss, D. & Oliveri, M. E. (1983). The family's construction of social reality and its ties to its kin network. *Journal of Marriage and the Family, 45,* 81-91.

Riley, D. & Cochran, M. (1985). Naturally occurring childrearing advice for fathers: Utilization of the personal social network. *Journal of Marriage and the Family, 47,* 275-86.

Roberts, B. (1978). *Cities of peasants.* London: Edward Arnold.

Rosenblatt, P., Johnson, P., & Anderson, R. (1981). When out-of-town relatives visit. *Family Relations, 30,* 403-409.

Rosenthal, C. (1985). Kinkeeping in the familial division of labor. *Journal of Marriage and the Family, 47,* 965-74.

Salloway, J. & Dillon, P. (1973). A comparison of family networks and friend networks in health care utilization. *Journal of Comparative Family Studies, 4,* 131-42.

Schneider, D. (1984). *A Critique of the study of kinship.* Ann Arbor: University of Michigan Press.

Segalen, M. (1985). Family change and social uses of kinship networks in France. *Historical Social Research, 34,* 22-29.

Shulman, N. (1972). Urban Social Networks. Doctoral dissertation, Department of Sociology, University of Toronto.

Sik, E. (1988). Reciprocal exchange of labour in Hungary. In R. Pahl (Ed.), *On Work,* pp. 527-47. Oxford: Basil Blackwell.

Soldo, B., Wolf, D., & Agree, E. (1986). Family, household and care arrangements of disabled older women. Paper presented to the annual meeting of the Gerontological Society of America, Chicago, November.

Sussman, M. & Burchinal, L. (1962). Kin family network: Unheralded structure in current conceptualizations of family functioning. *Marriage and Family Living, 24,* 231-40.

Tardy, C. (1985). Social support measurement. *American Journal of Community Psychology, 13,* 187-202.

Tilly, C. & Brown, C. H. (1967). On uprooting, kinship, and the auspices of migration. *International Journal of Comparative Sociology, 8,* 139-64.

Tsai, Y. & Sigelman, L. (1982). The community question: A perspective from national survey data—The case of the USA. *British Journal of Sociology, 33,* 579-88.

Unger, D. & Powell, D. (1980). Supporting families under stress: The role of social networks. *Family Relations*, *29*, 566-74.

Walder, A. (1986). *Communist neo-traditionalism: Work and authority in Chinese industry*. Berkeley: University of California Press.

Walker, A. (1986). Community care: Fact or fiction. P. Willmott (Ed.), *The Debate about Community*, pp. 4-15. London: Policy Studies Institute.

Walker, G. (1977). Social networks and territory in a commuter village, Bond Head, Ontario. *Canadian Geographer*, *21*, 329-50.

Warren, D. (1981). *Helping networks*. Notre Dame, IN: University of Notre Dame Press.

Wellman, B. (1979). The community question. *American Journal of Sociology*, *84*, 1201-31.

Wellman, B. (1982). Studying personal communities. In P. Marsden & N. Lin (Eds.), *Social structure and network analysis*, pp. 61-80. Beverly Hills, CA: Sage.

Wellman, B. (1984). Looking for community. *Environments*, *16* (2), 59-63.

Wellman, B. (1985). Domestic work, paid work and net work. In S. Duck & D. Perlman (Eds.), *Understanding personal relationships*, pp. 159-91. London: Sage.

Wellman, B. (1988). The community question re-evaluated. In M. P. Smith (Ed.), *Power, Community and the City*, pp. 81-107. New Brunswick, NJ: Transaction Books.

Wellman, B. (forthcoming). The quality of urban social relations. *Annual Review of Sociology*.

Wellman, B. & Berkowitz, S. D. (Eds.) (1988). *Social structures: A network approach*. Cambridge: Cambridge University Press.

Wellman, B., Frank, O., Espinoza, V., Lundquist, S. & Wilson, C. (1988). Integrating individual, relational and structural analysis. Department of Sociology, University of Toronto. Working Paper No. 201.

Wellman, B., Carrington, P., & Hall, A. (1988). Networks as personal communities. In B. Wellman & S. D. Berkowitz (Eds.), *Social Structures: A Network Approach*, pp. 130-84. Cambridge: Cambridge University Press.

Wellman, B. & Leighton, B. (1979). Networks, neighborhoods and communities. *Urban Affairs Quarterly*, *14*, 363-90.

Wellman, B., Mosher, C., Rottenberg, C., & Espinoza, V. (1987, June). The sum of the ties does not equal a network: The case of social support. Paper presented to the annual meeting of the American Sociological Association, Chicago.

Wellman, B. & Wortley, S. (1989a). Brothers' keepers: Situating kinship relations in broader networks of social support. *Sociological Perspectives* (July): in press.

Wellman, B. & Wortley, S. (1989b). Different strokes from different folks: Which types of ties provide which kinds of social support. Toronto: Centre for Urban and Community Studies, Research Paper.

Whyte, W. F. (1943). *Street corner society*. Chicago: University of Chicago Press.

Willmott, P. (1986). *Social networks, informal care and public policy*. London: Policy Studies Institute.

Willmott, P. (1987). *Friendship networks and social support*. London: Policy Studies Institute.

Wolf, E. (1966). Kinship, friendship and patron-client relations. In M. Banton (Ed.), *The Social Anthropology of Complex Societies*, London: Tavistock.

Wood, V., Traupmann, J., & Hay, J. (1984). Motherhood in the middle years: Women and their adult children. In G. Baruch & J. Brooks-Gunn (Eds.), *Women in Midlife*, pp. 227-44. New York: Plenum Press.

Young, C., Giles Jr., D., & Plantz, M. (1982). Natural networks: Help-giving and help-seeking in two rural communities. *American Journal of Community Psychology, 10*, 457-69.

Young, M. and Willmott, P. (1957). *Family and Kinship in East London*. London: Routledge and Kegan Paul.

Family, Religion, and Personal Communities: Examples from Mormonism

Marie Cornwall
Darwin L. Thomas

INTRODUCTION

There has been a renewed interest in the family-religion connection over the past decade (D'Antonio & Aldous, 1983; Thomas, 1988; Thomas & Henry, 1988; Thornton, 1988). Most of this work examines the interface between family and religious institutions without careful attention to the distinctive impact of the family's religious community. When studying the impact of religion, researchers frequently emphasize religious affiliation or levels of orthodoxy and participation. However, these are all aspects of institutional religion. Religion is also expressed and experienced within personal religious communities which are not necessarily defined by religious affiliation or congregational participation. Religious identities are sustained within these personal religious communities and the religion and family interface cannot fully be explored without careful attention to the distinctive impact of these communities apart from the impact of institutional religion.

Family and religion remain viable institutions in the modern world, although their defining characteristics may have changed. Families are smaller, more women work for pay outside the home, divorce rates are higher. Religious institutions have also changed considerably, but most social scientists agree that religion remains a significant element in the lives of most Americans (Caplow, Bahr, & Chadwick, 1983; Greeley, 1989; Roof & McKinney, 1987; Stark & Bainbridge, 1985). While some change has occurred — conservative churches are growing while others have lost a substantial number of their membership (Kelley, 1972; Hoge & Roozen, 1979) —

there appears to be much more stability than most social scientists predicted just a decade ago (Greeley, 1989, p. 8; Caplow, Bahr, & Chadwick, 1983).

Community remains a problematic construct in sociological discourse since it is used to reference both macro social structure and micro interpersonal relationships. The problem has plagued social science discourse and still illustrates confusion even in the most contemporary analysts such as Habermas (see Smelser, 1988). We use personal community as a concept which refers to extended family, friends, and associates which form the set of people with whom the individual is directly involved. It is no longer sufficient to define and study community in just the geographic or institutional sense (Wellman, 1979). Rather, personal communities are social worlds created by and centered around individuals or families. Despite the pluralism of modern society, individual identities are still created and maintained in face-to-face primary interaction and families are embedded in networks which provide emotional and social support (Fischer et al., 1977; Fischer, 1982; Gottlieb, 1981).

The continued viability of family and religion and new perspectives on the nature of personal communities begs for an empirical and theoretical exploration of the role of personal communities in the interface between family and religion. While few have addressed the issue in the recent past, a careful reading of Herberg (1955) and Lenski (1963) provides a preliminary foundation. We begin with a review of classical perspectives and then consider recent network research using both to suggest useful points of departure. The second half of the paper then examines the role of personal communities in the family and religion interface using empirical data from Mormon populations. Finally, possible implications for family and religion in the post-modern world are discussed.

RELIGION, FAMILY, AND PERSONAL COMMUNITIES

The Religious Community

Early American sociologists working in the classical tradition expected that urbanization would create a segmented society and dilute the moral order which depends upon intimate relations with extended family and neighbors (Thomas & Weigert, 1971; Park, 1916). Wirth (1938) noted that the large size of cities introduced a greater range of individual variation. Subsequently, heterogeneity of culture, occupation, and religion would give rise to a situation in which

> The bonds of kinships, of neighborliness, and the sentiments arising out of living together for generations under a common folk tradition are likely to be absent or, at best relatively weak . . . (p. 11)

Because of the large numbers of people living within the city, city dwellers would have contact over the normal course of a day with a large variety of people, only a small proportion of whom they would know. Urban relationships were characterized as being more superficial, anonymous, and transitory than rural relationships.

Herberg's *Protestant, Catholic, Jew*, is one of the first of many sociological treatises which questioned these assumptions. Herberg suggested Americans thought of America as one great community divided into three religiously defined subcommunities (1955, p. 38). This division was based on "three diverse representations of the same 'spiritual values,' . . . the fatherhood of God . . . brotherhood of man, [and] the dignity of the individual human being . . . (p. 38-39)." Herberg argued that religion had become the only identifying mark that immigrants were *not* expected to change as they became part of American society. Thus, religion became the one differentiating element and context of self-identification and social location. While it was, therefore, almost mandatory for an American to place herself in one or another of these groups, identification with Protestantism, Catholicism, or Judaism was not necessarily identification with a church or religious institution. It was identification with a religious community. Church attendance and participation in religious programs and activities at the local level were not necessarily indicators of identification with the religious community. Herberg's analysis suggested that religious groups provided communal identification and a sense of belonging which in some ways mitigated the effects of the "melting pot" as well as the urbanization of American life. Immigrants were expected to shed much of their culture and language, and were likely to have frequent contact with others who did not share the same ethnic heritage. Identification with the religious community saved them from the resultant anonymity of urban living and provided a sense of belonging required for successful identity formation (Herberg, 1955).

Herberg's treatment of religion is sometimes macro and sometimes micro analytic. For our purposes, however, the critical element is the individual's identification with significant others in her immediate social world of primary relations. Indeed, whenever identification occurs, the individual is seen as internalizing the normative expectations of significant others and thus "community" at that level is said to exist. In this sense, our use of community emphasizes the subcommunity of Herberg's analysis, not the connotations of Catholic, Protestant, Jew in the macro sociological sense.

Empirical evidence of the importance of religious communities was provided by Lenski (1963) in his examination of *The Religious Factor* in the formation of attitudes and the behavior of Detroit area residents. Lenski concluded "our theory leads us to think of contemporary American religious groups not only as associations, but as subcommunities as well; not merely as carriers of religious norms in any narrow sense, but as the carriers of complex subcultures relevant to almost all phases of human existence" (p. 334). Lenski found that religious communities played an important role in helping individuals maintain their unique beliefs (religious, political, economic or family oriented) in the heterogeneous and pluralistic world of urban living.

Using Herberg's distinction between religious institutions and religious communities, Lenski created measures of *associational* and *communal* religious involvement. Associational involvement was institutional participation. Thus individuals could be classified as "actively involved" in the churches, or as "marginal members" depending upon their participation in the religious organization. Communal involvement, on the other hand, was measured in terms of "the degree to which the primary relations of an individual (i.e., his relations with friends and relatives) are limited to persons of his own [religious] group" (p. 23). Individuals who were married to someone of the same socio-religious group and who also reported that all or nearly all of their close friends and relatives were of the same group were classified as being involved in the religious community.

In examining the correlation between associational and communal involvement, Lenski found very low correlation. High participation in the religious community was apparently not very predictive of high participation in the church organization, and vice versa. Furthermore, Lenski found that these two aspects of group involvement had a different impact on individuals depending on the outcome under study. The religious subcommunity was a distinct social order with its own roles and normative expectations. It did more than just reinforce the teachings of the institutional church, and in fact, occasionally came into conflict with the religious institution.

More recently, Welch (1981) has demonstrated the impact of religious group membership and involvement in a religious community on individual belief and participation. Using data collected in 1963 from church-going Protestants (10 different denominations are represented) in Northern California, Welch concluded "the survival of traditional [religious] commitment in modern America is explained by the survival of particular types of moral communities, and by the integration of individuals into those communities." He urged social scientists to look beyond individual-level characteristics, and pay more attention to the importance of "ties to the denomination or congregational community, as well as the nature of the community itself" (Welch, 1981, p. 91).

Cornwall (1989) has suggested that personal community relationships influence individual conformity to religious norms and expectations. Her study of the personal networks of 904 Latter-day Saints in the United States and Canada suggested an association between the composition of an individual's personal network and conformity to the norms and expectations of the religious group. Although she found a direct effect of personal community relationships on conformity, much of the impact was indirect. Personal community relationships influenced the level of religious belief and commitment which in turn impacted behavior. The number of in-group ties was associated with increased religious belief and commitment and the number of out-group ties was associated with lower belief and commitment. Belief in and commitment to the normative order of the personal religious community may be more important in predicting behavior than sanctions existing at the institutional level. The more integrated an individual or family are, the more likely they are to value the normative order and therefore behave consistently. As Etzioni has suggested, the power of religious institutions is limited when individuals do not value or are not committed to the normative order reflected in institutional arrangements (Etzioni, 1975). Individuals and families are more likely to adhere to the normative order if that order gives meaning to their life. While religious institutions have symbol systems, ritual, and leadership practices which encourage institutional commitment (Kanter, 1968), religious communities also encourage commitment by helping create individual identities which are attached to and affirmed by interaction with others in their personal world who also believe. The family and religion interface must, therefore, be examined along two dimensions. The impact of the social control and social support functions of religious bodies, for example, should be examined in terms of the institution (e.g., hierarchy, liturgy, official Church pronouncements, church programs for youth) and the personal religious communities which individuals and families create for themselves.[1] For some religious bodies, the institution may serve as an important context for creating personal religious communities. For example, Gremillion and Leege (1989) report that a Catholic's sense of attachment to the local parish is generally a function of opportunities to participate in parish functions, to take on responsibilities for various ministries, the caring nature of other parishioners and the local pastor, and the celebration of liturgies in a way that gives recognition to the importance of the religious community.

On the other hand, the fact that religious institution and religious community can exist apart from one another is clearly demonstrated in D'Antonio's recent description of the "gradual deinstutionalization of Roman Catholic religiosity" in the American church. American Catholics, he suggests, continue to identify themselves as Catholics while rejecting the formal teachings and formal authority of the institution. There is a shift "away from dogma and toward imagery; away from traditional authority emanating from Rome or the local bishop's seat and toward the gemeinschaft-like relations of

local parish life; away from threats of excommunication and punitive control and toward pastoral support, love, and friendship"
(1988, p. 102). These changes demonstrate less emphasis on associational involvement and more emphasis on communal involvement and personal religious communities among American Catholics. It is these communities that support and sustain individual
religious identities and at the same time make possible the rejection
of the traditional authority of the Pope.

Religious Communities and the Church-Sect Continuum

The relationship of family and religion and the amount of overlap
in associational and communal involvement is partly a function of
the religious institution to which the family relates (i.e., sect, denomination, or church). When defining the church-sect continuum
sociologists (Troeltsch, 1981; Weber, 1964) were quick to note the
radical element within Christianity which stresses breaking completely with the world including family (Lenski 1963, p. 246). For,
"I have come to set a man against his father . . . [and] he who loves
son or daughter more than me is not worthy of me" (Matthew
10:37). New religious movements in tension with society often find
it advantageous to radically revise existing relations as a way of
insuring greater commitment from new converts. Thus, Jim Jones'
defining his group as Family and himself as Father, Joseph Smith's
introduction of polygamous marriage, John Humphrey Noyes'
teachings and practice of group marriage, and the Shakers' insis-
tence on celibacy can all be seen as examples of new religious
movements' efforts to sever existing kinship ties and thereby increase group commitment and friendship ties. Individuals who participate in community cults and "greedy group cults" (Pescosolido
& Georgianna, 1989) are likely to have very dense networks and
these networks are almost totally defined by the individual's level
of associational involvement. But in other religious groups, as demonstrated by Lenski's findings, we would expect to find no correlation between associational and communal involvement.

Lenski suggested that "church-type religious organizations see
the kin group as an ally deserving support, whereas sect-type orga-

nizations tend to see it as something of a competitor" (1963, p. 249). The impact of the church-sect continuum is difficult to assess because most religious groups cannot easily be classified as one or the other. Johnson suggests religious bodies can be classified according to "the extent to which [it] accepts the culture of the social environment in which it exists" (1971, p. 128). Stark and Bainbridge emphasize the defining characteristic of a sect as the amount of "subcultural deviance or tension" with the social environment (1985, p. 49). Iannaccone (1988) has therefore suggested that sects demand the rejection of society and therefore must provide an alternative society of its own. For example, sects provide their members with most of their closest friendships, but churches do not. Furthermore, according to Innaccone, these friendships substitute for secular ones as suggested by sect members lower rates of participation in non-religious organizations.

The interface of family and religion is different depending upon the tension between society and the religious group to which the family belongs. In extreme cases, as mentioned, the religious group may actually infringe upon family ties in order to encourage solidarity within the group. But religious groups in less tension with society are less likely to threaten family ties (particularly the nuclear family), while still providing a relatively dense network defined almost entirely by the religious community. Such groups discourage contact with the broader society and encapsulate the family within both a protective and socially controlling religious community (e.g., Mennonite and Amish communities). The religious participation of individuals and families in these sect-like groups naturally increases the correlation between associational and communal involvement. Friendship choices not only arise out of religious participation, but also reinforce group norms. Moving further along the continuum towards church-type religious groups, a lower correlation between associational and communal involvement is expected. Friendship choices are less likely to be determined by religious participation when the density of personal networks is lower. Under this condition, the impact of the religious community may be less supportive and less controlling.

Olson's (1988) research on the networks of members of five Baptist General Conferences in the St. Paul-Minneapolis area demonstrates the interface between personal communities and religious group participation. The Baptist General Conference is an evangelical denomination, toward the high tension end of the church-sect continuum. Respondents were very involved in their respective congregations and reported highly traditional views of the Bible. While the results do not represent the general population of the United States, it suggests what the nature of religious communities may be like for families who belong to more conservative religious groups. Olson collected extensive information about the personal networks of his respondents, using methods designed by Fischer (1982). He found, that on average two-thirds of the respondents' personal networks were people from the same religious denomination. Even after controlling for multiplexity (the same associate is known in more than one setting), 45 percent of the respondent's personal networks were from the same denomination. Furthermore, church related settings were a primary source of respondent's associates, second only to kin. He concluded that church based relations play a very important role in the formation of personal networks.

As further evidence of the existence of a distinct moral community, Olson reports that respondents had significantly more intimate relationships (measured in terms of friendship, regular socializing, and sharing of personal matters, and as well as high valuation of associates opinion) with fellow church attenders than with persons known in nearly all other settings examined (e.g., neighbor, coworker, or membership in same voluntary organization).

Using multidimensional scaling techniques, Olson identified three unique sectors within the personal networks of his respondents which correspond to the categories of kin, fellow attender, and neighbor. The kin sector was characterized by relations with relatives, persons to whom the respondent feels especially close, has known for a long period of time, lives a far distance from, and with whom the respondent has infrequent contact. The fellow attender sector was characterized by relations which involve friendship, frequent socializing, sharing of personal matters, and a high valuation of the associate's opinion. Olson found a high degree of homogeneity among associates within this sector, particularly with regards to age and similarity of beliefs. The neighbor sector was characterized by persons who live nearby, who are more likely to oppose the respondents' religious beliefs, and with whom the respondent has frequent contact. This sector includes associates who are neighbors, co-workers, and members of the same voluntary organization. This data therefore suggest some degree of differentiation within personal networks as defined by kinship, church participation, and associations within neighborhoods and in the workplace. However, it also suggests that the consequence of such differentiation is not the loss of a common folk tradition, the decline of religious influence, or the privatization of religious beliefs (Wirth, 1938; Berger, 1967). Rather, it suggests the continuing viability of moral communities.

Further, research by Fischer (1982) suggests that urban living may actually contribute to the creation of these moral communities. In a study of the personal networks of people living in both urban and rural settings, Fischer (1982) reported that urban dwellers were less likely to report a religious affiliation, and that those who did affiliate placed less emphasis on religion. However, the data also suggested that among religionists (people who reported a religious identity and at least one person other than a blood relative who was of the same religion), urbanism was associated with more involvement in the religious community. Furthermore, for respondents who affiliated with minority religions, urban living actually increased contact with co-religionists. Compared with rural living, urban living apparently increases the likelihood of a person finding others who share common interests and beliefs simply because there are greater numbers of people from which to choose (see Blau, 1974).

Taken all together, it would appear that while family and religion become more differentiated at the institutional level in modern society, this differentiation may in fact favor the growth of religious communities, some of which will be in tension with society. A new religious movement which taps into communal relationships in kinship, neighborhood, and religious settings creates an alternative to the anomie generated by the modern differentiated and technological world. Movements will be successful if they provide necessary supportive relationships within personal religious communities which will sustain religious identities and group commitment.

EXAMPLES FROM MORMON FAMILY RESEARCH

The foregoing discussion of the family and religion interface raises questions about the role that personal religious communities play in providing families with needed resources, particularly when it comes to encouraging the development of religious identities, social competence in adolescents, and adult well-being. Data collected from Mormon populations provide some insights into the role of personal religious communities in these processes. While all findings from Mormons may not be generalizable to the total population, they would likely be generalizable to families who belong to more conservative religious groups that are in some tension with society.

Religious Communities and Religious Socialization

The significance of religious communities in the socialization process has been demonstrated among Jews (Himmelfarb, 1979), Catholics (Fee, Greeley, McCready, & Sullivan, 1981), and Mormons (Cornwall, 1988). In each case, parental religiosity, integration into a network of similarly religious peers, and church socialization influenced adult belief and commitment. But, more importantly, the research demonstrates that "parents socialize their children by channeling them into other groups or experiences [such as schools and marriage] which will reinforce [have an additive influence on] what was learned at home and will channel them further into similar adult activities" (Himmelfarb, 1979, p. 478).

Cornwall's (1988) study of adult Latter-day Saints furthers our understanding of this channelling process, and the role of religious communities in reinforcing religious beliefs taught in the home. A retrospective study of the processes of religious socialization, the research examined the impact of associational involvement (as measured by seminary attendance[2] and attendance at worship services) and communal involvement (measured by asking how many of the respondent's friends were active members of the Church of Jesus Christ of Latter-day Saints). The findings suggested that church and seminary attendance during the teenage years had little impact on adult religious belief and commitment. Maintaining a network of religious peers during the teenage and young adult years was, however, highly correlated with adult belief and commitment. Moreover, church and seminary attendance as well as a religious home environment influenced the extent to which an individual's peers were actively religious.[3] Contrary to Lenski's (1963) suggestion that associational and communal involvement are not correlated, this research suggests that associational involvement during the teenage years facilitated communal involvement during the young adult years which in turn influenced adult belief and commitment.

The data further suggest that the adolescent from a family where both parents were present and both were LDS were more likely to make friendship choices within the religious community. A high degree of emphasis is placed on family life within Mormonism and interfaith marriages and single parent families may face real challenges in religious socialization. Parents in interfaith marriages or single parent families may be less integrated into a religious network themselves and therefore less able to help channel their children into peer groups which support parents' religious values. In our judgment, the implications of these findings go beyond Mormonism. Parents in interfaith marriages may also (either intentionally or unintentionally) channel their children into experiences which do not foster identity with one particular religious group. Presented with the option to choose between two religions, they may opt for neither one. The increasing numbers of "unchurched" Protestants or "religious nones" (Hoge & Roozen, 1980, p. 17) may be partly a function of such interfaith marriages and the heterogeneous religious communities they produce.

Religion and Family Influence on Adolescent Social Competence

The relationship between well-functioning families and social competence in adolescents has been well established in the literature (Rollins & Thomas, 1979). More recent research has suggested that a religious home life and participation in religious communities also positively influence adolescent development (Thomas & Carver, in press).

Social competence is variously defined and operationalized but generally refers to the adolescent's ability to function adequately in her social world. Such things as self-esteem, development of social skills, and making plans for the future are often used to define the positive dimensions of a multidimensional concept. Those aspects of adolescent attitudes and behavior which are not valued in contemporary society such as involvement in the drug world, early pregnancy, and a variety of school problems (drop-out, poor grades) are generally seen as the negative side of social competence (Dryfoos, 1988; Blinn, 1988; Rollins & Thomas, 1979).

Research based on a sample of 934 adolescent Mormon males (ages 12 to 18) tested path models of religious influence to demonstrate the impact of home religious observance, and associational and communal religious involvement on the development of social competence (measured by the making of future plans) ("Home Cradle," 1987; Ensign, 1984).

Home religious observance—family scripture study, family prayer, and weekly family home evening activities—does not directly influence the making of future plans when other variables (personal religious behavior, attendance at worship services, and program participation) are included in the model. The strongest predictor of future plans is the adolescent's personal religious behavior (frequency of personal prayer, reading religious materials, and fasting). Attendance at worship services has only half the impact, producing a standardized coefficient of .27 compared to .49[4] for personal religious behavior. Participation in church programs and activities has little systemic effect on future plans. However, the importance of parental socialization is clearly demonstrated when we examine factors that influence the private religious behavior of an adolescent. The strongest predictor of private religious behavior is home religious observance.

By comparison, parental attendance at worship services have no effect on private religious behavior, although these parent variables do have some influence on the adolescent's attendance at worship services. In other words, parental associational involvement does seem to influence adolescent associational involvement, which in turn has some influence on future plans. But the more private aspects of family and individual religious behavior are far more predictive of future plans than the more public and institutional aspects. The most meaningful interpretation of the LISREL test of these path models is that primary face-to-face religious interactions within the family encourage the development of a religious identity and personal religious behavior, which in turn are the best predictors of future goals and values.

In addition to family influence on future plans, this research also shows the role institutional religion has on the development of adolescent social competence. Associational characteristics at the institutional level are not the important predictive variables. However, communal relationships established in the institutional setting have a significant impact. A close relationship with an adult advisor (measured by the degree to which the adolescent identifies with, trusts, confides in, and wants to be like this adult)[5] positively influences attendance at worship services, the private religious behavior of an adolescent, and future plans.

The relative importance of family and communal involvement in this model changes as young men grow older. For the younger adolescent (12 and 13 years old), the influence of home religious observance on private religious behavior is three times greater than the influence of the relationship with the advisor (standardized coefficients of .51 and .16 respectively). For the older adolescent (16 to 18 years old), the influence of the relationship with the advisor is sizably stronger than the influence of home religious observance (.46 compared to .31 coefficients).

As the adolescent's world expands, his relationships in his personal religious community become more important for creating a religious identity and making future plans. To be effective, the adult who represents the religious institution cannot just be any adult, but must be one who can connect with the adolescent in his world, present a world view with which the adolescent can readily identify, and then assist the adolescent in his efforts to navigate through his own personal family and religious world.

The last thing that this research demonstrates is the importance of the adolescent's personal religious community as he resolves ambiguities centering around whether he will actually go on a mission when the time comes. The social science literature has consistently demonstrated the problematic dimension of predicting behavior from measured attitudes (Cooper & Croyle, 1984). These Mormon adolescents were asked in 1981 whether they planned to serve a mission for their church. In 1986 those adolescents who were 16 to 18 years of age in 1981 were contacted again to determine how many had, in fact, served a mission. Indepth interviews were conducted to determine who or what had influenced their decisions. Future mission plans reported in 1981 were good predictors of actual missionary service. Of those who said in 1981 they probably or definitely would not serve a mission, only 5 percent changed their mind and in fact did go on a mission. In contrast, of those who said in 1981 they would definitely serve a mission, 90 percent went on missions.

The role of personal community relationships is clear when we examine those cases in which the adolescent changed his mind about missionary service. Those who decided to go talked about their relationship with significant other adults who represented the religious institution; for example, a seminary teacher who was particularly close to the young man or a lay church leader who was also a neighbor. These significant others were institutional agents, but it was the communal aspect of the relationship which was clearly most important. Conversely, those who decided to not go were influenced by friends (peers or adults) who thought it best that they not go on a mission. The most influential relationships are those which have become an integral part of the young person's personal religious community.

These data seem to indicate that decisions about missionary service is made fairly early in life as both public and private dimensions of a religious identity are created. The adolescent then structures a life that allows that identity to unfold and facilitates the later decision to actually serve or not serve a mission. The research suggests the primary importance of religious socialization in the home. But it also suggests the importance of personal community relationships which are created through institutional involvement. These relationships with peers and adults play a significant role in the formation of a religious identity, a pattern of private religious devotion, and, therefore, adolescent competence within the social order. While this research focused on the religious development of young men, we would likely expect to find similar patterns for young women.

Religion, Family, and Adult Well-Being

Further analysis of recent Mormon research (Thomas, 1988; Thomas & Roghaar, in press) underscores the significance of communal relationships in understanding the family and religion impact on adult well-being. In this cross-sectional research from 780 adults from intact Mormon families in the U.S., well-being is measured by the absence of depression and a general satisfaction with life. The findings from LISREL analysis demonstrates that private religious behavior is more a function of family influences than of associational involvement. Religious activities carried out in the home facilitate a sense of personal spiritual devotion manifested by desiring to live a Christ-like life, seeking the promptings from the Spirit of God, forgiving others, and seeking repentance.

As was true in the adolescent research, the associational variables do not play a dominant role. Parents' church attendance in the family of orientation does have a small effect upon religious observance in the home of an adult married child. In addition, a sense of belonging to the institutional church appears to have a suppressing effect upon the incidence of marital violence. This is an oft-reported finding and probably reflects the social control dimension of institutional religiosity. The important part of this research for our discussion is the significance of the personal spiritual devotion dimension in predicting adult well-being. Of all the religion and family variables analyzed in this research, personal spiritual devotion has the strongest overall effect on adult well-being. This is due largely because of the direct effect it has on adult well-being, as well as two indirect paths through both marital satisfaction and parental satisfaction. The significance of this variable was not anticipated, since it was expected that satisfaction with how family life was going in the form of marital and parental satisfaction would be the best predictors of adult well-being.

Our interpretation of these findings is that the communal relationships experienced in the religious world, as well as primary relationships in the family, are largely responsible for the development and maintenance of personal spiritual devotion, which in turn is strongly predictive of adult well-being. For those wishing to understand the religious institution, we are convinced that continued study of the nature of close relationships in the family and in the personal religious community will be the most productive. Research of this type will better illuminate the social supportive function of religion as opposed to the social control dimension emphasized in institutional analysis. In this sense we agree with Welch, D'Antonio, and others cited above. More research should be done which explores the importance of religious subcommunities and how they function as supportive agencies. Additional attention could then be given to the differential impact of associational and communal types of relationships and their consequences for individuals and families in our contemporary world.

RELIGION AND FAMILY
IN THE POST-MODERN WORLD

The reoccurring evidence of the last three decades in the social sciences demonstrates that the post-modern world has not witnessed the demise of religion nor the family as was anticipated. Indeed, some of the critiques of technological societies in the post-modern era argue for a growing need for religion and family. These two institutions, it is argued, are most able to address questions of ultimate significance that are left unaddressed by technologically-oriented social orders (D'Antonio & Aldous, 1983; Thomas, 1988; Schroll, 1988).

We use the term post-modern to designate a time period in the western world starting sometime in the first part of the 20th century. The first contribution of this time period (for our treatise) is the emergence of the paradigm shattering realization of the physical scientists that they could not describe the natural order in any absolute way. Their descriptions were dependent on the conceptual model overlaid on sensory data as well as the particular measuring instruments they used to produce the empirical data. With the demise of the possibility of the scientific world view offering general or universal knowledge, problems of relativity once again entered center stage (Thomas & Wilcox, 1987; Thomas & Roghaar, in press).

The second important aspect for our view of the post-modern world is the critique of post-modern philosophers and social scientists which underscores the fact that modern societies misuse *knowledge* in the pursuit of *power*. That is, the scientism in modern societies justifies itself on the basis of creating knowledge, when in fact, it also uses the pursuit of knowledge to justify its position of power in the society in terms of resource use and allocation. This problem of misusing knowledge in the pursuit of power has been especially severe in much of the western world which has, according to Aronowitz (1988), tended to recognize science as the only legitimate epistemology.

With the realization that scientists and philosophers were unable to describe the natural order in universal terms, and seeing that knowledge created by science was not free from the interests of those *creating* the knowledge, questions about morality and ethics have reappeared.

As Etzioni (1989) has persuasively argued, discussions of the moral order must be restored to center stage in social science discourse in order to address pressing problems of the day. He sees the "Me First" model informed by hedonistic and materialistic assumptions as being replaced by an "I and We" model which points to humankind's dual nature by underscoring the moral dimension of human behavior. The "We" aspect of Etzioni's model is required precisely because a "sense of morality is what separates human beings from animals." And the "We" dimension arises because the individual is not a "solitary person" but rather a "part of a community" (p. 44).

The failure of the scientism of the first half of the twentieth century to create a meaningful world through which humankind can maneuver has opened the door for alternative world views to re-enter (see Schroll, 1988; Jaki, 1988; Murphy, 1987; Fuller, 1987; and Gerhart & Russell, 1987 for typical discussions). Some of these alternative world views raise questions relevant to both religion and family which are experiencing increased interest. We see nothing on the horizon to stem the rising interest in the religion and family interface (Thomas, 1988) in the post-modern world.

When researchers and theorists take seriously the challenge confronting them in attempting to understand families in contemporary religious communities, we can then expect forthcoming answers for currently unanswered questions. What are the similarities and dif-

ferences in religion and family in our contemporary world? As social institutions, religion and family are repeatedly asked to support
and sustain people struggling to make sense out of basic life events
that demand answers. Birth, death, as well as some tragic events
(Weigert & Hastings, 1977) require family members as well as religious functionaries to attempt to give meaning to these events
which a technological, materialistic, and hedonistic social order
renders meaningless if not absurd. As this treatise has argued, communal relations will play a significant role in explaining how institutional influences get carried out in the lives of individuals in families and religions.

We expect the answers from future research and theory to show
that communal involvement in the religious sphere will have similar
effects as various family variables. We see the similarity of religion
and family influences coming from the social support functions of
each. For us the moral dimension is created and maintained in face
to face personal worlds.

However, we suspect that research focusing on the social control
function of families and religions will likely find significant differences. The study of the controlling dimension of families has for
decades proven unusually problematic (Thomas, Gecas, Weigert,
& Rooney, 1974; Rollins & Thomas, 1979). We expect associational influences along the control dimension in the religious sphere
as likely not resembling family influences on adolescent and adult
attitudes and behavior.

We expect some of the most significant payoff in future research
and theory to more correctly identify family and religious influence
in various socialization processes. Cues in the foregoing treatise
lead us to expect family and religion to be more similar to each
other than they are to other socialization influences from the economic, political, or educational spheres (Abrahamson & Anderson,
1984; Heaton & Cornwall, in press; Berger, 1967). However, we
expect that there is sufficient differences between religion and family to require that research and theory pull apart family influence
from religious influence, be it communal or associational. The research on the family's ability to channel its adolescent members
into peer relations which further reinforces basic family religious
values is very important. These findings help us better see how

religion and family come together in our contemporary world. Likewise, the increasing importance of the adult representing the religious institution in the life of the late adolescent compared to family influence points to the significance of the personal religious community in socialization outcomes.

With continued research and theory about personal religious communities, we may begin to understand the role of family and religion in our contemporary world. Hopefully we may encounter a social science discourse that more often asks about the place of the moral order in our "I" and "We" world.

NOTES

1. But what of the significant number of families who may be "unchurched"? Some might assume that these "unchurched" families are not a part of an identifiable subculture or community, but such assumptions await empirical verification. These families, in fact, may be a part of a subculture which is defined by their nonaffiliation and which effectively maintains their "unchurched" identity.

2. Seminary is a program of religious study offered to LDS students in the ninth through twelfth grades. In most areas of the United States students attend early-morning seminary prior to attending regular school. In Utah students are allowed "release time" from their regular studies to take a seminary course during the day.

3. These findings are based on path models created using LISREL. While it is difficult to assess causality with cross-sectional retrospective data, three studies based on data collected among three different religious groups (Himmelfarb, 1979; Fee et al., 1981; Cornwall, 1988) suggest similar conclusions. The authors are now involved in two different longitudinal studies which will provide the type of data necessary to identify and clarify causal relationships.

4. Only significant standardized coefficients are discussed. Since these are LISREL coefficients they represent the effect of the variable net the effects of all other variables in the model.

5. In the Mormon priesthood program, the deacons' (12, 13 years old), teachers' (14, 15 years old), and priests' (16, 17 years old) age groups have an adult advisor who meets weekly in religious instruction as well as weekly activities. Each respondent described his relationship with his advisor. Sixteen items factored together which defined this relationship variable. All items measured the degree to which the adolescent agreed or disagreed (5 point scale) with each statement describing his relationship. Such statements were: "We feel the same way, we have a lot in common, we have fun together, I want to be like him, I respect and admire him, I feel close to him, we share spiritual experiences, I turn to him with personal problems, I tell him about good things that happen to me," etc.

REFERENCES

Abrahamson, M. & Anderson, W. P. (1984). People's commitments to institutions. *Social Psychology Quarterly, 47,* 371-381.

Aronowitz, S. (1988). *Science as power: Discourse and ideology in modern society.* Minneapolis: University of Minnesota Press.

Barber, B. K. & Thomas, D. L. (1986). Dimensions of fathers' and mothers' supportive behavior: The case for physical affection. *Journal of Marriage and the Family, 48,* 783-794.

Berger, P. (1967). *The sacred canopy: Elements of a sociological theory of religion.* Garden City, NY: Doubleday.

Blau, P. M. (1974). Presidential address: Parameters of social structure. *American Sociological Review, 39,* 615-635.

Blinn, L. M. (1988). Stability and change in pregnant adolescents' perceptions of their future marriage and family life. *Family Perspective, 22,* 255-268.

Caplow, T., Bahr, H. M., & Chadwick B. A. (1983). *All faithful people: Change and continuity in Middletown's religion.* Minneapolis, MN: University of Minnesota Press.

Cooper, J. & Croyle, R. T. (1984). Attitudes and attitude change. *Annual Review of Sociology,* 395-426.

Cornwall, M. (1988). The influence of three agents of religious socialization: Family, church, and peers. In D. L. Thomas (Ed.), *The religion and family connection: Social science perspectives* (pp. 207-231). Provo, UT: Religious Studies Center, Brigham Young University.

Cornwall, M. (1989). The determinants of religious behavior: A theoretical model and empirical test. *Social Forces, 68,* 2.

D'Antonio, W.V. (1988). The American Catholic family: Signs of cohesion and polarization. In D. L. Thomas (Ed.), *The religion and family connection,* (pp. 88-106). Provo, UT: Religious Studies Center, Brigham Young University.

D'Antonio, W. & Aldous, J. (1983). *Families and religions: Conflict and change in modern society.* Beverly Hills: Sage.

Dryfoos, J. G. (1988). Using existing research to develop a comprehensive pregnancy prevention program. *Family Perspective, 22,* 211-224.

Ensign. (1984). Key to strong young men: Gospel commitment in the home. *Ensign* 14(December), 66-68.

Etzioni, A. (1975). A comparative analysis of complex organizations. New York: Free Press.

Etzioni, A. (1989). The "me first" model in the social sciences is too narrow. *The Chronicle of Higher Education* (February), A44.

Fee, J. L., Greeley, A. M., McCready, W. C., & Sullivan T. (1981). *Young Catholics in the United States and Canada.* New York: Sadlier.

Fischer, C. S. (1982). *To dwell among friends: Personal networks in town and city.* Chicago: University of Chicago Press.

Fischer, C. S., Jackson, M. R., Stueve, C. A., Gerson, K., Jones, L. M., &

Baldassare, M. (1977). *Networks and places: Social relations in the urban setting*. New York: The Free Press.

Fuller, R. C. (1987). Religion and empiricism in the works of Peter Berger. *Zygon, 22*, 497-510.

Gallup, G. (1985). *Religion in America: Fifty years, 1938-1985*. Princeton, NJ: Gallup.

Gerhart, M. & Russell, A. M. (1987). A generalized conception of text applied to both scientific and religious objects. *Zygon, 22*, 299-316.

Gottlieb, B. H. (1981). *Social networks and social support*. Beverly Hills: Sage.

Greeley, A. M. (1989). *Religious change in America*. Cambridge, MA: Harvard University Press.

Gremillion, J. & Leege, D. C. (June, 1989). Post-Vatican II parish life in the United States: Review and preview. *Notre Dame study of Catholic parish life* (Report No. 15).

Heaton, T. B. & Cornwall, M. (in press). Religious group variation in the socio-economic status and family behavior of women. *Journal for the Scientific Study of Religion*.

Herberg, W. (1955). *Protestant, Catholic, Jew*. Garden City, NY: Anchor Books.

Himmelfarb. (1979). Agents of religious socialization among American Jews. *Sociological Quarterly, 20*, 447-04.

Hoge, D. R. & Roozen, D. A. (1979). *Understanding church growth and decline, 1950-1978*. New York: Pilgrim Press.

Hoge, D. R. & Roozen, D. A. (1980). The unchurched American. *Review of Religious Research*, Supplement.

Home is cradle of gospel values: Mission choices nurtured. (1987). *Church News, 57*(10), 3.

Iannaccone, L. R. (1988). A formal model of church and sect. *American Journal of Sociology, 94*(Suppl.), 241-268.

Jaki, S. L. (1988). The three faces of technology: Idol, nemesis, marvel. *The Intercollegiate Review, 23*(2), 37-46.

Johnson, B. (1963). On church and sect. *American Sociological Review, 28*, 539-549.

Johnson, B. (1971). Church and sect revisited. *Journal for the Scientific Study of Religion, 10*, 124-137.

Kanter, R. M. (1968). Commitment and social organization: A study of commitment mechanisms in utopian communities. *American Sociological Review, 33*, 499-517.

Kelley, D. M. (1972). *Why conservative churches are growing*. New York: Harper and Row.

Lenski, G. (1963). *The Religious factor: A sociological inquiry*. Garden City, NY: Anchor Books.

Messer, S. B., Sass, L. A., & Woolfolk, R. L. (Eds.) (1988). *Hermeneutics and psychological theory: Interpretive perspectives on personality, psychotherapy, and psychopathology*. New Brunswick, NJ: Rutgers University Press.

Murphy, N. C. (1987). Acceptability criteria for work in theology and science. *Zygon, 22,* 279-297.

Olson, D. V. A. (1988, October). *Religious subcultural involvement in the personal networks of Baptist churchgoers: A deterrent to privatization.* Paper presented at the annual meetings of the Society for the Scientific Study of Religion, Chicago, IL.

Park, R. E. (1916). The city: Suggestions for the investigation of human behavior in the urban environment. *American Journal of Sociology, 20,* 577-612.

Pescosolido, B. A. & Georgianna, G. (1989). Durkheim, suicide, and religion. *American Sociological Review, 54,* 33-48.

Rollins, B. C. & Thomas, D. L. (1979). Parental support, power, and control techniques in the socialization of children. In W. Burr, Hill, R., Nye, F. I., & Reiss, I. L. (Eds.), *Contemporary theories about the family.* New York: Free Press.

Roof, W. C. & McKinney, W. (1987). *American mainline religion: Its changing shape and future.* New Brunswick: Rutgers University Press.

Schroll, M. A. (1988). Developments in modern physics and their implications for the social and behavioral sciences. In D. L. Thomas (Ed.), *The Religion and family connection: Social science perspectives* (pp. 303-323). Provo, UT: Religious Studies Center, Brigham Young University.

Smelser, N. J. (1988). Social structure. In N. J. Smelser (Ed.), *Handbook of sociology* (pp. 103-129). Beverly Hills: Sage.

Stack, S. (1988). The effect of domestic/religious individualism on suicide. In D. L. Thomas (Ed.), *The religion and family connection: Social science perspectives* (pp. 175-206). Provo, UT: Religious Studies Center, Brigham Young University.

Stark, R. & Bainbridge, W. S. (1985). *The future of religion: Secularization, revival and cult formation.* Los Angeles: University of California Press.

Thomas, D. L. (1983). Family in the Mormon experience. In W. V. D'Antonio and J. Aldous (Eds.), *Families and religions: Conflict and change in modern society* (pp. 266-288). Beverly Hills: Sage.

Thomas, D. L. (Ed.). (1988). *The religion and family connection: Social science perspectives.* Provo, UT: Religious Studies Center, Brigham Young University.

Thomas, D. L. & Carver, C. (in press). Religious influence on prosocial development of adolescents. In Thomas Gullota (Ed.), *Advances in adolescent development: Vol. III The promotion of social competency in adolescence.* Beverly Hills, CA: Sage.

Thomas, D. L. & Henry, G. C. (1988). The religion and family connection: Increasing dialogue in the social sciences. In D. L. Thomas (Ed.), *The religion and family connection: Social science perspectives* (pp. 3-26). Provo, UT: Religious Studies Center, Brigham Young University.

Thomas, D. L. & Roghaar, B. H. (in press). The conceptual and empirical emphases in postpositivist theorizing: The religion and family case. In Jetse Sprey (Ed.), *Family theory: Current perspectives.* Beverly Hills, CA: Sage.

Thomas, D. L. & Weigert, A. J. (1971). Socialization and adolescent conformity to significant others: a cross-national analysis. *American Sociological Review, 36,* 835-847.

Thomas, D. L. & Wilcox, J. (1987). The rise of family theory: A historical and critical analysis. In M. B. Sussman and S. K. Steinmetz (Eds.), *Handbook of marriage and the family* (pp. 81-102). New York: Plenum Press.

Thomas, D. L., Gecas, V., Weigert, A., & Rooney, E. (1974). *Family socialization and the adolescent.* Lexington, MA: Lexington Books.

Thornton, A. (1988). Reciprocal influences of family and religion in a changing world. In D. L. Thomas (Ed.), *The Religion and family connection: Social science perspectives* (pp. 27-50). Provo, UT: Religious Studies Center, Brigham Young University.

Troeltsch, E. (1981). *The social teaching of the Christian churches.* (O. Wyon, Trans.). Chicago: University of Chicago Press.

Weber, M. (1964). *The sociology of religion.* (E. Fischoff, Trans.). Boston: Beacon Press.

Weigert, A. J. & Hastings, R. (1977). Identity loss, family, and social change. *American Journal of Sociology, 82,* 1171-1185.

Welch, K. (1981). An interpersonal influence model of traditional commitment. *The Sociological Quarterly, 22,* 81-92.

Wellman, B. (1979). The community question: The intimate networks of East Yorkers. *American Journal of Sociology, 84,* 1201-1231.

Wirth, L. (1938). Urbanism as a way of life. *American Journal of Sociology, 44,* 1-24.

INTERACTIONS ACROSS SETTINGS
AND OVER TIME

A Theory
of Competencies × Settings Interactions

Luciano L'Abate

The purpose of this paper is to present a theory that defines personality as a set of competencies in different and diverse settings. This paper serves as a link between two viewpoints concerning personality development in the family. The first is based on a perspective of family functioning that is reductionistic. It attempts to derive family functioning from individual characteristics, a perspective that is contiguous with psychology. The second viewpoint, expressed mainly by systems thinking, attempts to deal with the family as an irreducible whole. Individual behaviors are understood and described as solely the result of transactions among family members. These transactions are separate and independent from individual contributions to those transactions. This view sees itself as being discontinuous from psychology as a science and as a profession.

The field of personality development and psychological theory has been strongly influenced by what has been called "interaction-

The author is grateful to Donald G. Unger for his meticulous editing and to Marcia Cooley for her helpful reworking of one draft of this paper.

ism" (Ekehammer, 1974; Endler & Magnusson, 1976). In the field
of family therapy, the field has been dominated by so-called systems thinking (L'Abate & Colondier, 1987). Both movements need
to be reconsidered for the primary purpose of reconciling individual
and family constructs and seeing the family as being *in part* the
outcome of individual determinants.

This paper presents a model of family functioning that is derived
from individual characteristics that were developed from the original family context. Two individuals start a family by conceiving a
child and, usually, living under the same roof. Both individuals are
the products of contexts from their families of origin. Both carry
these influences with them into their new family of procreation.
These individual characteristics must adapt to new demands from
different settings, which in turn influence family functioning. How
can one reconcile family functioning with psychological constructs?
This theory straddles individual and family system perspectives by
viewing individual development within the context of the family.
This task requires keeping the importance of the family context primary, relating individual determinants to family functioning, and
using a relational rather than a systems language. If the family is a
unit(y) of interacting personalities (Burgess, 1926, 1927), then we
need to define personality within its context, or, as we shall see,
within various contexts or settings.

DEVELOPMENTAL COMPETENCIES

This theory of developmental competence in the family acknowledges the importance of specific developmental competencies as a
function of interactions with specific settings. The acquisition of
personal and interpersonal competence is a developmental process
that acknowledges the importance of specificities that are peculiar
and particular to a given setting. This theory maintains that these
personal specificities are peculiar and particular to the interaction
between specific task characteristics and demands in settings that
interact with specific skills and abilities in individuals (L'Abate,
1976, 1983, 1985, 1986, 1987; in press, a, b, c; L'Abate & Bryson,
in press; L'Abate & Colondier, 1987). A theory of developmental

competence in the family would need to meet at least three requirements: (a) to redefine personality according to relational and contextual concepts; (b) to reduce such relational and contextually relevant concepts to known and accepted psychological constructs; and
(c) to verify these concepts empirically as well as applicatively.

This theory, summarized in Table 1, is made up by *assumptions*,
postulates, *modalities*, *resources*, *skills*, and *models*. These components go from the general and the abstract to the specific and the
concrete. Competencies underlie two assumptions, abilities underlie two postulates, while three modalities underlie six resources
classes, which, in turn, are basic to the development of skills.
These skills are defined by testable models. COMPETENCIES
AND ABILITIES underlie modalities of BEING, DOING, AND
HAVING that are made up by six resource classes: STATUS and
INTIMACY, INFORMATION and SERVICES, and MONEY and
GOODS. These resources are summarized by testable models
which require different sets of skills. Skills related to BEING are
basic to the ability to LOVE, while the skills of DOING and HAV-
ING are basic to the ability to NEGOTIATE. The way the different
sets of skills are applied pertains to the concept of SETTING. The
importance of the interactions within these settings is understood
when one uses the concept of PRIORITIES among settings interacting with individual's priorities among the modalities of Being, Doing, and Having.

Assumptions

Space and time are the two basic assumptions of the theory.
Space subsumes a dimension of distance defined by extremes in
approach-avoidance. Extremes in approach-attachment produce
symbiotic conditions ending up in abuse and apathy. Extremes in
avoidance produce rejections, neglect, abandonment, and aggression. Somewhere in the middle of this dimension, there is the
proper balance of distance, ultimately culminating with closeness
and intimacy.

Time subsumes a dimension of control defined by extremes in
discharge-delay. Extremes in discharge tend to produce hyperactiv-
ity, impulsivity, and acting out, while extremes in delay tend to

TABLE 1. A Developmental Theory of Interpersonal Competence

256

produce obsessive compulsive thinking and behavior as well as withdrawals.

Postulates

Both of these assumptions underlie the concept of COMPE-TENCE. Ever since White (1959) brought forth this concept, it has captured considerable attention in motivational and personality theories (Brody, 1980; Ford, 1985; Marlowe and Weinberg, 1985; Phillips, 1968; Wine & Smye, 1980). It seems more relevant, specific, and concrete than concepts of personality and environment. The concept of competence implies an interaction of something with something. One cannot talk about competence without specifying the context in which such competence is manifested.

Ford (1985), for instance, in reviewing past and present definitions of competence, referred to it as: (a) capabilities to formulate and produce effortful, persistent goal-directed activity, (b) one's behavioral repertoire of specified and specifiable skills and abilities, and (c) effectiveness in relevant contexts. Consequently, we need to specify the nature of the contexts where these sets of capabilities, effectiveness, and skills are manifested and used. Competence can be specified and even assessed in a specific setting much more easily than personality. While personality seems to encompass a wide range of traits and states, most of them internal and difficult to measure, competence is limited to a finite and definite number of settings. It may be a more restricted term than personality. However, it may be also easier to define and measure it because of a more specific interaction than just person × situation. Instead of a person × situation interaction, I am suggesting a competence × setting interaction.

Competencies need to be differentiated from abilities and skills, instead of using them synonimously. Competencies lie on the subjective, experiencing side (input), while skills lie on the expressive side (output). Abilities lie in the middle of this continuum (throughput). Assumptions, then, subsume the notion of competence to regulate distance, an internal, developmental process, which eventually transforms itself in the ability to love. This ability to love is shown, manifested, and expressed on the output side by very specific skills. The competence to modulate and modify control over oneself transforms itself developmentally into the ability to negotiate, which is also shown, manifested, and expressed through specific skills. The abilities to love and to negotiate are the two postulates of the theory.

Modalities

Each modality of BEING, DOING, and HAVING subsumes two classes of resources exchanged (Foa' & Foa', 1974). BEING, the modality for the expression and sharing of the ability to love, is defined by *status* and *intimacy*, evidenced in emotional availability and presence. DOING and HAVING are the two modalities necessary for the expression of the ability to negotiate. Doing is defined by the resource classes of *information and services*, as evidenced in performance. Having is defined by the resource classes of *money* and *goods or possessions*, as evidenced in production.

In summary, personal and interpersonal competence is defined by what an individual *is, does, and has*. From the two sets of abilities to LOVE and to NEGOTIATE; the three modalities of BEING, DOING, AND HAVING, and six resource classes of STATUS, INTIMACY, INFORMATION, SERVICES, MONEY, and GOODS, one can derive various testable models.

Skills and Models

From the ability to LOVE and its modality of BEING, two models can be derived. The resource class of STATUS produces a model of selfhood, self-definition, and identification based on the attribution of importance to self and to significant others (spouse, child, parent, friend, etc.). This attribution can produce four different interpersonal outcomes: (a) *selfulness,* attribution of importance to self and other ("I win, you win, we both win"); (b) *selfishness*, attribution of importance to self and denial of importance of other ("I win, you lose"); (c) *selflessness,* attribution of importance to other and denial of importance of self ("You win, I lose."); and (d) *no-self*, denial of importance of self and of other ("I lose, you lose"). Most psychopathologies and levels of functionality align themselves according to this model. Selfulness is equated with equality, reciprocity, and intimacy in relationships. These qualities make up personal and interpersonal competence as well as marital and familial functionality. Selfishness is the major characteristic of acting out character and personality disorders. Selflessness is the major characteristic of most self-defeating, dependent, and depressed personalities. No-self is the characteristic of most severe psychopathologies, abuse, and apathy (borderline, psychotic, schizophrenia, etc.).

The resource class of INTIMACY yields another model defined by four processes of: (a) seeing the good, (b) physical, practical, and financial caring, (c) forgiveness, and (d) intimacy (L'Abate, 1986). Intimacy is defined as the sharing of hurts and of fears of being hurt. The ability to LOVE, being present without demands for perfection, performance, production, or problem-solving, is related to skills in the attribution of importance and in the skill to develop intimate (close and prolonged) relationships. Being is not negotiable. Our attributions of importance and our emotions are based on how we feel subjectively. What we chose to attribute and to affirm to ourselves and to those we love and who love us, is based on feelings and emotions. Neither are negotiable. Both are sharable if and when they are expressed positively. The skills necessary for Being are defined by *presence,* and that is, the skill to be available emotionally to oneself and to selected others in the time of need, i.e., when we are hurting.

The ability to negotiate requires different skills and yields, therefore, different models. Both DOING and HAVING are negotiable commodities. Doing requires skills of *performance*, while Having requires skills of *production*. Together these skills represent *power*. Power is negotiable in democratic families, where all the members count as equally important, though each member may have different functions. In dysfunctional families, power is misused, abused, or unused. Family members cannot show and share their love in enhancing ways. Dysfunctionalities take place when families (and some family therapists!) confuse issues of self-importance, presence, love and intimacy (BEING) with issues of performance (DOING) and production (HAVING), i.e., *power*: "If you loved me you would do. . . ." "If you loved me, you would buy. . . ."

The ability and the skills necessary for negotiation yield two major aspects of the same process, and they are: *structure* and *process*. The structure of negotiation is made up by: (a) authority (who makes the decisions) versus responsibility (who carries the decisions out); (b) orchestration (once in a life-time decision, like marrying, moving, etc.) versus instrumental decisions ("What shall we eat tonight?"); and (c) the content of the decisions, having to do with either performance and/or production. The process of negotiation can be broken up into three different models: (a) *styles* in negotiation among intimates, or the level of dysfunctionality-functionality at the time of negotiation, going from dysfunctional styles, like *A*busive-*A*pathetic to *R*eactive-*R*epetitive to functional styles, like *C*onductive-*C*reative, the ARC model (ILL); (b) *the skills* required by the process of negotiation, and that is, *E*motionality, *R*ationality, *A*ctivity, *A*wareness, and *C*ontext, the ERAAwC model (SKILL); and (c) the *motivation* necessary for negotiation, as defined by one's priorities, as discussed further below (WILL). Thus, the ability to negotiate is made up by a multiplicative function of ILL × SKILL × WILL.

SETTINGS

Competencies and abilities vary as a function of the task requirements of each setting. There are a finite number of settings. In order of functional importance, they are: home, work, leisure, transit (going from one to other settings) and transitory ones (shopping stores and malls, bars, barbershops, beauty salons, etc.). Of course, there may be overlaps among all five settings. For instance, leisure time activities may take place in the home, or, in some instances, in work settings. Competence in one setting does not necessarily predict competence in another setting. One could be a terrific parent at home but a mediocre employer at work. By the same token, one could be a strong athlete during leisure hours, but not function as well at either work or at home. Further study is needed to determine whether there may be a general "g" factor that predicts cross-setting transfer of certain, yet to be specified, competencies (Bem & Allen, 1974).

Home

This setting has task requirements related to the maintenance of a family as an emotional unit and, the home as a physical entity. Most of the responsibilities can be broken down into four specific roles: caretaker, provider, partner, and parent. Each of these roles demands certain specific skills. For instance, the responsibilities of the *caretaking* role are of two kinds. One kind refers to nurturant qualities that deal with love, being present and available emotionally. The other kind refers to instrumental qualities that deal with the physical and material well-being of the home, like cooking, cleaning, purchasing, repairing, etc. The role of *provider* deals with the economic aspects of family living. Salary, income, credit rating, mortgages, etc. are aspects of this role. How much money comes into the home and how is it spent? Both the caretaker and provider roles depend a great deal on what kind of person one is. How well one functions as a *partner* depends on a variety of personality competencies that can be summarized in the selfhood model presented above. In this role, both abilities to love and to negotiate are necessary. The fourth role of *parent* is probably one of the most difficult and most demanding in our lives. Often, this is the role for which we have received little if any training except for what we automatically learned as children by watching our parents. Most of us perpetuate their errors and may forget their assets because the task requirements of today are different from those of a previous generation. Both the ability to love and to negotiate become crucial at this stage. Consequently, a proper and appropriate developmental sequence would require first of all the development of personhood as being basic to partnership. Being able to be a partner is basic to being a parent. Unfortunately, very few of us are lucky enough to follow such a sequence in an orderly fashion.

Work

Work requires two separate but interwined sets of skills. The first set consists of specific occupational skills that are necessary to perform a job, such as filing, typing, drawing, writing, ditch-digging, etc. The second set of skills is extra-job, consisting of interpersonal skills to get along with co-workers, authority figures, clients, customers, etc. This set of skills may require interpersonal sensitivity, political gamesmanship, contextual awareness, etc. It may have little to do with substantive job skills necessary for success. Yet, these skills may make the difference between promotion or stagnation on the job!

In the western culture, many people identify themselves according to their occupational role (Crandall, 1984; L'Abate, 1986). In fact, this role often may provide the major source of gratification and, therefore, it may require greater energy investment than would take away from other roles. We identify ourselves by what we *do* or what we *have* in possessions, instead of who we *are* as human beings and persons. What happens to us when we lose our jobs or retire? Do we have any self left? How does this role (unemployed or retired) interfere with other roles?

Other Settings

Under these categories are the left-over skills that are neither home- or work-related. There are fewer demands and requirements here. These skills may be considered more discretionary than obligatory.

Leisure Settings

Leisure activity is sometimes spent at home, sometimes in other settings. It takes place in company of others or it can be solitary. It can be active or sedentary, indoor or outdoor, or oriented toward people or towards things. Working in one's basement on a hobby, participating in the Elks Club once a week, watching TV, going to church, or running a marathon are all examples of activities in this setting. Leisure time activities are important for the enjoyment of life and personality development (Franken & Van Raaij, 1982; Hirschman, 1984; Stamps & Stamps, 1985). They are an integral part of how we function as individuals. These activities define specifically how much value we put on friends and relationships in our lives. Leisure settings require skills that are specific to the activity being performed in a particular setting as well as skills to develop and maintain relationships that are formed within each setting.

Transit

These settings may have not been as important in the past as they are today, with our capacity to travel long distances in short periods of time. This capacity has the effect of increasing the number and variety of transit settings within which we interact each day (highways, airports, cars, buses, etc.). With changing perceptions about distance and time allotment towards transit settings, time and activities spent in these settings may take on its own identity. Increased time spent in commuting to and from various settings requires the acquisition of skills to learn to commute and to make the best of it. But the ease of commuting within various settings may also increase the chance of overlap among settings. For instance, having an office in the home may be more comfortable way of reducing commuting time. However, it may produce conflicts in fulfilling responsibilities one may not be required to fulfill if one had an office away from home. Lee and Kanungo (1984) noted that: ". . . it is clear that there are new problems and opportunities in coordinating work and personal life and achieving personal well-being. There is clearly a need for theory and research that might offer insights and guidelines that would be helpful to those most affected by these (social and economic) changes" (p.6).

Transitory

These settings are temporary and variable in importance from one person to another. Purchasing goods and services, shopping in a mall, going to a beauty salon, or attending a bar, may require different time and energy requirements depending on how important one thinks that activity is. Getting the oil changed at the corner garage, waiting in an unemployment line, completing the requirements for automobile registration, buying a bottle of aspirin, take us to different settings. Each of these settings has its peculiar role demands and codes that need to be observed. They may seem less important than other settings. Yet, our ability to transact in these settings allows us to survive in the most important setting, the home.

PRIORITIES

To understand how we allocate time and energies from one setting to another we need to invoke the concept of PRIORITIES. This concept is motivational in nature (L'Abate, 1976, 1986). These priorities stem from definite choices we make about what is important in our lives. How important a person, an object, or an activity is to us? How important is one's self in relationship to others? How important are BEING, DOING, AND HAVING?

Priorities can be divided into *vertical and horizontal priorities.* Vertical priorities can be differentiated into the three modalities of BEING, DOING, and HAVING. Personal, familial, and interpersonal priorities, are all ranked according to the relative importance given to self and to significant others. Vertical priorities are developmental, while horizontal priorities are structural, that is, they exist regardless of anyone's level of development. One may value DOING more than HAVING or BEING, stressing the work setting at the expense of the home and leisure settings. This emphasis, for instance, could define the great American workaholic man. By the same stereotypic token, of course, a woman may be described by her stress on BEING present emotionally in the home. Work and leisure settings may be considered secondary to her emotional availability. In other words, vertical and horizontal priorities intersect and interact with each other.

How successful one is in any of these settings depends a great deal on the priorities of that particular individual. If one defines oneself primarily in occupational terms ("I am an engineer") rather than domestically ("I am a husband and a father"), it will follow that that individual may be more successful at work than at home. By the same token, avocational pursuits sometimes may overshadow both domestic and occupational roles. We all need to balance modalities and settings so that no one modality or setting is stressed at the expense of the others.

The salience and satisfaction derived from each modality and setting remains an individual prerogative that determines how each modality and setting is ranked in respect to the others. Each one can be reduced in importance by increasing the importance of the others. For example, activities in the leisure area can become direct antidotes for the negative effects of stresses at work or at home. How this juggling and counterbalancing demands and difficulties takes place to maintain balance in one's life is reflective of one's priorities. Priorities motivate people to negotiate with themselves and significant others important issues in their lives.

These priorities can be measured easily by time analysis. How much time does one spend in each of the settings? What modality of expression among BEING, DOING, or HAVING is being used primarily, secondarily, and tertiarily (Juster & Stafford, 1985)? BEING, of course, is much more relevant to the home setting than to the modalities of DOING and HAVING. The latter two modalities, on the other hand, are more relevant and primary at work and in leisure settings.

THEORETICAL AND PRACTICAL IMPLICATIONS

The primary purpose of this theoretical framework is to link individual with family psychology (L'Abate, 1976, 1983, 1987), in both functional and dysfunctional aspects. A secondary purpose is to link and bridge inevitable gaps between theory and practice, between theory building and theory testing, and between theory and levels of prevention. To fulfill both purposes, this theory attempts also to meet two additional formal requirements, that is: reducibility and verifiability.

Reducibility

This first requirement is met, first, by using psychological terms that are at the same time interactional and relational. Love and negotiations, for instance, imply the presence of another partner to love and to negotiate with. Both sets of abilities are necessarily vital for individual, dyadic, and familial functioning. In fact, most family dysfunctioning is the outcome of deficits in the either/or both abilities. This framework also draws from and links to developmental and cognitive psychology, personality, social and stress theory (L'Abate, in press, a).

Verifiability

To fulfill this second requirement, a theory needs to develop methods that are derived from and are isomorphic as much as possible with the theory itself, or models derived from the theory. Methods, not techniques, are needed to verify this or any other theory. A method is a step-by-step sequence of verifiable procedures. Over the years, a variety of paper and pencil self-report tests were validated to verify some of the models derived from the theory (L'Abate, 1976; L'Abate & Wagner, 1985, 1988; Stevens & L'Abate, in press). The theory can be verified also processionally through content-analyses of verbal family interactions derived from the very same models of the theory. More dynamically, this theory can be tested according to different levels of prevention. In primary prevention, the theory can be evaluated through structured enrichment programs, some of which were also derived from the same models of the theory (L'Abate & Weinstein, 1987; L'Abate & Young, 1987). In secondary prevention, the theory can be evaluated through the use of theory-derived and theory-independent para-therapeutic workbooks (L'Abate, in press, a & b; L'Abate & Cox, in press).

Both humanistic and behavioral approaches can be integrated in this theory (Gesten & Jason, 1987). The ability to love, stressed by the humanistic school, is related to the support received in *empowerment*. The importance of negotiation, stressed by the behavioral school, is related to *enablement*, that is, learning of problem-solving skills (Dunst, Trivette, & Deal, 1988).

CONCLUSION

A theory of developmental competence derived from assumptions of space and time postulates two sets of abilities necessary and sufficient for functional family living: ability to love and ability to negotiate. The sets of skills derived from both abilities interact with five different settings: home, work, leisure, transit, and transitory ones, according to one's developmental and structural priorities. From both postulates various relational models can be derived that describe the attribution of importance to self and others. Loving and intimacy and the ability to negotiate with others are essential skills for living. These models are reducible to psychological constructs and can be verified directly and indirectly at various levels of prevention. Personal competence can be understood if one looks at the setting in which it takes place and the priorities one assigns and allocates to different modalities of expression in daily life.

REFERENCES

Bem, D.J. & Allen, A. (1974). On predicting some of the people some of the time: The search for cross-situational consistencies in behavior. *Psychological Review, 81,* 506-520.

Brody, N. (1980). Social motivation. *Annual Review of Psychology, 31,* 143-168.

Burgess, E.W. (1926). The family as a unity of interacting personalities. *Family, 7,* 3-9.

Burgess, E.W. (1927). The family and the person. *Publications of the American Sociological Society, 20,* 133.143.

Crandall, R. (1984). Work and leisure in the life span. In M.D. Lee & R.N. Kanungo (Eds.), *Management of work and personal life: Problems and opportunities.* New York: Praeger.

Dunst, C., Trivette, C., & Deal, A. (1988). *Enabling and empowering families: Principles and guidelines for practice.* Cambridge, MA: Brookline Books.

Ekehammar, B. (1974). Interactionism in personality from an historical perspective. *Psychological Bulletin, 81,* 1026-1048.

Endler, N.S. & Magnusson, D. (1976). Toward an interactional psychology of personality. *Psychological Bulletin, 83,* 956-974.

Foa,' U.G. & Foa,' E.B. (1974). *Societal structures of the mind.* Springfield, IL: C.C. Thomas.

Ford, M.E. (1985). The concept of competence: Themes and variations. In H.A. Marlowe, Jr. & R.B. Weinberg (Eds.), *Competence development: Theory and practice in special populations.* (pp. 3-49). Springfield, IL: C.C. Thomas.

Franken, D.A. & van Raaij, W.F. (1982). Satisfaction with leisure time activities. *Journal of Leisure Research, 24,* 337-351.

Gesten, E.L. & Jason, L.A. (1987). Social and community interventions. *Annual Review of Psychology, 38,* 427-460.

Hirschman, E.C. (1984). Leisure motives and sex roles. *Journal of Leisure Research, 16,* 209-223.

Juster, F.T. & Stafford, F.P. (Eds.) (1985). *Time, goods, and well-being.* Ann Arbor, MI: University of Michigan, Institute for Social Research.

L'Abate, L. (1976). *Understanding and helping the individual in the family*. New York: Grune & Stratton.

L'Abate, L. (1983). *Family psychology: Theory, therapy, and training*. Lanham, MD: University Press of America.

L'Abate, L. (1985). Descriptive and explanatory levels in family therapy: Distance, defeats, and dependence. In L. L'Abate (Ed.), *Handbook of family psychology and therapy*. (pp. 1218-1248). Homewood, IL: Dorsey Press.

L'Abate, L. (1986). *Systematic family therapy*. New York: Brunner/Mazel.

L'Abate, L. (1987). *Family psychology II: Theory, therapy, enrichment, and training*. Lanham, MD: University Press of America.

L'Abate, L. (In Press, a). A theory of family competence and coping. In B.N. Carpenter (Ed.) *Personal coping: Theory, research, and applications*. New York: Pergamon Press.

L'Abate, L. (In Press, b). Reconciling personal and professional priorities. In F. Kaslow (Ed.), *Voices in family psychology*. Newbury Park, CA: Sage Publications.

L'Abate, L. (In Press, c). *Primary and secondary prevention with families*. Newbury Park, CA: Sage Publications.

L'Abate, L. & Bryson, C. (In Press). *A theory of personality development*. New York: Brunner/Mazel.

L'Abate, L. & Colondier, G. (1987). The emperor has no clothes! Long live the emperor! A critique of systems thinking and a reductionistic proposal. *American Journal of Family Therapy*, *15*, 19-33.

L'Abate, L. & Cox, J. (In Press). *Programmed therapy: Self-administered interventions with individuals, couples, and families*. Pacific Grove, CA: Brooks/Cole.

L'Abate, L. & Wagner, V. (1985). Theory-derived, family-oriented test-batteries. In L. L'Abate (Ed.), *Handbook of family psychology and therapy*. (pp. 1152-1177). Homewood, IL: Dorsey Press.

L'Abate, L. & Wagner, V. (1988). Testing a theory of developmental competence in the family. *American Journal of Family Therapy*, *16*, 23-35.

L'Abate, L. & Weinstein, S. (1987). *Structured enrichment programs for couples and families*. New York: Brunner/Mazel.

L'Abate, L. & Young, L. (1987). *Casebook of structured enrichment programs for couples and families*. New York: Brunner/Mazel.

Lee, M.D. & Kanungo, R.N. (1984). Work and personal-life coordination in a changing society. In M.D. Lee and R.N. Kanungo (Eds.), *Management of work and personal life: Problems and opportunities*. New York: Praeger.

Marlowe, H.A., Jr. & Weinberg, R.B. (Eds.) (1985). *Competence development: Theory and practice in special populations*. Springfield, IL: C.C. Thomas.

Phillips, L. (1968). *Human adaptation and its failures*. New York: Academic Press.

Stamps, S.M. & Stamps, M.B. (1985). Race, class, and leisure activities of urban residents. *Journal of Leisure Activities*, *17*, 40-55.

Stevens, F.E. & L'Abate, L. (In Press). Validity and reliability of a theory-derived measure of intimacy. *American Journal of Family Therapy*.

White, R.W. (1959). Motivation reconsidered: The concept of competence. *Psychological Review*, *66*, 297-333.

Wine, J.D. & Smye, M.D. (Eds.) (1980). *Social competence*. New York: Guilford.

Paradise Through the Sands of Time: The Human Yearning for Community

Kris Jeter

It is not . . . government that (the hu)man wants . . .
It is life . . .

> — Arthur Maurice Hocart
> Anthropologist, 1883-1939

What life have you if you have not life together?
There is no life that is not in community . . .

> — T. S. Eliot
> Poet, 1888-1965

INTRODUCTION

In the 1989 movie, *The Field of Dreams*, baseball players of 60 years past are redeemed from accusations of foul play as they re-create a community on a diamond constructed in a cornfield by a passionate man who has the courage to follow the commands of an unknown voice. The ballplayers walk through rows of corn to arrive on the diamond and inquire, "Is this heaven?" They are told, "No, this is Iowa." The ballplayers are then asked in return, "What is heaven?" One replies, "Heaven is where dreams come true."

Heaven, indeed paradise, lies deep within the dreams of individuals and within the mythologies of societies. "Religions, philosophies, arts, the social forms of [the] primitive and historic [hu]man, prime discoveries in science and technology, the very dreams that blister sleep, boil up from the basic, magic ring of myth" (Campbell, 1968, p. 3). Fundamental among dreams and myths is the yearning for paradise.

THE DESERT

Go to the desert alone and you will find community.
Go to the desert with others, and you will know solitude.

— Bedouin Expression

The desert and arid lands have been the birthplace and home for major mythological, philosophical, and religious systems. In the barren wilderness of the desert, humans are especially challenged by ominous energies. Images of paradise arise. As sand blows into every pore and cell of a desert dweller, the remembrances of hungers and thirsts that never get quenched arise. Many persons yearn for a place of abundance, beauty, ecstasy, immortality, integrity, liberty, radiance, rectitude, and tranquility. Countless humans pine to communicate as respected friends with animals, plants, and deities. Unity with mother and father is desired. Unity with generations of the past and future is wanted. A sense of true family and community, a brotherhood and sisterhood with all life is desired.

It is easy to become lost in the desert. Within minutes, sands slide and float through the air; within hours, dunes deflect and divert upon the earth. The high dunes are unreliable milestones. Rather, it is the windswept tree, the massive stone, the forgotten oasis, the watering hole which fills the heart with hope and ignites visions of paradise. Today, as humans live in a desert of cities, there are lessons which may be learned from those who have for centuries lived successfully in the desert of sand.

In this analytic essay, I examine how the yearnings for community have been expressed in the interconnecting arts of architecture, art, history, literature, mythology, philosophy, and psychology. I focus on images which have arisen from the desert to fuel the concepts of paradise and community in Judaism, Christianity, and Islam.

NEXUS POINTS AT THE DESERT CROSSROADS

Historically, the desert has many times been at the passageway and intersection of diverse cultures. It has been the site of combat dethroning potentates and rotating power bases; the scene of oases replete with communal life with cultural traditions flowing and exchanging. With each turn of the wheel of power, people adopt thoughts and incorporate them into their view of paradise.

Mesopotamia

Between ten and seven thousand years ago, the ice cap was increasingly melting, the earth was slowly warming, and the mammoth was becoming extinct. Hunters who had until now migrated from cave to cave, from warmth to warmth, while following the great herds of herbivorous mammoths, needed to develop a new life style. As the great Pleistocene grasslands dried out, the areas within the latitudes closest to the equator developed unique identities. Likewise, the settlers of each new region created a distinctive culture appropriate to the environment. The more recent Holocene cultures exhibited greater regional differences and faster rates of adaptation than the preceding Pleistocene Age. Two Holocene age developments in particular — animal domestication and plant cultivation — transformed the history of humankind.

The Near East is one of the first areas where the Holocene age developed. The core highlands to the north and east of the Fertile Crescent became the home for the wild animals and plants. The hill peoples moved according to the season and complemented their diet of wild foods with foods they were learning to cultivate. In northern Iraq, sheep were domesticated approximately 9000 BCE (Before the Common Era). Before 7000 BCE, in southwestern Iran, barley and wheat were cultured. As the nomadic hill peoples migrated to the lowlands, they were motivated by the harshness of the dry lands and lessened rainfall to utilize to the best advantage the domesticated animals and seeds they had brought with them. As food supplies and populations increased, cities formed in which individuals of varied skills and status established their identities within political and religious structures.

From approximately 4500 BCE, dark-headed peoples from Persia traveled down the Tigris and Euphrates rivers to colonize the land, approximately the size of New Jersey, between and on the outer sides of the lower courses of the rivers. Living at first on wild dates in the autumn and native barley in the spring and through democratic cooperation and long patience, the persons built up and cultivated the marshlands into terraces of flora, foliage, grains, herbs, trees, vegetables, and vines, a virtual horticultural Tower of Babel. Around 3300 BCE, the Sumerians developed and utilized a cuneiform script to bureaucratize a union of twelve cities. They wrote the first known narration on paradise.

> Once upon a time there was a pure, pristine, and brilliant land named Dilmun. Dilmun's inhabitants were immortal deities who lived gentle lives without illness. Alas, Dilmun had no fresh water. Thus, Enki, the God of Sweet Water, commanded Utu, the God of the Sun, to dispense water from underneath the earth. Utu complied and Dilmun was transformed into a paradise of edible delights.

In a society where donkeys were the swiftest mode of travel, empires came and went while localities endured. Between 2700 BCE, and 1000 BCE, Mesopotamia, "the land between the rivers," changed hands from the Sumerians, to the Akkadians, to eastern barbarians, to the rulers of Ur, to the Elamites, to Hammurabi of Babylon, and to Cassite warlords from the Zagros Mountains. Each conqueror's utilization of the Sumerian cuneiform script to note holdings and business transactions unknowingly accorded them the power to connect cities.

The deities that humans relate to are imaged by the human mind. It is humans who observe the powers of nature, assign them anthropomorphic images, then name them deities. With time, deification, and the creation of tools to harness natural powers, tribulation and trepidation are replaced by respect and reverence. Thus, for instance, in Mesopotamia, water in the form of a raging flood is feared as the destroyer of life. However, water in the form of a flowing river is loved as the provider of life itself. Trees both bear fruit and clasp the soil along human made canals, dikes, and terraces. Today, there are pieces of ancient Mesopotamian art which survive to provide us with images of their paradise.

Early Sumerian tablets picture Inanna, goddess of love and fertility, the reservoir of the vital blood of the land. A magnificent human size goddess of 2125-2025 BCE, Mari holds a vase through which water was channeled up from a cavity in the foundation. Babylonians believed that the tree is given life by the four-faced mother goddess Tiamat, who clasps a vase against her breast from which water flows on two sides. An ivory plate of 1243-1207 BCE, Assur depicts a god as a mountain with four rivers of life surrounded by trees and sun symbols. As we identify other images of the garden paradise, we find the Meopotamian themes of the four rivers of life, mountains, palm trees, and springs woven into other cultural contexts.

The Mesopotamians created paradise upon their land during a significant and explosive era of human evolution. The family and tribe were being absorbed by the community and the city. With urbanization came a new economy. Early tribes lived from day to day, gathering and hunting for foods; with the development of agricultural skills and trade, it was now possible to accrue goods. A monarch with a centralized bureaucracy was required to regulate the saving and distribution of commodities. The development of writing was necessary for keeping records in the new economy.

With this swift movement toward a new social form, fresh mythological stories and ritual patterns were required to accommodate the psychological and spiritual well being of the community members. The Mesopotamians created a living paradise of community, government, mythology, and ritual which all mirrored each other. The center of the land was established and made into the home for the monarch. The monarch's vigor was required for the very health of a community. When the fertility of a community was threatened, the monarch would be ritually slain and replaced. Mythological stories about Adonis, Aliyan, Baal, Attis, Dumuzi, Marduk, Osiris, and Tammuz told of the dying and rising god who regenerates the earth and changes the seasons of the year.

Archaeological excavations, art, and cuneiform tablets tell us of the successful efforts by the ancient Mesopotamians to create a paradise on earth. In tenth century BCE Mesopotamia, 10,000 square miles of soil were cultivated.

Old Persia

The word, paradise, is derived from the old Persian word, "pairidaeza," which is a combination of two words: "pairi" (around) and "daeza" (wall). Paradise is defined as an enclosure of cultivated land such as a hunting ground or imperial park. Pairidaeza is also the holy virgin who will bear the future redeemer of the world, the "Mahdi." Even today, Shi'ite Arabs wait for the advent of the Virgin Paradise, the next blessed mother.

The Greek historian and writer, Xenophon, accompanied the Greek mercenaries in the early fourth century BCE to Persia. In Xenophon's Socratic Discourse in the "Oeconomicus," Socrates describes the Persian king as a noble and skilled warrior and gardener.

> In whatever countries the king resides, or wherever he travels, he is concerned that there be gardens, the so-called pleasure gardens, filled with all the fine and good things that the earth wishes to bring forth, and in these he himself spends most of his time, when the season of the year does not preclude it. (Xenophon in Moynihan, p. 1)

Socrates then elaborates on the concept of the paradeisai and describes an interview conducted by Lysander, the Spartan commander of the Peloponnesian fleet and winner in the war, with the opulent and ornate Persian, Cyrus the Younger, in his estate garden at Sardis.

> Lysander has wondered at it—that the trees should be so fine, the plantings so regular, the rows of trees so straight, the angles so finely laid, and that so many pleasant scents should accompany them as they walked—marveling at these things, he spoke, "I, Cyrus, am full of wonder at the beauty of everything, but much more do I admire the one who has measured out and ordered each kind of thing for you." On hearing this, Cyrus was pleased and spoke, "All these things, Lysander, I measured out and ordered myself, and there are some of them," he said, that "I even planted myself." (Xenophon in Moynihan, p. 1)

Egypt

The Egyptians, living under the searing sun and on the scorched edge of the desert, developed their concept of paradise as the lavish "Fields of Yalu" translated as the Fields of Offerings and Reeds. The Fields of Yalu are the genesis of dynamic opulence where the dead could live happily forever and be reborn. Here, the dead theoretically continue their professions; actually, servants do the real work. Priestesses are bare-breasted so that their milk is readily available to the dead.

JUDAISM

Judaism, a term not found in the *Talmud*, was articulated by the Hellenistic Jews through their unique customs of communicating with and serving one God. Through the legal concept of the Covenant, Jews have believed that they are chosen by a stable and enduring God, not associated as other deities of the time with familial roles or forces of nature.

The creation myth of the Garden of Eden contains an image of paradise which serves as a beacon throughout the evolution of the Jewish, Christian, and Muslim communities. Each year in the Jewish calendar, the story of Adam and Eve is ritually told as a reminder of the community's origins. However, throughout the history of Judaism, there have been eras of extreme social adversity and agony which have demanded another view of paradise. It is during these times that the community strives to redeem itself and dreams of the coming Messiah and the new heaven and earth.

The Garden of Eden

Eden in Hebrew means "a place of delight." Ancient Jews located the original, lost, rural Garden of Eden on Mount Saphon in Syria. Hebron, the site of an oracular temple in a fruitful valley was considered to be paradise. During the Babylonian captivity, the Persian Gulf was considered to be another site for paradise because it was watered by the Choaspes, Euphrates, and Tigris rivers and the Pallakopas Canal. The Garden of Delight, wherever its archeological site, is rich in mythological and psychological meaning.

Once upon a time, beyond the place where the sun went to sleep each night, there was a Garden of Eden, a paradise of delight. Here lived an androgynous being named Adam, or Red Earth. Adam was to care for the garden and never to eat of

278 *Families in Community Settings: Interdisciplinary Perspectives*

either the Tree of Good and Evil, or the Tree of Life and Death.

With time, Adam longed for mutuality, a fully human help-mate, a fitting companion. Thus, Adam was split into a woman and a man. The male notes that "bone for bone, flesh for flesh," they were not so different after all. The male and female engendered each other and met as friends.

One day, a serpent told Eve that if they would eat from the Tree of Good and Evil or Knowledge, they would become as the Deity. Eve, followed by Adam, chose the frightening action to enter the cycle of life. They must now toil forever to regain harmony with animals, plants, and each other that they had known in the Garden of Eden. The snake still slithers above and below the earth, searching from the Tree of Life and Death, for the immortality of the deity.

This story of Adam and Eve, based on the account in Genesis 1:1-27, has been interpreted by Waskow, Cady, and Raines (1989) to be a developmental history of the human community. At first, Adam and Eve were as infants, unconscious and unable to shape their destiny. Eve, by taking the bite out of the apple of conscious-ness became the obvious adolescent at an earlier time than Adam. For the past 4,000 to 5,000 years, humans have been adolescents, afraid of the Mother-Father Deity. Individuals have searched for unique differences, and have hurt each other through the knowing of each other as different. The developmental task for youth is to separate from their parents and to learn the use of nurturing skills with the varied forms of life. The developmental task ahead for humankind is to know the association between the Tree of Good and Evil and the Tree of Life and Death, the interrelationship of knowledge and immortality.

In the Jewish calendar year, celebrants move from the horror over the loss of the Temple to Rosh Hashana ceremonies for the new year to Passover acknowledging the liberation of the people to the death of Moses, who, after all his effort and toil, cannot enter the paradise of the promised land to commemoration of creation story. Celebrants honor the great spiral of life and death, good and evil. There is no progression—rather, life is a spiral in which humans go back and forth, however each step is with new eyesight and hearing. In the spiral, there is no space to linger; in the calendar, there is no time to loiter. Within the annual repetition of the rituals of remembrance, there are the opportunities to reflect upon the myth in a personal and collective way and to progress on the spiral of life. In communal re-living and remembrance, individuals get closer and closer to the paradise of the promised land. The story of Adam and Eve reaffirms the values of balance, harmony, and partnership.

The Messiah and the New Heaven and Earth

Approximately 800 BCE, Jews developed into a community bound to the concept of one God, the creator and sustainer of all life, who never fatigues, dies, or rises again. This omnipotent God was the antithesis of the Mesopotamian and Mediterranean concept of the dying and rising god. As the Jewish community was dispersed from the land of Israel, they were united in their belief in the one, ever-living deity.

With each adverse loss, the community began to think of paradise as a future home and the Messiah as its herald. From 587 to 586 BCE, the First Temple was destroyed and the Jews were dispersed to Babylonia. Cyrus, who allowed the Jews to return home, was considered to be a Messiah. From 175 to 165 BCE, the community suffered despotic torture under the Syrian Seleucid potentate, Antiochus IV. During this time, the hope for a Messiah to lead the community to paradise was recorded in the Book of Daniel. Some thought that the Messiah was to end Syrian domination, reinstate the reign of the Kings of David, reassemble exiles, and reconstruct the Temple as a paradise for the community. Others felt that the Messiah was to end the Syrian rule with an explosive calamity, inaugurate the Day of Judgement, revive the departed, and start a fresh era and paradise, a new heaven and earth.

The paradise ordained by the Messiah had two polarities: One was seen as an immediate, practical, realistic intention, and the other was seen as an ominous, spectacular, apocalyptic desire. Today, these opposing thoughts can be observed in modern-day Israel. The Prayer for the State written by Zionists describes the nation as "the beginning of the sprouting of our Redemption." There are Israelis who believe that the messiah and paradise are to come in the future, at the end of all days.

Map makers, philosophers, and psychologists have utilized Jewish texts to determine the site of the Days of the Messiah and the World to Come. Some have placed the crafted urban paradise of Jerusalem that David had originally built in Mesopotamia, near Baghdad, in the rich land between the Tigris and the Euphrates Rivers. For philosophers, the Future to Come addresses both a resurrected and rejuvenated earth and heaven. Analytic psychologists have described the temple, the center, the temenos, the source, as that place where the ego meets with soul and spirit.

CHRISTIANITY

It was out of the despair of the Jewish community and its need for a Messiah that Christianity was born. Josephus Flavius and the author of Acts 5 refer to several individuals who assumed the role. Yeshua ben Yussef was the individual who grew out of the political desire; he acted without concern to the political situation and named himself the Son of Man. It was the authors of the Gospel of Matthew who wrote the genealogy linking Jesus to King David in order to justify his Hebrew title of Messiah, the anointed one, translated into the Greek name, Christos.

Christianity, as an outgrowth of Judaism, adapted many artistic images and some philosophical concepts of paradise, presenting additional layers of meaning to the Garden of Eden and the Future to Come. The Christian understanding of Adam and Eve has accentuated the human "original sin" and alienation from God. Christianity bases its concept of an eschatological paradise on three verses in the New Testament: Luke 23:43; 2 Corinthians 12:3; and Revelations 2:7. Paradise is an ethereal heaven achieved through euphoria. During the final events of the world's evolution—the second coming of Christ, the Last Judgment, and the resurrection of the dead— persons who are forbearing, especially those who suffer and die for the greater good, will be bestowed with the gift of the fruit of the Tree of Life. Christianity, as a conquering way of life, absorbed international mystery rituals along with Greco-Roman and Gnostic philosophies. The Christian arts depict vivid images of paradise which have served to yeast the imaginations of humans yearning for utopian communities in life and heavenly communities in the after-life.

Mystery Rituals

By 323 BCE, Alexander the Great had marched eastward to the Indus River, northward to the Aral Sea, and southward to the Indian Ocean. With the dismantling of monarchies and urban bureaucracies, human faith in deities, rituals, and royalties, the very safeguards of the community, faded. The need for a new mythology and ritual to combat the loss of community led to the spread of mystery rituals. During a mystery rite of passage, a deity would be revered and secret wisdom regarding triumph over death would be disclosed to the initiate. From Asia Minor came the worship of Cybele, Dionysius, and Sabazius. From Egypt, the mysteries of Isis and Serapis were hailed. From Persia, came the ritual for Mithra. From Syria, the worship of the ancestors, Attis and Ishtar, was expanded.

In a world which had lost the stability of the ancient monarchy, the mystery rituals presented a way for humans to establish community. The objective was deification, the realization of the venerable longing of the human to become divine. The mystery rituals were abundant in ethics and dictums, yet were based on mythological deities, not actual humans. The allure and stimulation of early Christianity has its beginnings as a mystery ritual, founded on a human being. In fact, this human being was imperative to nourish and support humans in the worldwide scope of the Roman Empire.

Early Christian

Early Christian rituals mirrored Orphic mysteries in which the initiate entered a womb-like building and drank milk. Christians likened themselves to young goats and said, "As a kid I have fallen into the mystic milk." Orphics said, "Beneath the bosom" and "Into the womb of the Lady, Queen of the Underworld, I have sunk."

In early Christian art, the young lamb symbolizes not only Jesus but the faithful — Abraham, the Apostles, John the Baptist, and

Moses—who have been separated from the goats. Jesus exemplifies both the sacrificial lamb and the good shepherd. The palm tree represents the tree of paradise, the tree of life and death, the Eucharist, the victory of life over death.

Although there is no concise Christian text describing paradise, there are independent passages. The Christian paradise is a garden or a walled city with four rivers. Jesus sits on a throne surrounded by angels and saints. There is no concept of time. Thus, the individual is pictured as an eternal youth or a wise elder. The mature man is in the likeness of such powerful Greco-Roman deities as Jupiter, Neptune, and Pluto, with a full-bearded face.

Early Christian art expressed ecstasy. Paradise was reached through the euphoria of martyrdom, persecution, and torture.

Medieval Christian

Medieval arts expressed the gamut from Eden to Jerusalem, exposure to enclosure, seclusion to society, and nature to craft. *Divina Commedia* by the Italian Dante and *Pearl* by an anonymous English poet differentiate the paradise as garden and city.

In *Pearl*, a melancholy man has misplaced an unequaled, exquisite pearl in a garden. While dreaming, the man discovers the pearl crystallized in the shape of a woman. The pearl represents paradise, a community of righteous folk who live in a magnificent city. When the man attempts to enter paradise, he awakens from his dream.

In both *Pearl* and *Divina Commedia*, anticipation for the heavenly paradise occurs in an earthly paradise, a waiting room in the suburbs of the real thing. Dane proceeds from the garden to an apparition of a river of illumination whose sparkles are ruby crystals which light upon the golden flowers at the river's edge. Then, the river vanishes and a celestial city of architectural delight emerges which is at the same time in the shape of a rose.

Early Renaissance Christian

The Flemish painter, Hieronymus Bosch, painted several panels on the polarities of paradise. In "Earthly Paradise," God presides from the clouds while Eve and Adam are tempted by a humanoid serpent coiled around the tree of knowledge of good and evil. In the companion panel, "Hell," demons are for the first time in history portrayed as animals, humans, and vegetables. In a second series, paradise on earth and in heaven is contrasted. In "Earthly Paradise," there is a valley of trees with a hill crowned by a fountain. Bosch replaces the physical concept of medieval paradise with an introspective mystical vision of the soul. In "Heavenly Paradise," ecstatic humans accompanied by angels leave the darkness of the firmament and approach the everlasting light at the end of a circuitous tunnel.

In 1667, Milton wrote *Paradise Lost*. Milton utilizes symbols of paradise — a fountain, four rivers, a mountain and trees — expressed almost 5,000 years before in Sumer.

The New World

Paradise, the new world, has been a goal for explorers of the outer world and inner self. Upon first seeing the American continents, Europeans labeled them as both Eden, a fertile land pregnant with possibilities, and Jerusalem, a city on a hill with gold paved streets. Likewise, America has been called, the "land of the free" where the body, mind, and spirit can expand as desired.

ISLAM

Islam means "to surrender to God's law and thus to be an integral whole." The Muslim is the person who surrenders. Islam grew out of the code of honor of life in the desert. The code, "muruwah," meaning manliness, urges men to honor courage, hospitality, covenants, retribution, and women. Islam developed in 622 CE and the Qur'an was codified in the eighth century CE. Today, Islam is the faith with the largest number of followers in the world.

The Arabic word for garden, "janna," is indicative of both the paradise of the Garden of Eden and the Garden of Delight for the righteous dead. According to the Qur'an, every Moslem will ultimately live in paradise. The door of paradise is closed to the infidel. The story, most told and retold is the ancient story of Layla and Majnun recorded by the Persian poet and the founder of the Persian romantic epic, Nizami. Layla and Majnun are chaste so that they may live apart in their community and together in paradise.

Once upon a time, there was a Bedouin chief who had all of his heart's desires except for a son to remember his life when he was dead. Eventually, his prayers were answered and a boy child, Quays, was born. The boy learned devotion, fidelity, and mercy.

At age ten, Quays was sent to a school for the children of Bedouin chiefs. He was attractive, talented, and popular. A new pupil, Layla, of great loveliness and gifts also arrived, and they instantly fell in love. Their instructors and families became embarrassed by their behavior and urged them, without success, to withhold their love. Layla's family removed her from school and sequestered her. Quays became a Majnun, a mad man. Quays roamed the desert, composing and singing ghazals, songs on the loss of love, which were heard and repeated throughout the land, even within Layla's compound. Quays became known as the herald of secrets that hold no reason.

Quay's father attempted to arrange a marriage between Layla and his son but was denied because Quays was a mad man. Layla's parents presented Layla to Ibn Salaam. She married him, saying she would die if the marriage were consummated. Ibn Salaam had such love for her the he agreed.

Majnun lived in the desert and became at one with his environment. Animals lay with him. Vultures shaded him with their wing span. Lions guarded him. Likewise, Layla, in her own home, became unified within her spirit.

An elder arranged for Layla and Majnun to communicate with letters and then to meet in a garden. Their intensity was such, however, that they could not touch. They left the possibilities of the garden, knowing that they could only be truly together in paradise.

Ibn Salaam, broken hearted that he would never have the love of Layla, passed on. Layla entered the prescribed two years of mourning and before it ceased, she passed on. Majnun learned of her death, went to and tightly embraced Layla's blue grave stone whispering, "You, my love." His soul passed from his body. Now, at last, Layla and Majnun live forever in paradise.

Throughout the ages, Layla and Majnun have been held as role models in the Islamic community. Layla is admired and desired by many men. Yet, Layla chooses to own her soul and to live her destiny. Layla and Majnun each attain a spiritual unity between the self and the environment. Both know that paradise is the reward for their love and endure as best they can within the norms of their community.

CONCLUSION

You will go to new places —
Your eyes will always go backward . . . toward home.

                              — Cochese, Apache Chief
                                "Broken Arrow"

Recently I asked the Venerable Khenpo Palden Sherab Rinpoche and the Venerable Khenpo Tsewang Dongyal Rinpoche, Nyingma lamas in exile from Tibet since 1960, what were the lessons they had learned as refugees. They responded that upon going into exile, they took with them a roadmap, the teachings of the Vajrayana tradition to use as their guide. This guide teaches and reminds them to live with love and compassion. The exile has forced them to leave their retreat in Tibet to live and teach their ways throughout the world. They have learned that their home is within their hearts and that they are at home, in paradise in their lower Manhattan apartment and wherever they reside on this planet. The diaspora, the scattering, the sowing of seeds across the earth, nourishes paradise on earth.

We stand at the crossroads of history. When we can feel ourselves to be at home and share our visions of paradise with others, humanity can enter a new phase of development. Community can be strengthened by the recognition of the lessons of exiles, the sharing of paradise, and the embracing of home. Joseph Campbell ended his four volume series of *The Masks of God* with this statement and challenge: "But in the end, as in the case of Parzival, the guide within will be his own noble heart alone, and the guide without, the image of beauty, the radiance of divinity, that wakes in his heart 'amor,' the deepest, inmost seed of his nature, consubstantial with the process of the All, 'thus come.' And in this life-creative adventure the criterion of achievement will be, as in every one of the tales here reviewed, the courage to let go of the past, with its truths, its goals, its dogmas of 'meaning,' and its gifts: to die to the world and to come to birth from within" (pp. 677-678).

We actualize community with each act. When we catalyze the nobility, the paradise in others, we can create a new community.

REFERENCES

Addison, J.T. (1932). *Life beyond death in the beliefs of mankind*. Boston, MA: Houghton-Mifflin.

Arberry, A.J. (1950). *Sufism: An account of the mystics of Islam*. London: Allen and Unwin.

Armstrong, J.H.S. (1969). *The paradise myth*. London: Oxford University Press.

Ashe, G. (1970). Paradise: A good place, blessed and happy, heavy is the final beatitude, the ultimate goal. In R. Cavendish (Ed.), *Man, myth, and magic*. New York: Marshall Cavendish Corp.

Boies, J.J. (1983). *The lost domain: Avatars of the earthly paradise in western literature*. Lanham, MD: University Press of America.

Campbell, J. (1968). *The hero with a thousand faces* (2nd Ed.). Princeton, NJ: Princeton University Press.

Campbell, J. (1984). The earthly paradise. In J. Campbell (Ed.), *The masks of God: Creative mythology*. New York: Penguin Books.

Cavendish, R. (1977). *Visions of heaven and hell*. London: Orbis Publishing.

Cohn, N.R.C. (1957). *The pursuit of the millennium*. Fairlawn, NJ: Essential Books.

Dante, A. (1948). *Divina Commedia* Norton Translation. New York: Oxford University Press.

deFord, S. (1967). *The pearl* (S. deFord, Translator). Northbrook, IL: AHM Publishing Corporation.

Duncan, J.E. (1972). *Milton's earthly paradise: A historical study of Eden*. Minneapolis, MN: University of Minnesota Press.

Eastham, S. (1983). *Paradise and Ezra Pound: The poet as shaman*. Lanham, MD: University Press of American.

Eliade, M. (1954). *The myth of the eternal return*. Princeton, NJ: Princeton University Press.

Esquizel, J. (March, 1980). They have threatened us with resurrection. Cited by

H.S. Tomkins. Personal communication. Pottstown, PA: Fellowship Farm, August, 1989.

Gordon, E.V. (Ed.) (1953). *Pearl*. (I.L. Gordon, Reviser). Oxford, England: Clarendon Press.

Jacoby, M. (1976). Der mythos vom verlorenen paradies—heute [The myth of paradise lost today]. In *Analytische psychologie: Zeitschrift fur analytische psychologie und ihre grenzgebiete*, 7(1), 36-47.

Jacoby, M. (1985). *The longing for paradise: Psychological perspectives on an archetype* (M.B. Gubitz, Translator). Boston, MA: Sigo Press.

Jeter, K. (1989). *Images of paradise across the sands of time: An illustrated lecture and photo essay*. Newark, DE: Beacon Research Associates.

Kaufmann, U.M. (1978). *Paradise in the age of Milton*. Victoria, BC: English Literary Studies, University of Victoria.

The King James version of the Bible. New York: American Bible Society.

King, R. (1979). *The quest for paradise: A history of the world's gardens*. New York: Mayflower Books.

Kirkpatrick, R. (1978). *Dante's paradiso and the limitations of modern criticism: A study of style and poetic theory*. Cambridge, England: Cambridge University Press.

Kramer, S.N. (Ed.) (1961). *Mythologies of the ancient world*. Garden City, NY: Doubleday and Company, Inc.

Lewis, R.W.B. (1955). *The American Adam: Innocence, tragedy, and tradition in the nineteenth century*. Chicago: University of Chicago Press.

Lincoln, A.T. (1981). *Paradise now and not yet*. Cambridge, England: Cambridge University Press.

Lindenbaum, P. (1986). *Changing landscapes: Anti-pastoral sentiment in the English renaissance*. Athens, GA: University of Georgia Press.

Manuel, F.E. & Manuel, F.P. (1979). *Utopian thought in the western world*. Cambridge, MA: Belknap Press of Harvard University Press.

Marshall, R. (1979). *William Morris and his earthly paradises*. Tisbury, England: Compton Press.

McClung, W.A. (1983). *The architecture of paradise: Survivals of Eden and Jerusalem*. Berkeley, CA: University of California Press.

Milton, J. (1953). Paradise lost. In J.H. Hanford (Ed.), *Poems of John Milton* (2nd Edition). Glenview, IL: Scott, Foresman and Company.

Nizami. *The story of Layla and Majnun*. R. Gelpke, Editor and Translator. Boulder, CO: Shambhala.

Partin, H.B. (1987). Paradise. In M. Eliade (Ed.), *The encyclopedia of religion: Vol. II*. New York: Macmillan Publishing Company.

Rinpoche, K.P.S. & Rinpoche, T.D. (August, 1989). *Buddhist psychology*. Wilmington, DE: Padmasambhava Meditation Center.

Robinson, P.A. (Writer and Director). (1989). "Field of Dreams." Adapted from W.P. Kinsella (1982), *Shoeless Joe*. Boston, MA: Houghton Mifflin.

Sanford, C.L. (1961). *The quest for paradise*. Urbana, IL: University of Illinois Press.

Schimmel, A. (1978). *The triumphant soul*. London: East-West Press.

Sewell, D. (1985). *A way in the desert*. Nashville, TN: Thomas Nelson Publishers.

Smith, H.N. (1950). *Virgin land*. Cambridge, MA: Harvard University Press.

Stevens, H.B. (1951). *The recovery of culture*. New York: Harper Brothers.

Sylvia, M. Sister (1965). *Nostalgia for paradise*. London: Desclee.

Waskow, A., Cady, S., & Raines, J. (August 1989). "A second look at the first couple." Broadcast on *Dialogue*. Philadelphia, PA: WPVI Television.

Williams, G.H. (1962). *Wilderness and paradise in Christian thought*. New York: Harper.

Xenophon. The oeconomicus (C. Lord, Translator), *Xenophon's socratic discourse. An interpretation of the oeconomicus*. Ithaca, NY: Leo Strauss, 1970, pp. 19-22. Quoted in Moynihan, E.B. (1979). *Paradise as a garden in Persia and Mughal India*. New York: George Braziller.